The Metaphysics of Terror

About the Series

The **Political Theory and Contemporary Philosophy** series stages an ongoing dialogue between contemporary European philosophy and political theory. Following Hannah Arendt's and Leo Strauss's repeated insistence on the qualitative distinction between political *theory* and political *philosophy*, the series showcases the lessons each discipline can draw from the other. One of the most significant outcomes of this dialogue is an innovative integration of 1) the findings of twentieth and twenty-first century phenomenology, existentialism, hermeneutics, psychoanalysis and deconstruction (to name but a few salient currents) and 2) classical as well as modern political concepts, such as sovereignty, polity, justice, constitution, statehood, self-determination, etc.

In many instances, the volumes in the series both re-conceptualize age-old political categories in light of contemporary philosophical theses and find broader applications for the ostensibly non- or apolitical aspects of philosophical inquiry. In all cases, political thought and philosophy are featured as equal partners in an interdisciplinary conversation, the goal of which is to bring about a greater understanding of today's rapidly changing political realities.

The series is edited by Michael Marder, Ikerbasque Research Professor in the Department of Philosophy at the University of the Basque Country, Vitoria-Gasteiz.

Other volumes in the series include:

Deconstructing Zionism by Michael Marder and Santiago Zabala

Heidegger on Hegel's Philosophy of Right edited by Peter Trawny, Marcia Sá Cavalcante Schuback and Michael Marder

Politics of the One by Artemy Magun

The Negative Revolution by Artemy Magun

The Metaphysics of Terror

The Incoherent System of Contemporary Politics

Rasmus Ugilt

Political Theory and Contemporary Philosophy

Michael Marder, Series Editor

B L O O M S B U R Y

NEW YORK • LONDON • NEW DELHI • SYDNEY

Bloomsbury Academic
An imprint of Bloomsbury Publishing Plc

1385 Broadway	50 Bedford Square
New York	London
NY 10018	WC1B 3DP
USA	UK

www.bloomsbury.com

Bloomsbury is a registered trade mark of Bloomsbury Publishing Plc

First published 2012
Paperback edition first published 2014

Library of Congress Cataloging-in-Publication Data
A catalog record for this title is available from the Library of Congress

ISBN: HB: 978-1-4411-8252-4
           PB: 978-1-6289-2056-7
           ePDF: 978-1-4411-7053-8
           ePUB: 978-1-4411-6472-8

Typeset by Newgen Imaging Systems Pvt Ltd, Chennai, India

Contents

Introduction: Much Ado about Nothing

Philosophy sets itself apart from any other academic discipline by its *lack* of discipline. In all other areas of academia one will be able to at least give a negative definition of what counts as a relevant object of study. Philosophy, on the other hand, is exactly that discipline which cannot point to any object of *no* interest. The interest of philosophy is, at least in principle, equally aroused by the structure of subatomic particles, ancient Greek poetry, cats on mats, unicorns, money, terrorism and love. In the words of Hegel: 'the truth is the whole' (Hegel, Werke III, 24).[1]

But while philosophy has always had some aspiration towards totality, the totality was always too large or too unfathomable to grasp. Indeed, how does one *say* the whole? In the end, it seems as if the only adequate description of the whole would be the whole itself. And so, more often than not, philosophy ended up in some sort of reduction of everything to *one* thing (i.e. water, nature, discourse, the will to power, spirit, matter, substance, etc.). This manoeuvre of explaining, understanding, reducing the chaotic and unruly multiplicity of the whole to the more manageable *one*, has often been described as the kernel of metaphysics. Metaphysics has long been known as the discipline which searches for the one principle through which the world, or the whole if you will, can be explained as a system.

In the so-called School-Philosophy of the eighteenth century, in which philosophers such as Christian Wolff and Alexander Baumgarten were prominent, this notion of metaphysics was perfected and developed in great detail. On one hand, one would ask the general question of *what* being is, that is, what is the one through which we can explain everything else; on the other hand, one would ask the more specific question of *which* beings could be said to exist. The first type of questioning was termed *Metaphysica Generalis*, and the second was called *Metaphysica Specialis*. General metaphysics could also be termed ontology as it concerned itself with the question of being in its most general aspect. Particular metaphysics was in the hands of the scholastics turned into three distinct disciplines that concerned themselves with the questions of the specific beings of the human soul, the world and God in the subdisciplines of psychology, cosmology and theology respectively.[2]

As awkward as the idea may seem, the proposal of the present investigation is that one should understand our current predicament and the great political questions of our time under the heading of the metaphysics of terror, in this scholastic sense. We should in other words be investigating the ontology, the psychology, the cosmology and the theology of terror.

Such an approach surely requires an explanation. It is the objective of the introduction to give it. I will therefore in the following pages present my overall view of how metaphysical investigations should be conducted. It should be clear that this can only be done by engaging in some way in metaphysical discussions – at least in the form of a prolegomena. The discussion of how metaphysical investigations should be conducted is undertaken therefore by following the development of metaphysics from Kant, to Hegel and in the end, to Schelling.

While the division that guides the present study is scholastic in origin, taking these three as one's guides means that the contents of the four parts are not. If metaphysics traditionally can be defined as the search for the one that provides the founding principle of the whole, the claim I make here is that the one is not simply one. The one splits into two. The paradoxical nature of this claim should be embraced in full. Whatever is posited as the one principle through which the whole can be interpreted as system, that one will reveal an internal incoherence or a split; not in the sense that it turns out to be two separate ones (i.e. spirit and nature, form and matter, real and ideal, body and mind), but in the sense that the one as such is ambiguous. The philosophers who most brilliantly have pursued this idea are precisely the German Idealists, who followed in the wake of Kant's critical philosophy. Of particular interest here are the philosophies of Schelling and Hegel, who, despite their differences, had common ground in a certain notion of dialectics that can be expressed by the notion that *Identity is the identity of identity and difference* (Hegel, Werke II, 39; Werke V, 74; Schelling, AotW, 63).

This basic ontological claim means that the whole, which as we recall is the truth, cannot be put to any final formula. Not even the whole itself will serve as a description of the whole – it does not fit itself – exactly because being itself does not fit itself. The consequences for the disciplines of particular metaphysics are radical. There is no coherence to the subject in psychology. There is no coherence to the world in cosmology. There is no coherence to God in theology. While these are important claims, it is imperative that the point about the lack of coherence is not simply understood as an effort to deconstruct these disciplines. It is the crucial point of metaphysics to conceptualize this incoherence as such, not in order to overcome metaphysics, but instead to further it. This means, however, that metaphysical enquiries should be understood in a particular way. Most importantly, it means that metaphysics cannot be an ahistorical discipline. If there is no a priori coherence in being, subject, world or God, then these notions must undergo some kind of historical change. While philosophy on one hand is characterized by the search for the totality of a system, it is also 'its own time captured in thoughts' (Hegel, Werke VII, 26).[3]

This idea about the conflation of metaphysics and history is helpfully ambiguous in the sense that on one hand it expresses the notion that any time has its own metaphysics, and on the other hand sets a task for philosophy (or what I shall here term metaphysics as 'last philosophy'). If the basic truth about being is that it is a notion of incoherence and lack, then history in turn could be described as a development that takes place as we try to fill the gap that is thus opened. The metaphysics of any given time will therefore be the particular way in which it tries to close the gap in being. As Schelling is keen to observe, there is nothing which disturbs human beings as much as inconsistencies and contradictions (see, e.g. Schelling, AotW, 28; SW VIII, 219). Metaphysics in the traditional sense was precisely the theoretical endeavour that sought to overcome all such disturbances. Whether it in some way conceptualized the notion of being, subject, world or God, this form of metaphysics typically tried to install one specific theoretical entity as being completely free of internal contradictions, and thereby as the thing which should be able to guarantee the consistency of other beings.

Rejecting this notion of metaphysics does not, however, mean that metaphysics as such is rejected. One can set another task for philosophy or the science of metaphysics, namely to investigate the specific ways in which a particular time, that is, its own time, deals with the fundamental lack at the core of being. Does it always take the shape of postulating the specific thing which can fill the gap? In which ways does this filling function? Can it be done correctly? Can it be overdone? It is with the task of approaching such questions that the investigations of the present work set out.

The metaphysic of our time

So what are these times in which we live? Remaining still at the level of sweeping generalization, it has often been said that the twentieth century was one that fundamentally changed our perspective of ourselves and the world we inhabit. During this century, it gradually became clear that no thing, God or idea could fill the gap in being. As the story of postmodernism goes, History became histories. There is no longer one all-encompassing tale about humanity that each individual must find a place in. Postmodernism is characterized, as Jean-François Lyotard put it, by 'incredulity towards metanarratives' (Lyotard 1984: xxiv). The 'grand narratives' of religion, politics and spirit were discredited through the critique of metaphysics, and the ideological disasters of the twentieth century.

The crucial point here is that even after the announcement of the death of God, we should not just yet hasten to announce the end of metaphysics. A common reaction, to the condition Lyotard described, became to assert the individual narrative as the only legitimate measure of validity. Each person has his or her story. The most basic right after the fall of the great narratives of the just and equal society was therefore widely held to be the right to narrate about *oneself*.

The crucial consequence of the developments of the twentieth century was therefore the introduction of one last theoretical entity to fill the gap in being: the individual. Not the infinitely capable universal man of modernity, who triumphantly set out to shape the world in his own image, but the finite individual – everyday man. In this way, the end of the grand narratives became a grand narrative in its own right; after the metaphysics of God, Nature and History, we were given the metaphysics of *finitude*, to borrow a term coined by Alenka Zupančič (Zupančič 2008a: 43ff.). She writes:

> The range of this metaphysics of finitude is considerable; it stretches from very complex and highly elaborate philosophical enterprises to an utterly commonsense 'psychotheology of everyday life', [. . .] in which finitude appears as consolidation for, and explanation of, our little (or not so little) disappointments and misfortunes, as a new Master-Signifier summoned to make sense of our ('acknowledged') senseless existence, as a new Gospel or 'good news': You're only human! Give yourself a break! Nobody's perfect! (Zupančič 2008a: 48)

From Heidegger's destruction of metaphysics to Derrida's deconstruction, from Adorno's negative dialectic to Habermas's discursive reason, in most forms of American philosophical pragmatism, and in most forms of French post-structuralism, a common trend has been the idea that one should refrain from making the grand metaphysical gestures of the infinite and the absolute. And most often there was the explicit or implicit conclusion that one should instead seek truth (and only with a minor t) in the finite realm.

The crucial metaphysical point that is being made here is that metaphysics never simply produced the Truth with a capital T. It is not the case that there once was a coherent God above, a complete world below and a coherent subject acting somewhere between them; nor is it the case that these grand narratives suddenly became false at a certain point in history. Instead, metaphysics was always structured around a gap in being. The term 'metaphysics', in so far as it is taken to denominate a specific story about the fundamental structure and coherent ground of the whole, should always be taken to describe the reaction of a specific time, a concrete historical formation, to the fundamental metaphysical incoherence; all grand narratives were stories told in order to help us forget that there can be no coherent grand narratives.

This point throws important light on the idea of the end of all grand narratives. This so-called end cannot be seen as a radical change in the *way* stories are being told; it does not mean that narrations are no longer 'grand'. Rather, it means that the fundamental impossibility of coherent narration itself has become the theme of the narration. The metaphysics of finitude is the curious formation that takes place at this precise moment where the notion that God is dead becomes a part of the commonly accepted narratives. Instead of a disappearance of the grand narratives altogether, the narration of finitude was turned into the last overarching grand narration.

The result is that a paradoxical move is undertaken in the metaphysics of finitude. It consists in telling the story of the end of all grand narratives, in order to *hide* the fact that there cannot be any coherent grand narratives. In this way, the metaphysics of finitude is a grand narrative hiding in plain sight. It is accomplished exactly by installing a lack – of coherence and order – to cover the lack that is found at the core of every coherent order. In the metaphysics of finitude the human subject finds comfort in the idea that there ultimately is nowhere, one can find comfort. There is only this very simple human existence, which can never aspire to anything universal, infinite or absolute.

It is in this specific historical situation that we must evaluate the metaphysical functioning of terror. From the perspective of the finite individual, who is living under the absolute rule that there must be no absolute rules, the terrorist immediately sticks out as an *excess*. The terrorist, as he is known by the finite individual, is the one who is willing to sacrifice both his own life and the life of others, for some kind of overarching universal cause. This is a completely incomprehensible move to the everyday man of the metaphysics of finitude, because while this individual is certainly willing to kill, he can only accept killing if it is done with reference to, and reverence, for finitude. In the metaphysics of finitude, it is quite acceptable to invade other countries, but only if it is done to combat those who aspire to challenge this metaphysics – that is, the terrorists, fundamentalists and fanatics of the world.

Terrorist killings, on the other hand, are by definition excessive from the point of view of the metaphysics of finitude, not because they are excessively violent, but because they appear be in direct confrontation with finitude. Not only because the terrorists seem to adhere to the type of universal cause which the metaphysics of finitude prohibits, but also because terrorism seems to target precisely the finite individual. One thing that is repeated again and again about the terrorists of today is that they are targeting and killing innocent people with no relation at all to their terrorist cause. Accordingly, the story of the terrorist threat is a story about a potential threat against anyone and everyone. Not because of the capacity of every one of us to pose a threat against the cause of the terrorists themselves – whatever it may be – but simply because of the capacity of everyone to die. The understanding of terrorism which arises under the sign of the metaphysics of finitude is exactly a threat against the very thing which is positioned at the centre of this metaphysics itself: the finite individual. What better guarantee could one find for the validity of the idea that 'I' am really and fully an individual, than the idea that there is someone out there looking to destroy 'me'? In these ways, the excess of terrorism fits the lack at the core of the finite individual like an ideological glove.

This understanding of terrorism as excess will play a crucial role in the present investigations. As a result there is one possible misunderstanding which should be settled from the start. With the predicate 'excess', I do not seek to describe a form of excessive violence, which is often associated with the term. As we will come to see, the physical violence of terrorism is in general not at all excessive. Instead, the excess of terrorism should be understood as a specific way in which the concept works in language. For finitude, 'terrorism' is a concept that is overloaded with meaning – it means too much, it is meaningfulness-as-excess.

This very brief characterization of our own time provides no conclusions, but it does set a target for our investigations. What we should be searching for, in order to deepen our understanding of the times in which we live, is the metaphysics inherent in the ways in which we relate to terror. Especially, we should take care to notice the lacks and excesses which emerge in this regard.

The concepts of terrorism and politics

Since metaphysics is tied to its own time in the way I describe, it is surely also a political science. That is all the more so here, as we are dealing with an exemplary case of a political concept. If anything, it is terror that would today be the political concept par excellence. As a famous proverb goes, 'one man's terrorist is another man's freedom fighter'. This is an idea, which has been propagated by many, with great enthusiasm (see, e.g. Rees 2005), and which has been scorned upon by equally many (see, e.g. Netanyahu 1986). What is important to note about this point, as it is made here, is that it is not meant to introduce a moral relativism – I do not simply wish to say that it all adds up to the same in the end. The point which is assumed from the start is rather less ambitious; I simply observe that the concepts of terror and terrorism themselves are sites of intense political struggle.

In this regard the historical development of the concepts is of some interest. The concept of terror has quite a long history, but it was during the French Revolution, with the *regime of terror*, that the concept rose to the prominence it enjoys today in our political vocabulary (Walther 2004: 336ff.). It is of course particularly interesting to note how the concept of terror at this time was given a distinctly positive meaning. Especially, Robespierre has become famous for the position, made clear in a speech from the 25th of December 1793, that 'terror is nothing but justice, prompt, severe and inflexible' (see Walther 2004: 345–6). The concept of terrorism on the other hand was not coined until after the end of the Jacobin rule, where it was introduced to condemn the past and as a useful way of rhetorically defaming one's political enemies (Walther 2004: 348). Since then both of the concepts have changed their positive and negative connotations several times, but in the end this process led to the situation we are in today, where terror, terrorist and terrorism in general political discourse are simply used as derogatory concepts (Walther 2004: 324, 439). Calling someone a terrorist means not only to describe him in a certain way, it also means to condemn him. This political dimension is the reason why research on terrorism has not yet been able to agree upon a common neutral definition of terror and terrorism and probably never will be.[4] Or to put it differently, the day it is possible to say what a terrorist is, in a definitive manner, and without immediately putting oneself in a political minefield, will be the day when terrorism has lost its specific interest and meaning. Because the concepts of terror and terrorism are in this way crucial sites of political struggle, and because it is this very struggle itself which is of interest, I do not draw any line of distinction between terror and terrorism in the investigations that follow. Instead I argue that both of them designate a political *excess*. They are precisely concepts which designate something which is simply too much. Therefore an important task to be dealt with below consists in the development of a proper conceptual framework within which we can describe and understand such a thing as an excess.

The notion of politics at stake here is very closely linked to the notion of metaphysics presented above. Politics is fundamentally about the community – where there is no community there can be no politics – but just as there can be no *coherent* system of soul, world, God and being in our notion of metaphysics, there can be no community without conflict in our notion of politics. Politics is about communities and their conflicts. This is a notion of politics, which has been intensely discussed with reference to Carl Schmitt in recent years. Chantal Mouffe has among others insisted upon the necessity of paying close attention to the *Challenge* (e.g. Mouffe 1999, 2005) posed to liberal democracy by Schmitt's idea that politics ultimately is founded in enmity (Schmitt 2007a: 26).[5] We will get back to the discussion of Schmitt's notion of politics in the chapter on political theology below, but for now the crucial point lies simply in the link between the notion of politics as conflicting communities, and the notion of metaphysics as a systematic whole, which revolves around a crucial incoherence. It is precisely because we can claim that these two are to be viewed in this particular way, that we can make sense of a metaphysical enquiry into contemporary politics. It is because both metaphysics and politics can be seen as systems which function around a crucial and fundamental incoherence or lack that the investigations into the metaphysics of terror can and must be an investigation into the incoherent system of contemporary politics.

Metaphysics as last philosophy

The conflation of politics and metaphysics prescribes a certain degree of involvement with scientific inquiries that lie beyond the scope of traditional philosophical inquiry. This in turn necessitates a very careful consideration of what a metaphysical enquiry can at all amount to be. The present investigations are metaphysical in nature, but not in the sense of *first philosophy* that has traditionally been the understanding of metaphysics, at least since Aristotle famously gave form to the science that deals with the notion of being as being (Aristotle 1003a). Instead, to use a term coined by Michael Theunissen, my aim is to conduct *last philosophy* (Theunissen 1991: 26).

Where first philosophy was the kind of intellectual endeavour that sought to describe being as such through a set of a priori determinable categories, which subsequently would be handed down to other sciences and human life in general, last philosophy takes up the task of investigating a metaphysical thought that is revealed through a critical engagement with other sciences, with politics, with art – in short: with historical developments at every level. Last philosophy is the form of metaphysics that becomes available to us once we have realized that there is not and cannot be any final fact of the matter regarding the question 'what is being?', but where we at the same time realize that there is still an important investigation to be made regarding the functioning of being in history. This means that while last philosophy gives up on the notion that the study of metaphysics can be conducted as an a priori science, it insists that the classical metaphysical questions must still be asked and answered. Even though the whole cannot be given any absolute, a priori description, last philosophy retains the whole as the ultimate object of study. But as a last philosophical endeavour this investigation is obliged to engage seriously in the concrete phenomena that are relevant to the problem at hand. Metaphysics as last philosophy is not applied philosophy. It is the polar opposite in fact. Where applied philosophy takes philosophical thinking and exports it in a sense to a non-philosophical reality, last philosophy insists that the concrete, natural, political, social, cultural (etc.) world we inhabit is already metaphysics in action. Last philosophy conducts the manoeuvre from reality to philosophy rather than the other way around.

Our investigations should therefore be divided still in a general and a particular metaphysics. But given the specific focus upon a crucial political phenomenon of our time, they should at the same time be understood as political investigations. We can thus line out the four central tasks at hand. We must construct a political ontology of terror, a political psychology of terror, a political cosmology of terror and a political theology of terror.

The political ontology of terror takes seriously the problem that there can never be given a non-political definition of terror. This is done by engaging in concrete examples of both well-known and less well-known incidents of terrorism, but that is not all. We must also consult various strands of scholarly work, journalistic articles and governmental reports on terror. This engagement with these various forms of events and texts has the dual task of showing *that* terrorism is to be understood as a particular kind of excess and of showing *how* this excess is to be conceptualized. Prefiguring what is to follow it can be said that the excess of terror lies not with the actual terror that happens, but rather with the terrorism that could happen. The basic excessive structure of terrorism is hence one of potentiality. What is interesting to us in terms of terror is argued to be its potentiality rather than its actuality. In this precise way 'terror' always means more than whatever concrete terrorist incidents we are discussing. All discourse on terror involves a prefiguring or promise of the potential threat. It is the ultimate task of the investigating into the political ontology of terror to conceptualize this kind of excess of language. In a similar way each of the disciplines of the particular metaphysics of terror are taken up in a last philosophical manoeuvre.

1. The political psychology of terrorism deals with the way we relate to the excess of terrorism psychologically. It takes its starting point in the notion of the *Politics of Fear* that has gained a lot of currency in recent work in sociology and cultural studies on the subject matter at hand (see, e.g. Massumi 1993, 2005, 2007; Furedi 2005; Bigo & Tsoukala 2008; Closs Stephens & Vaughan-Williams 2009). From the discussion of the politics of fear it is argued that our emotional response to the excess of terror is best understood by drawing upon the ontological terms of potentiality and actualization that were introduced in the investigation of the ontology of terror. Furthermore, we will see that boredom is an often overlooked but crucially important emotion with regard to terror.
2. The political cosmology of terror deals with the political world in the time of the war on terror. This means that it takes up the discussion of the nature of war. Especially interesting in this regard is the theory of the generations of warfare that has been developed by American historian of war William Lind (e.g. in Lind et al. 1989, 1994; Lind 2001). What we can learn from the study of the history of warfare is a lesson about the ways in which space and time is transformed by the ways in which we conduct wars. We will see that there is a crucial difference between the ways in which terrorism and state militaries operate in, and indeed construct, space and time. And we will learn that this difference is again best understood by drawing upon the ontological distinction between potentiality and actualization.
3. Finally, the political theology of terror takes up the study of political sovereignty in societies that see terrorism as a crucial threat to public

safety and order. It takes up a debate about the rule of law and the state of exception that has been going on among legal scholars with great intensity since the 9/11 attack and the legal and political responses that followed in its wake (see, e.g. Scheppele 2004; Vermeule 2005, 2009; Gross & Ní Aoláin 2006; Scheuerman 2006a,b). A central figure in this regard is the aforementioned Carl Schmitt, who first coined the term 'political theology'. The political theology of terror does not deal with the religious notion of God, but exclusively with the political 'God', the sovereign who Schmitt defined in a famous way. 'Sovereign is he who decides on the exception' (Schmitt 2007b: 13). Since many of the debates about the state of the law in the time of terror relates to the question of what kind of exceptional legal measures (if any) can be legitimately used in combating the threat from terrorism, it should be no surprise that these Schmittian ideas have been a central part of recent legal debates. The argument I present is (again) that it is by introducing the concepts of potentiality and actualization that we will be able to get to the bottom of what is going on in these discussions.

This very brief way of presenting what will follow in the pages below is meant first of all to illustrate the scope of the argument and the method of making it. What I will be doing is to construct a philosophical system of utmost antiquated fashion. I will attempt to complete the move from prolegomena to systematic whole. But in doing so I will not simply proceed by way of general a priori principles and ideas, instead I will take the concrete political reality that we are facing in the time of terror and try to extract the metaphysics already at work in it. This is a precarious manoeuvre indeed. But it is the manoeuvre of last philosophy, which to my mind is the only one available to a philosophy which seeks to strive for systematicity, while at the same time insisting upon an engaged interpretation of the times, we live in.

The critique of ideology and the critique of metaphysics

This kind of philosophical project is far from innocent. Indeed, it could well be argued to be atrocious. Given the political character of the phenomenon of terror, there seems to be an obvious problem in addressing it in the language of metaphysics. From a certain political perspective, it would be claimed that such idle speculation could get in the way of the very real political action that (at least according to that perspective) needs to be taken to stop the threat of terrorism. But from a rather different point of view, metaphysics is not only problematic in virtue of its functioning as idle speculation. Indeed, was it not the lesson of the post-structuralist theory of the latter part of the twentieth century that metaphysics as such is one of the greatest political evils conceivable? Here the core problem of metaphysics is found in its tendency towards essentialism, and essentialism in turn is equated with the political power discourse of the dominating societal position – generally that of wealthy white Western heterosexual males.

According to such a critique, what is needed is not a new metaphysics of terror, but a critique of the ideology of terror, that is, the ideology that tells us that terror is the most crucial problem facing our societies, and that we accordingly should spare no costs, be it in terms of economy, justice or human life, to fight the threat from terrorism. As much as I sympathize with the ambition of providing a critique of the ideology of terror, it will be argued that such a critique of ideology is hopelessly lost, if it does not also engage in a metaphysics of terror – only this metaphysics of terror should be understood exclusively as *last* philosophy, never as *first*. This is a point which becomes all the more pertinent as the academic studies on terrorism recently have seen the emergence of its very own specific area of formalized critique of ideology – complete with professed agenda and an international academic journal.[6] The development of this field of research stems from a deep dissatisfaction with more traditional forms of terrorism research, which, according to the critical agenda, lack theoretical refinement and more than anything a critical reflection on the role played by research on terrorism in public discourse on the theme. Thus, typical objects of interest to this new field of research will be the articulation of crucial societal concepts in relation to the notion of terrorism, that is, how does the usage of the concept of 'terrorism' influence the use of concepts like Muslim, Jew, Western, woman, man, democracy, war, freedom, French, etc.?

Faced with such an agenda it is easy to see the problem one could have with a metaphysical study, such as the present one. Would not metaphysics simply result in the reification of the ideological structures that the critique of ideology is trying to combat? The answer to this problem is found in the specific approach that is undertaken here. The crucial point about the present project of metaphysics as last philosophy is that there can be no such metaphysics without a critique of metaphysics. The suggestion I should like to make in the rest of the introduction is that the right way of positing the relation between metaphysics and the critique of metaphysics can be found by following the road from Kant to Hegel to Schelling. Each of these classic German thinkers conceived of a new way of conducting metaphysics by founding it in a critique of metaphysics. *A metaphysical thought, thus goes the wager of the present investigations, which incorporates its own radical critique of metaphysics in the manner we can learn from Kant, Hegel and Schelling, provides some invaluable and to a great extent forgotten resources in dealing with the problems of political thought that confront us at the outset of the twenty-first century.*

This way of doing metaphysics through the guidance of a radical critique of metaphysics does not only serve to reformulate the metaphysical agenda. It can hopefully also help revitalize the critical one. The problem inherent in the ideology-critical approach to the study of terror is that such an agenda tends to adopt an epistemological stance towards the ideology of terror. A typical way of studying the problems listed above would consist of a discourse-analytical study of the ways in which the concept of terrorism is constructed in public discourse. Do we generally tend to associate terrorism with certain religious ideas or racial profiles? Do we generally construct an image of terrorists as enemies of war, as criminals or as diseases that are to be exterminated? What one would typically aim to do is, in so many words, to investigate a certain field of discourse and unmask the ideology at work therein, the critical ambition being contained in the hope that once the ideological constructs are revealed as such, they will lose their power.

The poverty of this hope has been most adequately rendered by Slavoj Žižek in his early work *The Sublime Object of Ideology* (Žižek 1989), where he, inspired by Peter Sloterdijk's *Critique of Cynical Reason* (Sloterdijk 1983), describes the working of current ideology as a particular form of cynicism. What is encountered in cynicism is the paradox that even though the postmodern self-narrators know very well that their practices are based on an ideological construct, they nevertheless keep on doing what they do. Ideology incorporates its own unmasking. We already know that our political and social practices entail and to a great extend foster global inequality, oppression of women, racism, ecological catastrophes, and so on, but we still keep on acting as if we did not know. If the classic Marxist formula for ideology was 'they don't know it, but they do it', then the new cynical form of ideology would be captured in the idea that 'they know very well what they are doing, but still, they are doing it' (Žižek 1989: 28–9).[7] In the current investigations this can be translated into the claim that we know very well that there are problems inherent in the way we relate to terror. We know very well that we are in a sense wildly overreacting, when we are dealing with terror, for example, in the form of public panic, wars of aggression and laws of exception, but nevertheless we continue doing what we do, as if we did not. For this reason it does not suffice to show that fear of terrorism is irrational or that it, so to speak, is founded in nothing at all, because the problem regarding terror is precisely that this nothingness works.

With this in mind, the thing which metaphysical reflection in the tradition from Kant, Hegel and especially Schelling has to offer to the critical agenda is a set of conceptual tools which can help describe *how* nothingness itself functions. The present investigations cannot give room to a full discussion of the philosophical programmes of these German thinkers, but what can be done is to spell out how the relation between metaphysics and a radical critique of metaphysics at stake in them provides the adequate background for our theoretical approach. In the end we will see that we will find the theoretical resources needed for these investigations in the unfinished philosophical project that Schelling undertook in the years following his most famous work *Philosophical Investigations into the Essence of Human Freedom and the Things that Relate to It* (hereafter the *Essay on Freedom*).

Kantian critique and the Hegelian critique of Kant

It was a crucial insight of Kant's critical philosophy that any attempts at theoretically determining the essence of the whole – and in line with that any attempt at tackling the problems of metaphysical psychology, cosmology or theology – would overstep the boundaries for what can legitimately be known by human reason. This is a fundamental point about the notion of metaphysics at stake here. One cannot know the essence of the world. Likewise one cannot know whether God exists, or whether human beings have an eternal soul. For anyone who accepts the Kantian arguments regarding metaphysics, it is an impossible endeavour to ask and answer a metaphysical question, in the same way as one would ask any other question, for example, 'Do terrorists predominantly rely upon religious or political arguments in their attempts to justify their actions?', or 'Do certain very restrictive laws introduced to combat terrorism generally become permanent after the perceived threat has disappeared, even though they have been introduced as exceptional and or temporary measures?'

This point is accepted by all the thinkers discussed here, and it is a point which will not be affected in the least by the proceedings that follow below. The crucial thing is, however, that this does not mean that the metaphysical questions stop making sense to us, or simply lose their meaning. Quite to the contrary, it is one of Kant's most famous ideas about human reason 'that in one species of its knowledge it is burdened by questions [i.e. metaphysical ones] which, as prescribed by the very nature of reason itself, it is not able to ignore, but which, as transcending all its powers, it is also not able to answer' (Kant, CPR, Avii). What is interesting to us given this predicament is how one undertakes an investigation into such questions, without ending up in a position where one simply makes no sense at all.

Here the Kantian solution would be to insist on the primacy of practical reason and argue that even though we cannot know the whole, and even though we cannot answer the metaphysical questions, we can still make sense of moral action through recourse to the notion that we should act *as if* these questions could be given positive answers. Indeed, one of the great discoveries of Kantian philosophy is the point that exactly because we cannot give any definitive theoretical answer to the classical metaphysical questions, therefore, and only because of that, can we have a truly practical relation to them.

Hegel in particular was sceptical of the epistemological foundation of the Kantian critique. While Hegel would agree with Kant that a limit has to be posited, and that the kind of philosophy, which simply assumes that it can in some way deduct, infer or gain access to the whole, is doomed to fail, he is nevertheless sceptical of the notion that the limit should be posited within the realm of knowledge. For Hegel it is wrong to say that it is because of our limited *knowledge* that we cannot gain access to the whole as a whole. Rather, it is because being itself is structured in such a way that there is something lacking in the whole itself.

A famous argument can tell us why: The setting of a limit, the drawing of a line, does in itself entail and postulate knowledge about what is to be found at both sides of the line. In other words there is a hidden contradiction in the Kantian setting of final limits within the realm of knowledge, because setting a limit between what we can know and what we cannot know, necessarily entails *some form* of knowledge about what is at both sides of that limit; in other words we both know and do not know what lies beyond the limits of our knowledge, once we draw such a definitive line of demarcation. Marcus Gabriel has put this idea to the point arguing that 'if the in-itself is inaccessible then it would not even be inaccessible' (Gabriel & Žižek 2009: 36). The Hegelian conclusion to the argument, and as such the crucial result of the *Phenomenology of Spirit*, would be that whatever is posited as the in-itself, it can only be in-itself as an in-itself-for-us. Whatever reality may turn out to be it cannot be the case that there is a part of reality, which is constitutively hidden from human reason. But the 'philosophical price' that is paid for this access to the in-itself is that 'in-itself' must be the name for a negativity. We can know the in-itself, but the in-itself that can be known is itself a lack.

While this Hegelian phenomenological argument establishes that there cannot be a part of reality which is constitutively hidden from human reason, this argument meant that the conception of reality itself was crucially altered. Instead of the Kantian split within the realm of knowledge, between noumenon and phenomenon (Kant, CPR, A 238/B 298) we get an ontological split in being itself. There is no part of the whole that is hidden from reason, but the whole itself is broken, split and does not fit itself. Being is the name for the lack at the core of the whole.

At this point we find agreement in the philosophies of Schelling and Hegel. Both of them retain the ambition that philosophy should strive towards the whole, but they also take the Kantian critique into account together with the Hegelian point regarding this critique. Thus it is the case for both of them that the whole cannot be a complete, finalized and closed system; as such the whole is not in sync with itself. Following this line of thought we can also determine the precise difference between the two. It lies in the interpretation of the founding negativity. In Hegel we find that focus is being put on the notion that the very failure of the system, to be and incorporate the whole, is what illuminates being and makes it accessible to systematic reasoning. In Schelling on the other hand we find that focus is placed on the notion that the failure of the system remains a failure; to Schelling, Hegelian illumination is never complete. There remains a certain indivisible remainder of negativity, which continues to haunt and threaten the systematic whole. This slight but crucial difference will become much clearer once we have taken a closer look at each of these philosophical systems.

Hegel's system

In *The Science of Logic* Hegel completes the move away from Kant's epistemologically founded thought and instead goes directly to the ontological consideration of the notion of being. As should be evident by now, Hegel does not simply posit a new formula for being, in the sense of giving a definitive articulation of what being is. Instead, his first move of the *Logic* consists in showing that being is nothingness. The argument takes the form of assuming that being could be considered to be being. That would seem to be a tautological assumption, but as Hegel will show it is exactly in the nature of the concept of being that it is incoherent; it defies tautology. If being is *merely* being, then it should be clear that nothing can be said about it to determine what being is, other than that it is being. In that case the concept of being is the emptiest concept conceivable; it is the concept of *emptiness as such*, because as soon as one adds content to it, saying what it is, or what it is the being of, one would fill something into that emptiness, and that something would be an extra determination, it would be something more than simply being. In other words, if we reflect stringently upon the notion of being, we necessarily end up with the conclusion that the disavowed background of being is that it is pure nothingness (Hegel, Werke V, 82–3).

From this first move Hegel goes on to consider notions of becoming, existence, finitude, infinity, quantity, quality and measure, but with each move he shows how the proposed concept cannot provide a stable foundation for being. The point of the first part of the *Science of Logic* (The Doctrine of Being) is thus to show the incoherence of being. It shows that whatever one should choose as a basic concept to determine being, one will always end up revealing an inner incoherence, which necessitates a step beyond the boundaries of that concept. The second part of *The Science of Logic* (The Doctrine of Essence) takes the step beyond merely showing *that* being as such is incoherent. It takes it upon itself to investigate *how* the incoherence at the heart of being works. (This way of reading the *Logic* with the focus on *The Doctrine of Essence* and especially the chapters on the logic of reflection is of course greatly inspired by Dieter Henrich's ground-breaking work, see e.g. Henrich, 1971: 104–5.)

Hegel accordingly begins the Doctrine of Essence with the claim that 'Being is Illusion' (Hegel, Werke VI, 19), but the point is not simply to say that the notion of being is false. The illusion of being that has been revealed in the Doctrine of Being goes beyond merely 'not being true'. The illusion of being works somehow. Illusion does something; it is effectuating something. The German term for illusion is 'Schein', which can also have the meaning of that which lightens or perhaps even illuminates. This is a crucial point of the Hegelian Doctrine of Essence. While it has been revealed that 'Being is illusion', it is also the case that 'The truth of being is essence' (Hegel, Werke VI, 13).

Being as such is illusion, but there is truth in being nonetheless. This truth, which is called essence, is not, however, a stable substance always hiding behind the scene of the illusory play of appearance. Rather, the truth of being is found in the very illusory work that lies at its core: 'Essence is its own illusioning in itself' (Hegel, Werke VI, 23).

Essence is not something behind appearances, but instead it is the very working of the incoherence at the heart of being. In other words if we go looking for the essence of the world, we end up finding mere negativity, nothingness, illusion, but *that itself* is exactly the working of essence, which in the end structures the logic that makes the whole accessible as a system. In this way illusion *reflects* something. As Hegel argues: 'The illusioning of essence in itself is reflection' (Hegel, Werke VI, 17). This means that the structuring that takes place around the empty core of being is not only illuminating. It has a certain structure. A structure which Hegel then sets out to unfold in the various forms of reflection: positing reflection (Hegel, Werke VI, 25ff.), external reflection (Hegel, Werke VI, 28ff.) and determining reflection (Hegel, Werke VI, 32ff.). And this structure is in turn something which can be known by human reason. The point is therefore that exactly *because* there is no transcendent principle that is ordering the world, *for this very reason* it is possible for us to give meaning and structure to it. Only this meaning and structure is, because it is founded on pure nothingness, itself incoherent. There is no final fact about the whole or the world or God or the soul. There merely is the structuring that takes place around the emptiness at the core of the whole.

Where Kantian philosophy still bears with it the notion of a thing-in-itself behind the appearances, about which we can never assume to know anything, the specific move of Hegel consists in saying that there is nothing 'out there' behind appearances except for the very negativity we discover once we embark on the road to uncover it. One could say that precisely because there is nothing out there, therefore there is precisely a nothingness to be found. There is no part of the whole which is constitutively hidden from philosophy, but the whole itself is broken, flawed, contradictory and does not fit itself.

These Hegelian reflections should give us some crucial pointers with regard to the way we should conduct our last philosophical investigations. Last philosophy should not look for the stable concepts of being. The task is not to find the coordinates of orientation through which the rest of the world can be mapped. Instead, what should interest us are the curious moments of emptiness. What we should be looking for, as we conduct our investigation of the ways in which society reacts to terror, is not specific beings, general ideas or clear concepts which continue to guide our practices, but rather enigmas, gaps and the concrete ways in which they appear. What we should be looking for in the metaphysics of terror is nothingness at work. It is in this sense that we should understand the metaphysics of terror as 'Much Ado about Nothing'.

This point brings us quite some way towards answering the challenges mentioned above that our last philosophical investigations face. As we recall, two problems were foreseen. On the one hand there was the problem that metaphysics traditionally has been viewed as *the* ideological discourse par excellence. The claim of the present investigations is that this problem is avoided by making metaphysics the study of being as lack, rather than of being as foundation. Precisely by understanding being as the name for the gap in the whole, one can argue that there can be no such thing as an ultimate order of beings. There can be no metaphysical closure of the world, but there must be a metaphysics of the lack of a closure.

On the other hand we foresaw a problem inherent in an epistemological program for the critique of ideology. The danger to this program was argued to be that simply unmasking the ideology of terror can prove to be utterly impotent, since this ideology already includes its own unmasking. The problem with the ideology of terror is not only that many of the concepts, through which we organize our collective political imaginary, are empty constructs. If that were the problem all that would be needed would be an analysis which could prove that they are indeed empty. The problem is rather that they work precisely *because* they are empty constructs. While the Hegelian insight into the notion of being may not provide an easy way of dissolving the ideology surrounding the concept of terror – in the end this may be impossible – it can at the very least help us gain a better understanding of the way that ideology works, precisely because it offers a systematic logic which is centred in a nothingness which works.

This idea of a nothingness which works is certainly as much a Schellingian idea as it is Hegelian, and I will argue that there are a few crucial points which ennoble the Schellingian approach. Still, while I therefore, in the investigations that follow, will refer to the idea of a working nothingness as a Schellingian idea, it should be kept in mind that this all-important idea is as much Hegelian as it is Schellingian. Even though Hegel and Schelling certainly had their philosophical differences, they did see eye to eye on some of the most essential issues.

Schelling

Let us turn our eyes towards Schelling's dialectics. Since Schelling did change position throughout his career, it is important to note the stage we are focusing on. That will be the stage which is announced with the ground-breaking assertion from the *Essay on Freedom* that 'Willing is primordial being' (Schelling, SW VII, 350). It is with this essay and the subsequent philosophy of the *Ages of the World* that Schelling develops a philosophy of potentiality and actualization, and of lack and excess, which is best suited for our purposes here.

The argument in the *Essay on Freedom* is driven by a conceptual distinction that is as radical as the notion that willing is primordial being: The distinction between ground and existence (Schelling, SW VII, 357). This is the distinction between that which is, the essence in so far as it is full concrete existence, and the ground of that which is, the essence in so far as it is not yet full concrete existence. This relation between existence and ground is somewhat paradoxical. Existence is the whole, one could say. There *is* nothing more than existence. But still there is ground and ground is not existence. Ground is the nothing which is not existence. Or to be precise: it is 'Longing' for existence (Schelling, SW VII, 359). Ground is the 'not quite there' which is not something additional with regard to the whole, but it is nonetheless the 'thing' which means that the whole, in so far as it is the truth, cannot simply be the whole.[8]

The distinction between ground and existence can be said to be a distinction between that which is, on the one hand, and what it was, before it came into being. In this way it mirrors the Aristotelian distinction between potentiality and actualization. Ground is precisely merely potential existence, whereas only existence itself is actual existence. This Aristotelian tendency in the philosophy of later Schelling has been given a powerful examination in Thomas Buchheim's *Eins von Allen* (Buchheim 1992). Buchheim's basic point is that Schelling is an Aristotelian at this point in his philosophical development, which to my mind is going too far,[9] but it is an important point that the Schellingian notion of ground does have some similarity with the Aristotelian notion of potentiality; in so far as it is conceptualized as longing for existence, it is precisely also that which *could become* existence (Schelling, SW VII, 359). Yet as we will come to see below (ultimately in the political ontology of terror) the Schellingian idea of potentiality does contain some very radical differences from the Aristotelian one.

The importance of the notion of potentiality is further accentuated when we turn our eyes to the *Ages of the World*, where Schelling reintroduces the *potenz-lehre* that played a crucial role in his earlier philosophies of nature and identity. The notion of potency at work in the potenz-lehre is from the start helpfully ambivalent in the sense that it on the one hand designates the potential, in the Aristotelian sense of a possible actualization, while it on the other hand designates something which is potent, in the sense of a force in its own right. In the *Ages of the World*, the potenz-lehre gains a further twist as it is formed against the background of the distinction between ground and existence and the notion that willing is primordial being that were introduced in the *Essay on Freedom*.

The dialectic of the 'potenz-lehre' in the *Ages of the World* is best described as consisting of three stages or *potencies*, with a primordial 'non-stage' preceding the entire dialectic. The primordial 'non-state' of being is described as *indifference* by Schelling. This state is pure blandness and inactivity. It is the 'will that does not will anything'. In order for anything determinate to arise out of this prior state of pure inactivity, Schelling argues that there must first be what he calls a contraction. This is the will that actively wills nothingness. The first potency as something other than pure indifference is pure destruction. Only as a consequence of the will that actively wills nothingness, is it conceivable that there could be a will to will something. The will to will something is the second stage of the Schellingian dialectic. His technical term of this second will is expansion. But where the will that wills nothing is pure wanton destruction, the expansive will is pure excess. From the maddening destructive anger of the first will, we get a pure counteraction in the form of excessive love, desire and expression. Finally, Schelling argues that one can conceive of a third stage where the two potencies of contraction and expansion keep each other in check. This is a stage of stability, or what Schelling in the *Ages of the World* refers to as spirit.

In the terms of the *Essay on Freedom* this third potency corresponds to existence. Both of the first two potencies on the other hand are formations of the ground. The ground as longing is precisely that which pulls itself towards excessive expansion and love for existence, while at the same time constantly being pulled back by contraction. In this sense the ground is both too much and too little for it to be able to fully be. In the words of Slavoj Žižek ground is like a wild animal caught in a noose. It is constantly trying to break free, but the more it tries to break out of the trap the tighter becomes the noose (Žižek 1996: 23). In more Schellingian terms, where the existence of God is constantly at stake in the dialectic, the two first potencies should be understood as the labour God must go through in order to give birth to himself (!). It is crucial, however, to note that the third potency consists of the very same principles as the former two potencies. Existence is not essentially different from ground. It merely distinguishes itself from ground by the organization of the principles of contraction and expansion. In ground these two are at the same time too much and too little, whereas in existence they find their proper balance.

Wolfgang Hogrebe uses a very striking analogy to describe this dialectic. Think of a film reel in the cinema. In order for it to be possible to follow the storyline in a movie, the film reel must be spun at a certain pace. If it is spun too fast the viewers can only perceive a blurred mix of colours; if it is spun too slow, they only get a static image. To Schelling, being exhibits very similar qualities. It can be in synch, as it is the case when we see around 24 images per second at the movies, but it can also spin excessively out of control, and it can be protracted into a standstill (Hogrebe 1989: 100).

Schelling's three potencies should thus be seen as his way of trying to conceptualize the odd situation we find ourselves in, once we accept the Hegelian argument against Kant, and draw the conclusion that being as such is the name of inconsistency and incoherence; it is an attempt to make sense of ontology after we transpose the Kantian epistemological split into an ontological one, and conclude that being does not fit itself and that the whole is broken and incomplete. The point is that if being in this way is incoherent, it must at least be the case that we can say something about this incoherence. It can be both excessive and lacking, but sometimes it can also be in synch – coherence in being is something that can emerge in the midst of incoherence.

The concept of potency also serves quite nicely to distinguish between Schelling and Hegel. We have already seen the importance of the Aristotelian categories of potentiality and actualization for how Schelling understands ground and existence. The point where Schelling most clearly distinguishes himself from Aristotle is the point where the merely potential is considered to have a reality of its own. Ground, that is, potential existence, is precisely not actualized existence, but it is nonetheless real. There is longing in being, and this longing has a reality, which is of a different kind than the "normal" actuality of ordinary beings. Again this difference between Schelling and Aristotle will be covered in more detail below, but what is interesting here is that the point that separates Schelling from Aristotle also separates him from Hegel. The Hegelian stance towards such a notion of potentiality as real potentiality, would be to argue that it only amounts to an empty abstraction (Hegel, Werke VI, 202ff.),[10] at least in so far as the notion of potentiality intervenes in logical development.[11] In Schelling this intervention is precisely accentuated: the longing in potency carries with it a force that constantly threatens to pull existence of its rails so to speak.

These considerations leave us with a generic conclusion about the relation of the thought of Schelling and Hegel. Both Schelling and Hegel locate in the concept of being that which means that the world as such is out of synch with itself. But the ways in which they come to a conclusion regarding this incoherence are strikingly different. Hegel's focus is always on the ways in which this crucial lack breaks up, functions, develops and in the end *successfully* makes something happen in concrete. Schelling's focus on the other hand seems to be more turned towards the possible *failures* that can arise from the fact that being is out of synch. For Hegel the Schellingian position with its emphasis on the (un)ground and on contraction would amount to the 'dark night of knowledge, in which all cows are black' (Hegel, Werke III, 22). Conversely the Schellingian would counter against Hegel that one sees equally little where everything is illuminated, as one does where everything is dark. In order to see things clearly, we need contrasts (Schelling, AotW, 51).

In the present investigations these considerations of ground, being, reflection, potency, etc. are not merely introduced in order to discuss fundamental philosophical issues. They are introduced to help us diagnose the metaphysics of terror. Given this focus on a phenomenon, which is interpreted as an exemplary way in which being remains out of synch, it seems natural that we should take the Schellingian approach. Doing so enables us to take a decisive step towards constructing the theoretical framework that governs our investigations. It has been said above, that the knowledge we can have about the whole and about the lack at its centre, must be of a different sort than the kind of knowledge, we can have of for instance the motivations behind certain terrorist act, or of the workings of the various penal codes in function around the globe. Given the crucial Schellingian point that the lack and the excess are *potencies*, we can say that the knowledge we are constructing over the present investigations will be knowledge of the kind of objects that are subsumable to this curious ontological notion. The objects of our investigation are the potencies that arise around the lacking centre of the whole of our current situation. These potencies can themselves be either excessive or lacking, and the way they work will have to be investigated accordingly. This kind of investigation is what I propose as a scientific metaphysics, as an investigation of our own time captured in thoughts, in the form of last philosophy. That we are focussing on potencies could in a certain Hegelian light mean that we are dealing merely with abstractions. In the Schellingian approach these are nevertheless abstractions that have a very real and concrete way of functioning.

In this way we are on track to answering the task that was set above for these preliminary manoeuvres. In Schelling's notions of potentiality-as-excess and potentiality-as-lack we have the initial form of the conceptual tools that are necessary for the science of the metaphysics of our time to take flight. At the present stage of the investigations they have not yet been fully developed. In a certain sense that is absolutely necessary, because the metaphysical concepts used here can only be legitimate if they are developed while taking the concrete reality in which they are to be used into account. This is what it means that metaphysics should be understood as *last philosophy* rather than *first*. Schelling's dialectic can thus be said to provide an overall theoretical framework within which our concrete analyses can be conducted. It does not determine a priori the structures of being that emerge, but it does give us a set of conceptual tools, with which we can carry out our investigations.

What I hope to have shown so far is that this kind of investigation accommodates the demand one should put on any science of metaphysics worthy of the name. It is founded in a fundamental critique of metaphysics, invented by Kant, and further developed by Hegel. It sets out from a set of ontological notions that take the critique of metaphysics and ontology into account. And it insists that there can be no ontology of the one (thing that explains everything else), but only of the split-into-two: Identity is only identity as the identity of identity and difference.

Hegel and Schelling on philosophy of history

Before we go on to directly investigate how the concepts of excess and lack of potentiality and actualization are at work in our time of the war on terror, we need to have some kind of understanding of how the Schellingian conceptual apparatus relates to history. Therefore, the final point of focus in this introduction should be on the different ways in which Hegel and Schelling each conceive of a philosophy of history and of the relation of history and ontology. The best way of expose these questions consist in taking up their separate understandings of philosophical theology. One of Hegel's most striking descriptions of the ontological logic that he unfolds in the *Science of Logic*, goes as follows: 'One can therefore express it in the way that this content [of the *Science of Logic*] is the presentation of God, such as he is in his eternal essence, before the creation of nature and a finite spirit' (Hegel, Werke V, 44).

What Hegel introduces here is not merely a conflation of ontology and theology, but rather and most crucially a distinction between God's being and his action, that is, creation.[12] This would be the more precise way of rendering the problem, than to simply say that we are dealing with a conflation of ontology and theology, which arguably is a necessary consequence of the approach in the present investigations, where we set out from a political ontology (Chapter 1) and end in a political theology (Chapter 4). Still, the conflation of theology and ontology is not uncontroversial, and deserves to be discussed. Indeed, it makes for an easy target for the protagonists of the metaphysics of finitude. The prime example here would be Heidegger with his striking critique of the history of metaphysics – that it would always end up as some form of onto-theo-logy. This history begins with Aristotle's *Metaphysics*, which Heidegger would praise for its formulation of the ontological question in book Γ (Aristotle 1003a), and on the other hand scorn for finding the answer to the question in the highest being – the unmoved mover – in book Λ (Aristotle 1071b). To Heidegger this highest being need not be identified with any particular God in order for metaphysics to be justly characterized as onto-theo-logy, it is merely the very resolution of the question of being in a singular being, that accounts for the onto-theo-logical. The argument against Heidegger's usage of this critique of philosophers such as Hegel and Schelling, for example, when he accuses Hegel of defining 'the highest being as the absolute in the sense of unconditioned subjectivity' (Heidegger 1969: 60), would consist in showing that neither Hegel nor Schelling identifies a particular determinate being which should function as the ultimate ground of being. Quite the contrary in fact: both of them conceptualize being as a concept of fundamental lack. Understanding the above quote from Hegel in the light of the distinction between God's action and God's being, rather than simply as a conflation of the science of being and the science of God, enables us to interpret it along these lines. What is at stake in the question of the relation between God's being and God's action is the relation of the lack to the workings of the lack. With Schelling and Hegel and against Heidegger it is possible to establish a metaphysical critique of the metaphysics of finitude, by showing how this lack in being allows for no security in the realm of finitude. To use Zupančič's formulation: 'Not only are we not infinite, we are not even finite' (Zupančič 2008a: 53).

In the Hegelian way of interpreting the relation of God's being and God's action, it is possible to examine being in full, outside of and prior to any understanding of action. This is exactly the task of *The Science of Logic*. In Schelling, on the other hand, we find that being is exactly not determinable outside of action. God's own being is at risk, so to speak, in his action. This means that there is a kind of dynamic available to Schelling's thought which is not available to Hegel. For Hegel ontology itself cannot be subjected to historical development, at least not in the same way as it can for Schelling.

As we remember from the famous quote above, Hegel perceives his logic to be the expression of the mind of God before he entertains the process of creation. This process of creation could then be said to be what Hegel describes in the philosophies of nature (Hegel, Werke IX) and spirit (Hegel, Werke X), where the ontological principles expounded in the logic find their application. To speak in classic Hegelese, Logic is God's being in-itself, Nature is God's being for-itself and Spirit is God's being in-and-for-itself.[13] But the crucial point is that nothing of what happens in the two later parts of the system, that is, nothing of what happens over the course of creation, can have an effect back upon the ontology as it was conceived in the Logic; whatever the for-itself or the in-and-for-itself may turn out to be, they do not retroactively influence the in-itself considered as it was merely in itself.

This does not mean that the new cannot happen at all in Hegelian thinking. History is certainly an open process. But it does mean that there is a limit to the depth at which the new can happen. It is quite possible to imagine with Hegel that something new could happen in history which would fundamentally change the rules through which *history* is understood or for how it further develops. But it is impossible to imagine that something new could happen in history, which would fundamentally change the rules of *ontological* development. The mind of God before creation is not changed by what happens over the course of creation. Therefore, the *ways* in which there may occur changes to the basic rules of historical development, are not in the end subject to historical change. The logic of reasoning and the reasoning of logic go through their development, indeed they *are* their own development, but this development is entirely their own. It is not influenced by historical development. There is communality between reason and history in the philosophy of Hegel, but in the end this communality favours reason.

According to this we can understand Hegel's philosophy of history as one of recuperation. History may take its course in whatever direction it sees fit, but at the end of the day reason will be waiting and it will be able to see what has happened. This means that we can now add another famous quote to Hegelian point that 'philosophy is its own time captured in thoughts' (Hegel, Werke VII, 26), namely: 'The owl of Minerva does not take flight until twilight sets in' (Hegel, Werke VII, 28). The Hegelian philosopher is always placed after the fact. He is a post-festum sage.[14] He occupies the position of reason from which he is able to see the development that led up to his own position.

This is all quite different in Schelling. In Hegel history is subjected to reason. With Schelling in the *Ages of the World*, we find quite a different and novel idea, namely that reason is required itself to be temporal or even historical. One should be precise here. The point is exactly not simply that philosophy or logic or science should be able to account for temporal developments; for this to be possible one does not need to undertake a Schellingian position. Instead, the Schellingian point would be that the very *form*, of the philosophy which attempts to understand history and time, must itself be temporal. As he puts it in the very first sentences of each of the drafts of the *Ages of the World*, 'The past is known, the present is cognized [erkannt], the future is sensed. The known is told, the cognized is presented, the sensed is prophesised'[15] (Schelling, AotW, 3, 111; SW VIII, 199). The point is that if science is ever going to be able to understand either past, present or future, then it must itself adopt the temporal movements undertaken by history as it undergoes the changes from past, to present, to future. Philosophical thinking should take shape in accordance with the time it is thinking.

In Hegel's system, God's action is subsumed to his being. In Schelling's *Ages of the World* we find that God's action, his freedom, conditions his being. However, this freedom is not yet, as it would be the case in the late philosophy of mythology and revelation, a freedom to decide freely whether he should create or not. Instead, God's freedom to create, which conditions his being is itself involuntary. At the heart of the abyss of Schelling's thinking in the *Weltalter*-period, we precisely find this curious notion of *involuntary freedom*. As we recall the first potency, that is, the first step in creation, is a pure destructive willing of nothingness. God discovers himself in the midst of creating havoc so to speak. And only as a reaction against this disruptive will is it possible for him to initiate the real work of creation. He himself lags behind in the process of creation. God's creation of the world is at the same time his own desperate attempt at coming to terms with himself as existence. The task which God has to accomplish in this process is first of all to separate himself from his own past. He has to make a cut once and for all between past and present, and again between present and future. When Schelling thus speaks of the *Ages of the World* the point is precisely to conceive of time as divided into *times* in this way. The division between past, present and future is therefore not a simple division of time as it is experienced by human beings, according to Schelling. Instead it is the world and the absolute itself, which is divided into times (Schelling, AotW, 182).

This means that to Schelling history is not simply a long row of events that run their course from one moment to the next, nor is it a completely cyclical. Rather it is the case that there can be breaks in time. One time, one moment in the history of time, can come to a completion, and another can begin. The past ends and the present begins. Schelling describes this break as a *second* creation (Schelling, AotW, 246). In Schelling's philosophy the job of creation cannot be completed in one act, because the being of God itself undergoes change over the course of this act. The breaks that happen over the course of creation are precisely the breaks in history. In a certain sense therefore Schelling's philosophical interpretation of the genesis of God does prefigure what Alain Badiou would later come to term the Event.

That being said there are of course many crucial differences between Badiou's and Schelling's separate ways of the Event. Badiou conceptualizes his notion of the Event against the background of a mathematical ontology, whereas Schelling takes the infinitely more obscure route of conceptualizing the madness of God before creation. However, this difference between the two is surprisingly less striking once we consider that Badiou introduces the notion of God in relation to the paradoxes of set theory. Cantor, to whom Badiou refers in constructing the set theoretical foundation of ontology, precisely associates the absolute and the inconsistent. He terms the multiplicities that emerge upon reflection of for instance Russell's paradox 'absolutely infinite multiplicities' or simply 'inconsistent' (Badiou 2005: 41). What lies at bottom of the mathematical ontology that Badiou unfolds is in so many words the inconsistency of the absolute, which seems to be an idea that lies very close to the Schellingian notion of the ground in God.

Having introduced in the present context the notion of an Event in this Schellingian/Badiouian sense, there is a very common notion that should immediately be dismissed – namely the idea that 9/11 stands for something radically new in our recent history. This can certainly be doubted. As we will come to see, for all the talk about how the world would never be the same again after those events (with a minor 'e'), 9/11 precisely does not count as a rupture or an Event in any deeper sense. But even if the time of terror is a time with a clear absence of Events this does not make it any less important to investigate it with regard to the potentiality for the emergence of Events. Investigating in this way the temporal movements of a time in which nothing definitive is happening, in which History so to speak is in intermission, precisely lends itself to the Schellingian perspective. What we should be doing is to investigate our own time with an eye for the ways in which ground, in the sense of the longing inability to form something definitive, is operative in it. We should be thinking our own time in terms of its excesses and lacks.

The crucial question concerning the philosophy which tries to follow the movement of time in its very thinking, and which in doing so attempts to account for the ruptures in being, is: what position does philosophy take in relation to these ruptures? The Hegelian position here is the one of having the rupture in the past.[16] No matter how history develops, the development of history being as contingent as it may, the Hegelian philosopher will always be able to understand what has happened, after the events of the day have taken place, exactly because of his positioning as a post-festum sage. The security God has in his being, above and beyond his action, mirrors the security the philosopher has in the cunning of reason. No matter how history develops, it may go poorly, it may go well, it may be that time forever will remain out of joint, philosophical reason will always be able to capture it in thoughts, exactly because philosophical reason is the reason of unjointedness as such. To Schelling, this means that Hegel is a philosopher of the past. This in turn means that he will have a hard time conceptualizing the transformation from past to present *as it takes place*.

In Schelling's own philosophy, on the other hand, the idea that the being of God is in some way exposed to the act of God himself, and the subsequent need for a notion of a second creation, exactly goes to say that it is a much more precarious manoeuvre to position ourselves in relation to a historical event, as if it were truly past us. Instead, the Schellingian philosophy tries to tackle the historical event in its becoming, or to be more precise: in its potency. Therefore the Schellingian philosopher is in danger of being captured between the past and the present.[17] He will always be hard pressed to say that the time and history he investigates is truly past him, because the moment he perceives them to be past, will be the moment he risks turning their potencies into actualities.

The divergent stances of Hegel and Schelling towards the notion of the potentiality gain a lot of clarity in this regard. Exactly because of Hegel's positioning as a post-festum sage, his view to potentiality is for better or worse determined by his capacity to see what became of the potential that was. From the point of view where the potential has become actual, the consideration of the potentialities that *were* does indeed seem very abstract. Conversely, because Schelling positions himself with the historical development as it takes place, therefore the potential becomes much more important in its state of being potential. Schelling's philosophy is a philosophy that tries to grasp potentiality without being able to determine which actualities should come of it, that is, in their curious ontological status of being real merely as potentialities.

This of course has crucial bearings upon the possible ways in which the present investigations will be structured. Given that we are we are studying the metaphysics of terror as a way of composing a philosophy as its own time captured in thoughts, we must ask ourselves the crucial question of how we position ourselves in relation to this time. Are we allowed to say today that the time of terror is effectively in the past? Or must we instead take the stance from where we say that we simply do not know yet? At the risk of making an all too abrupt short-circuit: If the first creation of the time of terror was the events of 9/11, does the election of Obama, or perhaps the financial crisis, or the climate crisis, then count as second creation, which, in Schellingian terms, would place the time of terror effectively in the past? The most prudent answer to this question 'we cannot really say yet' immediately places the present investigations in the Schellingian position.

This Schellingian position also draws an important line of distinction between philosophy and other forms of academic research on terrorism. Most standard ways of doing academic research, be it with statistical, discourse-theoretical, juridical or other methods, will be exclusively focused upon the past. While Hegelian dialectics is of course very different from statistics, they nevertheless share this point of view to reality. It is first and foremost investigated as past. This should not be taken to mean that statistical, or other types of evidence, are systematically banned from these considerations. It should, however, be taken to mean that the conclusions we are arriving at here will be much different from the conclusions that can be made using statistics. They are in a sense much more urgent.

So what does it mean to think with time in its movement from past to present instead of thinking about a time that has already passed? One could say that it means to ask the question: how does our own time think in us? And that precisely is the question of last philosophy.

We should therefore in our conduct of last philosophy take care to distinguish clearly between our methodological position and our historical position.

Last philosophy does not necessarily mean a philosophical investigation of the things that have already happened – of the things that are past us. It only means that philosophical reflection is a reflection upon logics that are already at work in history, but that does not at all necessitate that what is reflected upon belongs exclusively to the past – it might just as well be contemporary or belong to the future.

To take an example that will interest us below. The events of 9/11 are in a certain sense past us. In a chronological order they happened some ten years ago as I write. But we can also discuss whether 9/11 is truly past us in the sense that it no longer bears any meaning for us. In this sense we could argue that it is certainly still a part of our present, and perhaps even still our future. Are we still in a time where the consciousness of potential terrorist attacks is dominating our political reality? Are we in a situation where the future of political action is still determined by the exceptional logics of the time of terror? The movements that make 9/11 dominate our current political thought, as well as those that might make it a thing of the past, are the questions that we are after here. To write the metaphysics of terror means in this sense to ask in what way terror can still be said to think in us.

Given this perspective on the last philosophical investigation of the metaphysics of terror, one might question the very notion of systematic philosophy that is nevertheless being pursued here. Indeed, if it can be argued against a Hegelian perspective that the ontological foundation of the system makes impossible the kind of ontological openness that is necessary for it to be possible to investigate the how our own time, that is, the time of terror, is thinking in us, then how can we defend beginning our investigations with an ontology, and following it up with a subsequent psychology, cosmology and theology? After all that is a structure which more than anything seems to mirror what has just been criticized in Hegel.

The answer is that each of the four parts themselves has to be investigated in a somewhat precarious last philosophical manoeuvre, where the system of potentiality and potency has to be developed from scratch in each case. It is thus precisely not simply the case that the ontological insights that will be gained in the chapter on ontology below should simply be applied or handed on to the subsequent chapters on psychology, cosmology and theology. Rather, each of these chapters has to prove their own point in a specific last philosophical manoeuvre. This is indeed the only way in which it can be shown that there is an ontology of terror that is thinking in us, and furthermore that there is a psychology, a cosmology and a theology of terror that thinks in us in a similar fashion. The wager of these investigations, which puts them together in a systematic whole, is then that there will be certain elements to these logics which will reveal a form of conceptual communality. As we will see it is a certain notion of potentiality which turns out to be at work throughout the system.

Outline of the following investigations

That being said we can outline the task ahead. In the following we are to conduct an investigation of the metaphysics of our time, by putting focus on one specific political phenomenon which can rightly be said to dominate these times: terror. The specific method for these investigations consists in a metaphysical study in the form of last philosophy, which goes to say that we will start out by studying research on terror and the relevant phenomena surrounding it, that is, the notion of terror itself, the politics of fear, the history of war and the relation between sovereignty and law. The strategy we must follow in taking up these different fields should not, however, consist in a search for the governing principles, or the ground on which such scientific conduct rests. Instead, we should be looking for the enigmas and paradoxes which, thus goes the wager of the investigations, organize the conduct within those practices, often behind the backs of their practitioners. That does not mean that the aim of our research is to reveal the emptiness at the core of certain ways of understanding the phenomenon of terrorism. It is instead to investigate how such emptiness works. To this end the introduction has worked to develop a Schellingian dialectic which will serve as the theoretical frame that will guide our efforts. What we will be looking for in the investigation of the metaphysics of terror are the potentialities and potencies of the nothingness at the heart of our relating to terrorism.

Conducting this kind of research can in the end be said to serve two distinct purposes. On one hand we can further our understanding of ourselves and the politics of the times in which we live. By investigating the work of nothingness in our responses to terrorism, we can learn something crucial about our own time and our political reality. On the other hand the very metaphysical nature of the investigations we are undertaking can hopefully show that metaphysics is a field of scientific inquiry which is not only possible, but desperately needed.

Part One

Metaphysica Generalis

1

The Political Ontology of Terror

Uneventful terrorism

Let us begin by considering something that must come across as an ana-
chronism: Two rather unspectacular incidents of Indian terrorism from the
mid-1980s. To be specific we will take a look at the hijackings of Indian Airlines
Flight IC 405 on 5th July 1984, and Indian Airlines Flight IC 421 on the 24th of
August the same year. What is particular about these hijackings is the curious
fact that nothing really ever happened. Both were as uneventful as one could
possibly imagine, given the circumstances of hijacking an airliner in mid-air.
In the terms of Ashis Nandy, who has provided a rigorous interpretation of the
events, they display in all its peculiarity the 'The Discreet Charms of Indian
Terrorism' (Nandy 1995: chapter 1).

Both of the hijackings took place in the time between the attack on the
Golden Temple of Amritsar on 3–6 June 1984 and the assassination of Prime
Minister Indira Ghandi (who ordered the attack) on 31st October 1984 by her
Sikh bodyguards. The assassination resulted in very bloody retaliations: a 'large-
scale slaughter of Sikhs at Delhi, virtually organized by the ruling party under
the patronage of the Indian state' (Nandy 1995: 19). The point is of course that
these hijackings took place at a very specific point in time in a very specific
political situation, and that everything might have been completely different, if
they had happened a year later. Still, the point that I will take from them remains
the same; what Nandy's analysis calls out is the curious relation terrorism has
to language and discourse – his interest is the curious relation between being a
terrorist and being named a terrorist.

Nandy describes how the initial media reports from the incident on Indian
Airlines Flight IC 405 were dominated among others by journalist Ajay Bose,
who was on the plane as a passenger. According to Nandy, it seems as if Bose, at
the outset, believed himself to be reporting from a war zone, but soon thereafter

ambivalence would set in. Bose described how the terrorists beat up an army officer and left him bleeding with a fractured hand. However: 'The major himself later gave a less dramatic version of the event. He did not mention his fracture but said that the leader of the hijackers gave him a bandage and some cotton to tie over his swollen right hand' (Nandy 1995: 3). In all the stories told by the victims Nandy finds similar ambivalence. 'At night, the hijackers took over from the airhostesses and served the passengers. Next morning, the airhostesses were back at work' (Nandy 1995: 4). But, 'at 10 a.m. the following day, the hijackers threw a bombshell and announced that they had finally decided to blow up the plane in five minutes. "You can all say your last prayers now" ' (Nandy 1995: 5).

As it turned out it did not come to that fatal conclusion, and after some tense moments the hostages were all released.

> Young journalist Ajay Bose, who had earlier assumed the tone of a war correspondent, was by now thoroughly perplexed. He had to locate his experience beyond the range of normality and sanity. 'Suddenly passengers and hijackers were in each others' arms, crying like children as the tension of the past twenty hours visibly melted away. It was a crazy scene I shall not forget. Passengers who were hijacked, humiliated and beaten up by these nine desperadoes were actually jostling with each other to get the hijackers' autographs on the back of their air tickets. [. . .] The fearsome Sikh with an axe ran round hugging passengers while Pinkha Singh made it a point to shake hands individually with everyone in the cabin and the fifteen-year-old boy hijacker just sat down on the floor and cried his heart out'. (Nandy 1995: 6)

The same major, the victim of the assault described by Bose, later pointed out 'that he thought the hijackers only carried toy pistols, that the only deadly weapon they seemed to have was the pick axe picked up from the plane itself' (Nandy 1995: 7). If we follow the account given by Nandy, the hijackers aboard Indian Airlines Flight IC 405 would seem to be anything but dangerous assassins ruthlessly working towards a well-determined goal. Indeed, they were better described as boys, who simply did not know what they were doing, but who nonetheless made sure to mind their manners.

The editorials and analyses that emerged in Indian media after the events were in stark contrast to the ambivalent stories told by the people at the scene: 'Already however the press, especially the editorial writers and political analysts, were building up the hijacking as the act of a group of well-trained, well-armed, merciless commandos let loose on Indian soil by enemy countries and traitors, taking advantage of the poor security at Indian airports' (Nandy 1995: 7). In this narrative it mattered very little what had actually taken place. As soon as the idea of terrorism entered into media circulation, a rather predictable spectacle ensued.

Nandy's account of the hijacking of Indian Airlines flight IC 421 on 24th August follows the same pattern. In general the events that took place on the ground and in air precisely revealed the 'Discreet Charms of Indian Terrorism'. Just like in the earlier hijacking the terrorists took great care to ensure the comfort of the passengers and the crew. For instance they made sure to release hostages who were taken ill. 'All the passengers later spoke well of their captors. Mrs Singh claimed that the hijackers were "mild mannered and did not harm any passenger", and that six of them had behaved "very well", especially with children' (Nandy 1995: 11). It even came to joint singing!

> As the night at Lahore airport became a long-drawn-out one and the passengers got increasingly tense and bored, a young hijacker, the one called Kissie, began to sing melancholy love songs from the Hindi films. The songs included old favourites like '*Ham chod cale hai mehfil ko, yad aye kabhi to mat rona*' and '*Mile na phul to kanton se dosti kar li*'. Kissie also sang a classical *tappa*. Though it was past 1 a.m., the passengers pressed Kissie to sing more. A colleague of his also joined in with a political number, '*Bhindranwale sanch sipahi*'. (Nandy 1995: 12)

Just as in the former case, the media reports were quick to adopt the security angle. The dominant trend of interpretation in the newspapers studied by Nandy was the scandal of the weak security of airports, airlines and ultimately government, and the dangerous, bloodthirsty nature of the terrorists. 'At least one newspaper – predictably the *Indian Express* – advised the government to resign' (Nandy 1995: 15).

Nandy's interest in terrorism is first and foremost fuelled by a general interest in culture and politics – especially of the kind which he encounters in South Asia. He concludes that the terrorist incidents reveal a schism within Indian culture, politics and public life in general that is to be expected from having to live with a 'modern nation-state in a traditional, post-colonial society'. Nandy explains: 'In such a society, the westernized middle classes see themselves as guardians or custodians, trying desperately to protect the rest of the society – seen as inefficient, anarchic and irrational – through a hard-boiled law-and-order approach and the technology of the state, which is viewed as the major instrument of modern rationality' (Nandy 1995: 23–4). The division which Nandy is therefore diagnosing is one particular to the experience of Indian society, where two dialects, languages or narratives seem to be in conflict with each other. 'I have tried to show that the data I have marshalled can be cast in either of the two languages I have identified – the universal language of the modern nation-state, which shapes so much of the available theories of terrorism, and the vernacular in which the majority of those in the hijacked IC 405 and IC 421 spoke' (Nandy 1995: 23). Nandy sees it as his task to help create space for the second of the languages, the minor language which easily becomes discredited by the power-discourse of modern science and the modern state, in which the signifier's terror and terrorism fit all too well.

The crucial point which Nandy thereby establishes for us is the essential relation between terrorism and language. His argument is that the signifier 'terrorism' fits perfectly within a specific form of discourse. That is the 'universal language of the modern nation-state'; the language of rationality, science, and in particular of security. Whenever a terrorist attack occurs there are certain things, which simply must occur, it would seem. There will be a lot of discussion about how one should defend society, and there will be a plethora of condemnations.[1] Politicians and other public figures will stand in front of a camera and say things like 'This is a repulsive act of terror, which calls for unconditional condemnation from all sides' (Thomsen 2008).[2] There have of course been plenty of scholars to argue, as does Nandy, that this language is far from it a genuinely universal one. It is often argued that the language of terror serves those who, as politicians or entrepreneurs or others, are in the business of selling security (see, e.g. Herman & O'Sullivan 1989; Hughes 2007). While it can certainly be argued that a lot more terror-security is being sold, than what seems to be called for in terms of actual terrorist threats, the argument I will be making, once we get to a more in depth discussion of the language of 'terror' below, goes in a different direction. The problem with many of the investigations that are being made into the construction of the threat from terrorism or into the politics of fear in general, is that they make an, to my mind unfounded, assumption about the language in which this threat is being constructed; this assumption is in all its simplicity that language *works* – indeed this is an assumption which Nandy to a certain extent shared with the rationalistic language of the modern nation-state he abhors. What I will be arguing against this idea is that 'terror' and 'terrorism' are signifiers around which language stops working properly. As pointed out in the introduction

I will be arguing for the idea that 'terror' is meaningfulness-as-excess. This will be the focus of my argument once we go deeper into the discussion of the language of terror, but for now we should concentrate on the different ways in which academic work on terror approach the phenomenon.

Following Nandy's argument, the many condemnations of terrorism and the repeated statements that 'one must never negotiate with terrorists' would be adequately termed a (postmodern) rite, which as we have learned from Emile Durkheim not only serves to bind men and Gods together, but primordially to produce the Gods and to keep them alive (Durkheim 1981: 467). In the ritual condemnations that follow upon terrorist incidents we are not producing gods but rather terrorist. It is not through his actions that a terrorist becomes a terrorist. Instead it is in the very condemnation of something as 'terrorism' that it becomes terrorism. A specific branch of security studies, namely the so-called Copenhagen School, takes the crucial idea here as its basic premise: Security is a political issue that is always in the need of articulation is some language. 'There is not any brute fact of the matter which constitutes a security issue', would be one way of putting the crucial claim of the work of researchers such as Ole Wæver, Barry Buzan and Jaap de Wilde (see, e.g. Wæver 1995; Buzan et al. 1998). Instead, the thing which ultimately determines what is a security issue and what is not, is its being named as such. Being able to name something a security issue therefore constitutes a very powerful item of language, which can serve as a tool in political discursive struggles in a range of sectors that go widely beyond the traditional security sectors of police and military (Buzan et al. 1998: 196).

It is quite easy to find scholars who are fundamentally opposed to the Copenhagen School and Nandy and other kinds of constructivists. Such a line of thought is already present in Nandy's analysis in the shape of what he calls the rational discourse of the modern nation-state. In this discourse terrorism is seen as a genuine threat to security. Such an understanding of terrorism that denies that articulation has a crucial role to play in constructing the terrorist has its own theoretical agenda within terrorism studies. Indeed, by all accounts this is the mainstream approach. Here central figures are Jessica Stern, Walter Laqueur, Bruce Hoffman, David Rapoport, Paul Wilkinson and Alex Schmid.[3] These authors share many things, but crucial in comparison with scholars like Nandy or the Copenhagen School is that they take some notion of terror or terrorism at face value. The idea is that there really are terrorists out there seeking to terrorize us, and that it is the terrorists, their motives, their means, their methods and so on that should be the object of study within terrorism research. Scholars who take on this latter approach I will term *classical* scholars of terrorism. The former agenda pursued by people like Nandy I will call *critical* studies on terrorism.

These issues of language, articulation, realism, constructivism, etc. are of course underpinned by the political dimension of the term terrorism. Calling someone a terrorist is not simply to give him a name like any other. It is also to condemn him. As such it plays a crucial political role. Indeed, as Nandy's argument seeks to show, naming someone a terrorist can help reorganize the entire field within which that articulation takes place. In this regard, it should be no surprise that the central figures of classical terrorism studies have a rather strong political bias in their selection of subjects. In general these scholars will focus upon the perceived terrorist enemies of the West, as has been documented quite convincingly by scholars like Edna Reid and Edward Herman and Gerry O'Sullivan (Herman & O'Sullivan 1989; Reid 1993, 1997; Reid & Chen 2007). Conversely, critical scholars will often be just as critical of the policies of the West as they will be critical of their more classically oriented counterparts within terrorism research.

Nandy is writing long before 9/11 in the middle of the nineties about events that took place even further back in the middle of the eighties. Taking this fact into account we will often be met with two opposing yet strangely similar views. On the one hand we will be met by the realists of today, who will be arguing that a new kind of terrorism has become evident with the 9/11 attacks, which has ushered in a new world order and which requires a new form of response. On the other hand we will be met with the constructivists of today, according to whom 9/11 has meant the initiation of a new kind of discourse about terrorism, which has helped construct a view of the world, which in turn has resulted in grave political changes across the globe. In both cases I think it would be worthwhile to take a deflationist approach to the idea that 9/11 stands for something radically new. The very idea that 9/11 should have ushered in a new threat to Western political hegemony is probably misconceived, not so much because terrorism is not capable of achieving immense political results,[4] but rather because Islamic terrorism had been around for quite some time before 2001. Indeed, it was not even the first attack against the World Trade Center by Islamic terrorists – the towers had been attacked by Islamic terrorists using a car bomb already in 1993. In this light there is certainly more merit to the constructivist argument that it was the reactions to 9/11 across the globe that created a new situation. But this second argument is itself often overestimating the novelty of our situation. While the Bush/Cheney administration arguably was extreme in its antiterrorist policies, those policies were not out of the ordinary in comparison to the policies that have been pursued by Western states the last 30–40 years. The Bush National Security Strategy of 2002 (in)famously announced that the United States would undertake pre-emptive attacks, when it saw the need (Bush 2002), but the idea of acting pre-emptively against foreign terrorists had already been accepted by the Clinton administration (Dershowitz 2006: 157, 320). In 1988 the Thatcher-led Tory government in Great Britain introduced what Phil Rees calls 'one of the most serious restrictions on freedom of expression since the Second World War. Without a debate in Parliament, the Home Secretary announced that supporters of militant groups would be banned from speaking on television or radio' (Rees 2005: 194). Finally, as Wilkinson notes in his *Inquiry into Legislation against Terrorism* counterterrorism legislation in Italy was already quite severe in 1975. 'Perhaps most surprising to foreign observers, the time limit of preventive detention without trial was increased to ten years!' (Wilkinson 1996: 75). In general, there has been a long tradition for the use of heavy-handed measures in the struggle against terrorism.

It can thus be argued that regardless whether one accepts the realist or the constructivist argument for the novelty of our situation post-9/11, it would probably be more correct to say that certain structures became evident with 9/11, but that these structures had long been in place by the time of 9/11 itself. Still, that does not take anything away from the essentially political character of terrorism and its name. Nor does it take anything away from the point that research on terrorism is and has been deeply enmeshed with the politics of terrorism and counterterrorism.

One of the more comical connections between the academic research on terrorism and Western governments is found in what is often cited to be *the* place to start when one embarks on the road to study terrorism: *Political Terrorism* written by Alex Schmid and Albert Jongman. In this work the authors collected 109 different definitions of terrorism from various government and academic sources in the effort to make one that is as generally acceptable as possible. From what they term an *academic* source they cite the following definition 'Terrorism is the deliberate and systematic murder, maiming, and menacing of the innocent to inspire fear for political ends' (Schmid & Jongman 1988: 36). In itself an interesting definition because of the almost forced ideological intent – 'murder, maiming, and menacing' of the 'innocent' – but the real interest is the scholar, who coined it. It is none other than Benjamin Netanyahu, who was the Israeli Ambassador to the United States at the time of the publication of the book. Since then, Netanyahu has become much better known, as he has twice been the Prime Minister of Israel: from 1996 to 1999, and from 2009 to the present day (writing on 26 January 2012). Anecdotal as it may be, the fact that Netanyahu is cited as an academic source is surely evidence that research on terrorism is not politically innocent. Indeed, no matter how one chooses to speak about terrorism it seems impossible to avoid severe political implications.

Let us summarize the points that have been made so far. The things that the small-scale events retold by Nandy should make us aware of, are the necessary linkage between terrorism and language about terrorism and the conflictual political undercurrent to this link. We have furthermore seen how these connections and conflicts can be found at work in scholarly and journalistic work on terrorism. This puts us in a situation where we are in need of the right set of theoretical tools with which we can make sense of this entire field. It is in this regard that I suggest that we should take a look at the notion of potentiality. The reason for choosing that particular concept will be clearer once we have taken a closer look at the certain ideas that have been flourishing within terrorism research.

Terrorism and potentiality

Taking Nandy as our starting point of course places us in a very specific position, which should come as no surprise to the reader. It should already be clear that the present work has a much greater affinity with the critical agenda than the classical one, but as we will see, I have plenty of criticism in store for the constructivists and especially the anti-metaphysical tendencies of this approach.

It would not be hard to imagine a counterargument to Nandy's article following a more security-minded line of thought – a counterargument which is of great importance. Security-minded academics, politicians and people in general will be quick to point out that terrible things *could have happened* in a hijacking situation such as the ones described by Nandy. Indeed, given that 9/11 revealed just what can happen when planes are hijacked, one could easily find someone arguing that the very possibility for those kinds of amateur hijackings, as uneventful as they may have been, is enough for us to have a need for more security. Such a line of thought is in no way coincidental. Indeed, it reveals the necessity of the concept of *potentiality* for our understanding of terrorism. Terrorism is basically about potentiality. It is, however, important that we take our time to investigate in greater detail how this notion of potentiality is at work in certain forms of academic work on terrorism. Here the notion of *new terrorism* plays an important role.

The notion of new terrorism was an idea which was discussed in great detail in the second half of the 1990s within classical studies on terrorism. Two crucial features of the idea should concern us. With the idea of new terrorism it was first of all believed that the dominant form of motivation for committing terror was moving from a political to a religious register. Second of all there was the idea that religious terrorists might be able to get their hands on weapons of mass destruction (WMDs). These two features meant that the new kind of terrorism which was envisaged had a particularly destructive outlook, cataclysmic even. The fall of the Soviet Union was believed to potentially open up a black market for the trade of the most deadly of weapons and substances, and because of the religious motivations of the terrorists, it was argued that these groups would be less inclined to be stopped by moral or strategic impediments that could have prevented politically engaged terrorists from utilizing such deadly weapons. In their *The New Face of Terrorism: Threats from Weapons of Mass Destruction* Nadine Gurr and Benjamin Cole wrote about these new terrorists that 'they have no constituency apart from themselves, and neither are they in a bargaining relationship with the authorities, because they want nothing more than the destruction of existing society' (Gurr & Cole 2000: 143) (see also Hoffman 2006: 82–130).[5]

Regarding such a notion of new terrorism it is important to keep the political background of the 1990s in mind. This was a world in which the most significant threat to the security of the United States and its allies, namely the Soviet Union, had only recently disappeared from the map. This meant that the security industry, the intelligence community and others who were making their living keeping everyone safe, were faced with a fundamental problem. After the fall of the Berlin Wall, a lot of people started to think that it might not be necessary to continue spending on military defence and security in the same way as one had done during the Cold War. In a way this meant that the lack of a genuine threat to security could be perceived as the most dangerous threat of all. In *America's Achilles' Heel. Nuclear, Biological, and Chemical Terrorism, and Covert Attack* Falkenrath et al. (1998) precisely describe the eroding of national defences due to waning support from politicians and the general public as one of the greatest security threats at the time of their writing. As they say, even if the FBI and the CIA had been submitted to great criticism before the fall of the

Berlin Wall 'the environment of the Cold War meant that the *raison d'être* of the intelligence community was never seriously questioned. With the passing of the Soviet threat, however, the critiques of U.S. intelligence [had] become more fundamental' (Falkenrath et al. 1998: 283). In other words, regardless of its empirical merits the very notion of a new form of terrorism, with potentially catastrophic consequences, was bound to have been a very welcome one in the security industry, the military industry and the intelligence community. That being said we should briefly take a look at these empirical merits – at least in so far as it is possible here.

The work by Gurr and Cole, mentioned above, is interesting for several reasons. The first edition of the book was published in 2000. A second edition with added Introduction and Epilogue dealing with 9/11 was published in 2002. In other words the book provides some way of gauging the idea of new terrorism as it was conceived before the events of 9/11. In this regard, the book includes an appendix which is a 'Database of Chemical, Biological, and Nuclear, Terrorist Incidents'. The database is of course out of date, but precisely because of this, it will give us some kind of idea of what the world looked like to those researchers who argued for the notion that there was a new kind of terrorism about. Finally, the work makes for an interesting case study in the literature on new terrorism because it is, in the words of Paul Wilkinson 'Calm, measured in tone, fair and balanced in its assessment of NBC terrorism [terrorism using nuclear, biological or chemical weapons]' (Wilkinson on the cover of Gurr & Cole 2000). Wilkinson is right to call *The New Face of Terrorism* fair and balanced. The authors carefully avoid the kind of alarmist predictions of unavoidable catastrophes, which are found in some parts of the literature. Exactly because of the balanced tone of their argument, however, the predicament of the theory of new terrorism can be brought to light by looking at their work. This is the predicament of being wed to an argumentative structure, which in itself – no matter how fair and balanced the assessments of the individual researchers are – plays on notions of the *potential* catastrophe.

The defining historical moment for the theory of new terrorism was the Sarin gas attack carried out by the cult Aum Shinrikyo in the Tokyo subway in March 1995.[6] Before this incident, the world had seen very little in terms of NBC terrorism. Still, the Gurr-Cole database lists no less than 192 incidents involving NBC weapons. There is a sense in which this number itself serves to produce an argument about the seriousness of the NBC terrorist threat; 192 incidents are certainly 192 too many. The producing of this kind of database does in other words serve to indicate both the seriousness of the issue, and the seriousness with which Gurr and Cole are treating it. Yet as they say in the preface, 'The following database is a list of not only the most notable and successful terrorist incidents, but also includes unsuccessful attempts to acquire NBC, attempted use of such agents; threats to use NBC-weapons without any evidence of actual capabilities; threats of use involving actual possession of NBC agents; hoaxes; and near incidents' (Gurr & Cole 2000: 267). Having stated that much, it slowly becomes clear how they arrive at the number 192. On their account, what makes a NBC terrorist incident is quite wide indeed. Nevertheless, if one goes through the database it quickly becomes clear that they should have added some more reservations to the above list. The database includes a fair amount of empty allegations and random speculation. By going through the database one will find 67 cases that consisted of nothing but allegations, 'may-have-beens' and 'it-has-been-said-thats'. Some of the more outrageous are '1980: In 1980 there was an allegation that Hezbollah had tried to acquire CBW. This has not been confirmed' (That is the entire entry) (Gurr & Cole 2000: 279). Or the more comical: '1995: There was a reported use of tear gas against government troops, by the Tamil Tigers in Sri Lanka' (Also the entire entry) (Gurr & Cole 2000: 287). If we are counting the usages of *tear gas* as an incident of NBC terrorism, then the number of incidents where states are guilty of NBC terrorism would go through the roof. Most of the other incidents (apart from these 67 that are entirely hypothetical) consist of empty threats, hoaxes, people who have been accused of NBC terrorism but not convicted and so on. In total the database include 16 cases that involve actual harm to human beings. Of these seven involve deaths. Three of those are attributed to the Aum Shinrikyo sect (two being their famous attacks in Tokyo and Matsumoto using Sarin gas, and another being the murder of a lawyer using poison) (Gurr & Cole 2000: 287–90). One reports the death of eight government troops in Thailand due to poisoning by the Khmer Rouge (Gurr & Cole 2000: 286). One reports the murder of single individuals by the use of Sarin gas in Chile (Gurr & Cole 2000: 288–9). One involves the death of 19 police recruits in the Philippines in 1987 'in what military officials *believed could have been* a mass poisoning by communist rebels, Muslim separatists, or one of several insurgent terrorist groups on the island of Mindanao' (Gurr & Cole 2000: 291, my italics). Not only do Gurr and Cole here cite something 'that could have been' as a NBC-incident, but they cite what *others believe* 'could have been'. Finally one entry involves the death of 911 cult members in the mass suicide/murder at the hands of Californian cult leader Reverend Jim Jones on

18th November in Guyana (Gurr & Cole 2000: 294). Nine hundred and eleven dead is surely a lot, but would at least be highly debatable if this incident should be classified as terrorism rather than, for example, cultist mass murder.

Two things can be deduced from these points. 1. The attack by Aum Shinrikyo was extremely important for the idea that there was a new kind of terrorism forming. 2. Apart from the attack by Aum Shinrikyo the notion of new terrorism is mostly built upon speculation about that which *could* happen. I will discuss each of these points in turn.

A point that is often made about the Aum Shinrikyo attack is that it in some way involved dispelling a taboo, or overstepping a moral boundary (Brackett 1996: 5ff.; Hoffman 1999: 17–18; Gurr & Cole 2000: 26; Wilkinson 2001: 180). In other words, once such an attack had occurred it seemed more likely to happen again, because other groups would be less inclined to accept moral prohibitions against the use of the deadliest of weapons, now that they had been used by others before. Such a claim can be linked to the notion that terrorist attacks are getting increasingly lethal (Gurr & Cole 2000: 22–3), that the proportion of terrorist groups that are religious in their motivational core is increasing (Hoffman 2006: 86), that terrorists show a tendency towards greater indiscrimination in selection of targets (Wilkinson 1990). All these points put together seems to argue in favour of the notion that the Aum Shinrikyo attack of 1995 in some way inaugurated a new era of terrorism, where clandestine agents might carry out terrorist attacks of apocalyptic proportions.

Nevertheless, there are also very prominent facts about the Aum Shinrikyo sect, which point in the opposite direction. First of all, it was extremely well funded. Hoffman asserts that its assets exceeded $1 billion (Hoffman 2006: 123). Others put the number higher than that (Choy 2002). The cult ran an enormous operation, counting in its own estimate 65,000 members in several countries, as it was at its peak in 1995. Apart from Japan, the cult had a particularly strong base in Russia, where it owned Radio and TV stations (Choy 2002). Second of all, the members of the cult were very highly educated as the cult aggressively targeted universities for recruitment (Gurr & Cole 2000: 51; Choy 2002). In other words it had more than an adequate number of engineers, chemists, biologists and physicists, and all the necessary funding and equipment to produce or otherwise acquire and put to use the most destructive of NBC weapons. It even had a small factory that was to produce up to 2 tonnes of Sarin gas a day (Gurr & Cole 2000: 51).

The Aum Shinrikyo sect could thus be described as by far the most capable terrorist organization the world has yet seen, and still they only managed somewhat minor attacks using NBC weapons (with a combined total of 19 casualties (Gurr

& Cole 2000: 287–90)). Compared to the death toll of 9/11 (around 3,000 (Gurr & Cole 2000: ix)), which was conducted using conventional weapons (albeit in a very innovative way) the damage caused by this very wealthy and very capable terrorist organization using NBC weapons must be said to be unimpressive. In other words: while the attack by Aum Shinrikyo in the Tokyo underground has been said to inaugurate a new era of terrorism that might have cataclysmic consequences, the attack and the circumstances to it, are at the very least open to an interpretation which highlights how extremely unlikely such terrorist attacks really are.

It is interesting to notice in relation to this how terrorism research has developed in the years following 9/11. As Andrew Silke shows in a survey of all the articles in the two main journals of classical terrorism studies (*Terrorism and Political Violence* and *Studies of Conflict and Terrorism*), the proportion of research on NBC or WMD terrorism has more than doubled when one compares post-9/11 research to pre-9/11 research (Silke 2007: 87). The key point, however, is that 9/11 precisely proved how conventional terrorism can be far more destructive than NBC terrorism has ever been. Here, I think, it becomes quite evident just how important the notion of potentiality is for our understanding of terrorism. What does set NBC terrorism apart from conventional terrorism is the idea that the *potential* effects of NBC terrorism are much greater than the potential effects of conventional terrorism. Conventional terrorism has a much lower ceiling than does NBC terrorism. It would seem that it precisely is this potential which leads the interest of research in terrorism rather than any notion of likelihood or actuality.

Furthermore, it is interesting to note that the infatuation with the potentially cataclysmic forms of terrorism predates the weapons we see as WMDs today. During the time where all terrorism was called anarchist, that is, at the dawn of the twentieth century, there was a widespread fear of terrorists using the WMD of that time: dynamite. In 'The International Campaign Against Anarchist Terrorism, 1880–1930' Richard Bach Jensen argues that, in the eyes of the people of that time, dynamite possessed catastrophic possibilities that are eerily similar to the way we tend to think of nuclear, biological or chemical weapons today (Jensen 2009: 104). One Spanish periodical in 1908 described dynamite as follows:

> Its irresistible force, its formidable power. It seems that the spirit of Shiva, the god of destruction, eternal destroyer of life, resides in the depths of its strange composition. All the great phenomena of Nature resemble it in their effects: . . . it creates and it destroys, it annihilates and it gives life; it is chained Prometheus and angry Jupiter; it illuminates and darkens. From civilization's necessity, it becomes its chastiser . . . it has changed into a social anathema, into the dissident sects' weapon of terrorism. (quoted in Jensen 2004: 116–17)

Furthermore, just as the terrorists of 9/11 had much more success with box cutters and airplanes, than Aum Shinrikyo ever had with WMDs, so too did the anarchists of the nineteenth century fare much better with the dagger and the rifle than they ever did with dynamite (Jensen 2004, 2009: 104). Interest in the potentially most catastrophic, but in actuality least deadly scenarios regarding terrorism is far from anything new, it would seem. Indeed, it is as old as modern terrorism itself.

At this point it should be clear in what sense metaphysics is sneaking in through the back door in even the most rational and tempered accounts of terrorism. No matter how we view terrorism, the notion of potentiality seems to be crucial for our relating to it. We continually return to the potential dangers of terrorism instead of looking at the actual threats that are around.

Now, the point of drawing attention to this fact is not simply a call to restore some kind of idealized realism or rationalism about the subject matter at hand, but rather to insist that potentiality itself is the crucial issue. Potentiality is a notion of very traditional metaphysics. It has been discussed again and again by philosophers such as Aristotle, Leibniz, Kant, Hegel and Schelling among others. Still, the mere fact that traditional metaphysics in this way is at work in our way of relating to terrorism is not all that I seek to prove here. The truly interesting point is the question of what kind of potentiality we find to be at work in our collective understanding of terrorism. In order to answer this question we will be well advised to take a look at the politics of terrorism as it was conducted in the years following 9/11 – the politics of potentiality.

Politics of potentiality

As the United States was gearing up to go to war in Iraq, as the UN weapons inspectors in Iraq found no evidence that the regime was hiding WMDs, and as the greater part of the rest of the world was looking on in disbelief, Defence Secretary Donald Rumsfeld of the Bush administration gave an argument which has since then become legendary:

> Reports that say that something hasn't happened are always interesting to me, because as we know, there are known knowns; there are things we know we know. We also know there are known unknowns; that is to say we know there are some things we do not know. But there are also unknown unknowns – the ones we don't know we don't know. And if one looks throughout the history of

our country and other free countries, it is the latter category that tend to be the difficult ones. (Rumsfeld 2002a)

The idea behind the argument is quite obvious. To Rumsfeld there were certain things that we knew that we knew about Saddam Hussein's regime and their WMDs. We knew for instance that we knew that the regime at one point had an extensive chemical weapons programme and that it had made use of those weapons (Stern 1999: 106–17). Furthermore, we knew that we did not know what had happened to all the weapons that used to be in the possession of Saddam Hussein. But neither of these two forms of knowing were the interesting ones according to Rumsfeld. The crucial problems rather were the unknown unknowns, the things we did not even know that we did not know anything about. It could for instance be the case that Hussein had had secret weapon programmes, about which we had never had the slightest idea and about which we therefore did not know that we did not know anything about. It could be that he had bought weapons from the black market; it could be that he had produced weapons in secrecy; it could be that he had devised completely new ways of hiding them. Indeed, as far as the realm of the unknown unknown is concerned just about anything could be the case. In this way a key argument for going to war in Iraq was an argument of pure potentiality.

A parallel notion was formulated by Vice President Dick Cheney in the so-called One Percent Doctrine according to which 'If there's a 1% chance that Pakistani scientists are helping al-Qaeda build or develop a nuclear weapon, we have to treat it as a certainty in terms of our response. It's not about our analysis ... It's about our response' (Suskind 2006). Cheney's point was that the probability of future occurrences of the catastrophic sort is entirely irrelevant; their mere *possibility*, no matter how small, is all that should concern an administration which acts upon them. Not likelihood, but potentiality is the driving force.

These and other similar comments by Cheney and Rumsfeld were not simply rhetoric. Indeed, they indicated a specific strategy which was outlined in the now infamous National Security Strategy (NSS-2002) doctrine laid out by President Bush in 2002 (Bush 2002) and they served as a crucial part of the argument for the war in Iraq, as is evident from a reading of the Congressional authorization for the use of force in Iraq:

> Whereas Iraq continues to aid and harbor other international terrorist organizations, including organizations that threaten the lives and safety of United States citizens;

Whereas the attacks on the United States of September 11, 2001, underscored the gravity of the threat posed by the acquisition of weapons of mass destruction by international terrorist organizations;

Whereas Iraq's demonstrated capability and willingness to use weapons of mass destruction, the risk that the current Iraqi regime will either employ those weapons to launch a surprise attack against the United States or its Armed Forces or provide them to international terrorists who would do so, and the extreme magnitude of harm that would result to the United States and its citizens from such an attack, combine to justify action by the United States to defend itself. (Pub. L. No. 107–243, 116 Stat. 1498., Preamble)

The crucial point here is that the 9/11 attacks precisely did not show, in any way, how devastating a terrorist attack using a WMD can be, they rather showed just how devastating a terrorist attack using conventional means can be – that is, of course, unless one allows oneself to speculate on the *potential* devastation that might occur if terrorists like the 9/11 ones succeeded in smuggling a dirty bomb or a nuclear device. And indeed, since we did not know all about what went on in Iraq in terms of WMDs, since we did not even know what it was that we had no knowledge about, this speculation on potential consequences could play a crucial role in the legitimization of the attack on Iraq. It is the politics of this notion of potentiality, which we must now look into in greater detail.

The focal point of the NSS-2002 is a notion of pre-emptive action. Deterrence, it claims, is an ineffective defence against rogue states and terrorists alike (Bush 2002: 15). That the NSS-2002 envisages a world in which deterrence is ineffective does not mean however that it was the first time that a US president had considered pre-emptive action. Pre-emptive action had already been entertained and authorized by President Clinton, as he fired missiles at targets in Sudan and Afghanistan in August 1998 (Dershowitz 2006: 157). Furthermore, the allies of the United States, most notably Israel has on several occasions pre-emptive attacks – most famously in the case of the bombing of the Iraqi nuclear reactor in 1981 (Dershowitz 2006: 96). Still, there is something quite different at stake with the NSS-2002 and the subsequent war in Iraq. If not for anything else because of the sheer scope of the operation and because of the immense controversy involved. This controversy has not in the least been lessened by the fact that most of the claims that were made against the Hussein regime to justify the war have since then been proven false. There were no WMDs to be found in Iraq, and there were no links found between the regime and terrorist organizations such as al-Qaeda – although one should not overlook the irony of the fact that, as a direct effect of the war, Iraq has seen an abundance of terrorism.

While they are tragic in many ways, the consequences of the war are less important for our purpose. We should concentrate on the pronounced strategies and the arguments for going to war, if we are to make sense of what is really at stake in the doctrine of pre-emption. One crucial problem with the NSS-2002 is that it uses the terms pre-emptive and preventive interchangeably.[7] Indeed, one could very well argue that the Bush administration specifically sought to not make a clear-cut distinction between these two concepts. That being said a clear-cut distinction between prevention and pre-emption is hard to come by. Even Alan Dershowitz, who perhaps most famously has argued for the necessity of constructing a clear and effective jurisprudence of pre-emption, at certain times seems to distinguish between prevention and pre-emption by virtue of the kind of action taken – that is, 'a preventive war, as distinguished from a pre-emptive attack' (Dershowitz 2006: 157), while he at other times draws upon the difference in temporality, which seems to be more common: 'It is useful to distinguish between pre-emptive and preventive wars, with the former limited to imminent threats and the latter extending to longer-range but relatively certain dangers' (Dershowitz 2006: 59).[8] But even if we take for granted that imminence is the crucial issue for any distinction between the terms, this does not make the problem any easier to deal with. Simply saying that a pre-emptive action is one that is taken against an imminent threat, and a preventive one is taken against a longer-range threat does not help us much, as the question tags along: what indeed does imminence mean?

Imminence is one of the three basic criteria which have to be satisfied for a pre-emptive attack to be legal in terms of international law. Let us make a few remarks in this regard. In general, international law exerts a stringent prohibition on the use of force, both in terms of treaties such as the UN Charter and customary law (Schmitt 2002–3: 525). Today two exceptions are in general accepted: On the one hand there is the Security Council, which upon determining 'the existence of any threat to the peace, breach of the peace, or act of aggression' (UN Charter, art. 39), may decide upon measures to be taken to restore the peace including, as a last resort, the use of force according to article 41 of the Charter. On the other hand there is the right to self-defence. It is with regard to the right of self-defence that we find the three basic criteria mentioned above. These are: necessity, proportionality and imminency.[9] I will not go into details about the former two, but merely note that the criteria of necessity means that it must be absolutely necessary that the threat is met with force rather than other means, and that proportionality means that the force used must be proportionate with the threat, that is, it must be of a kind sufficient to neutralize the threat, but not any greater than that. Finally, there is the imminency requirement, which is at the crux of the matter regarding the distinction between pre-emption and prevention as we saw above. In the strict understanding of the imminency requirement, an act of self-defence cannot be legal unless it is countering an attack that is already underway. In a less strict reading the attack must be underway or certain to take place in the imminent future. In such cases a pre-emptive counter-attack can indeed be legal. If a neighbouring state has launched a military operation and is gathering forces in order to attack, one is not obliged to wait until the enemy has crossed the border, before engaging in a self-defensive counter-attack. Conversely, if an enemy is merely building arms, for example, if he is building factories with the purpose of producing weapons, it would not be possible to legally claim that an attack on the factories would be an act of self-defence. Given the temporal distinction between prevention and pre-emption introduced above, this latter form of an act of self-defence would be called preventive, which again is the reason why preventive war is often simply equated with an illegal war of aggression.

The prevailing argument against such abstract distinctions between pre-emption and prevention consist in claiming that war is evolving. In the modern world of hi-tech WMDs, so the argument goes, the imminence of an attack must be seen in an entirely new way. A new way which has an eerie resemblance to paranoid phantasies: a potentially catastrophic attack could be imminent, even if we have no way of knowing about it. Indeed, that is precisely the point of the 1 per cent doctrine formulated by Dick Cheney. In similar fashion Condoleezza Rice argued in a speech on 1 October 2002 at the Manhattan Institute for Policy Research that new weapons and new technology require a new thinking about imminency. And the very same point is of course made in the NSS-2002 which advocates pre-emptive action even where 'uncertainty remains as to the time and place of an enemy's attack' (Bush 2002: 15). In short, the fact that the NSS-2002 does not draw any clear line of distinction between pre-emption and prevention is far from coincidental; it seems as if this absence is quite intentional. The aim of the NSS-2002 precisely seems to have been to extend the legality and legitimacy of pre-emptive action as far as possible into the realm of preventive action.

The point which I will be making is that these arguments for the war in Iraq as well as the difficulties involved in distinguishing between pre-emption and prevention are underpinned by fundamental ontological concepts of potentiality. The fundamental ontological issue at stake in the debate about imminence is not one of temporality, but rather one of potentiality. In order to make evident this underpinning, we should consider the meaning of the notions of pre-emption and prevention in greater detail, as well as the notion of deterrence, which was argued to have become obsolete by the NSS-2002.

Prevention, deterrence and pre-emption

The analysis relies upon distinguishing first of all between the epistemological condition and the epistemological demand which are relevant to each of these concepts. From these distinctions the ontological points about potentiality can be made out. We begin with the notion of prevention.

Prevention is something one undertakes in order to prevent a threat from *fully* becoming a threat. An obvious example in the global political situation of today would be the measures taken by the United States and its allies (notably Israel) to prevent Iran from gaining nuclear capabilities. Another example could be poverty in the southern regions of the globe. Northern powers could consider it a potential security threat that the poor global South would eventually produce various kinds of resistance, violence, terrorism or perhaps even global revolution as a result of global inequality. Prevention is a strategy, which in such and similar cases tries to prevent the threat from fully forming as a threat. The specific measures taken could of course be vastly different, ranging from bombings of Iranian nuclear facilities, to various forms of diplomacy, to aid-programmes in sub-Saharan Africa.

The logic of prevention relies upon the futurity of the threat. When we are acting preventively, it is the possible future formation of a threat that is being acted upon. Even if the possible threat were some time in the future to become an actual threat (if Iran were to get the bomb), there will still be time to act against this actualized threat, because an actual threat of an attack is in itself still only a potential attack. This means that prevention is a strategy which one can undertake against what I will call *future potentialities*. Prevention is something one undertakes in order to prevent future potentialities from becoming present potentialities (i.e. actual threats).

If prevention is targeted at future potentialities, then it is nevertheless clear that it is a future which we are able to know certain things about. The US intelligence agencies can, for instance, *with an acceptable degree of uncertainty*, come to know the state of Iran's nuclear program. It can be learned through conventional means that the enrichment of uranium has reached a certain level in facility X, that delivery capabilities of Iranian missiles have a range of so and so many kilometres, etc. And in the same way, the state of poverty in sub-Saharan Africa is something about which information can be gathered. It can be known *with an acceptable degree of uncertainty* that so many children are dying before the age of 1, 2 or 3, that life expectancy is dropping by that much, that civil unrest in certain areas is rising, etc. The crucial thing in the logic of prevention is that because of the futurity of the threat, these degrees of uncertainty are entirely manageable. The epistemological condition of prevention is therefore one of *knowability* – it relates to threats that can be known. They need not be known with absolute certainty, however, which means that the epistemological demand is one of *relative certainty*.

Let us consider the notion of deterrence in contrast with this idea of prevention. Where prevention was a strategy which aimed at preventing possible future threats from becoming actual present threats, deterrence is a strategy which aims at preventing an actual present threat from being fulfilled in the form of an attack or similar catastrophic occurrence. In relation to the terms I introduced above, deterrence is directed towards a *present potentiality*, where prevention was concerned with a *future potentiality*. One could say that deterrence is the strategy which is available even after the strategy of prevention has failed.

This means that deterrence is faced with a different kind of emergency than prevention is. When the threat is fully formed – missiles are armed with nuclear warheads and ready to launch – one cannot rely upon knowledge which is gained after the fact. The moment it is known that the missile has indeed been launched, it is already too late. Therefore deterrence is dealing with a wholly different epistemological demand than prevention is. In deterrence there is *no room for uncertainty*. In the old days of the Cold War deterrence aimed at having a nuclear arsenal great enough to not only annihilate your enemy, but also yourself, through the precipitation of a nuclear winter. The idea was to force your enemy to mirror this behaviour, and the result was that only a mad-man would 'press the button'. The logic of deterrence relies upon the balance of terror that has often been known as MAD (mutually assured destruction).

The epistemological condition of deterrence is on the other hand no different than the one we are faced with in prevention. In order for the logic of MAD to work it is absolutely crucial that each side can know (and indeed does know) about the capabilities of the other side. Just like with prevention, the epistemological condition of deterrence is knowability. In deterrence, as it was conceived during the Cold War, we *must* be able to know that the attack will not occur, but this epistemological necessity was founded on an epistemological situation in which one could know first of all if the other side indeed was mirroring one's behaviour and second of all that he would never strike first because even a first strike was likely to result in self-demise.

It is against the background of these conceptions of prevention and deterrence that we should understand the logic of pre-emption (and its encroachment upon the realm of prevention) that was envisioned by the Bush administration, and which was given its most striking formulation with Rumsfeld's argument that the crucial threats faced by democracies were the unknown unknown ones. When comparing this idea with the ones we have dealt with in terms of prevention and deterrence, the difference is striking. Where prevention only demands relative certainty and deterrence demands absolute certainty, they are both posited in an epistemological condition of knowability. In both prevention and deterrence we find ourselves in a situation, where we can know (to a certain degree) what our situation is like. Pre-emption on the other hand is positioned in an epistemological condition of absolute uncertainty. An important feature of both prevention and deterrence is the fact that here we can presume to know whether or not prevention or deterrence is the adequate strategy. One can presume to know whether the threat is of a present or of a future potentiality. It is this possible knowledge about the threat – the knowability of the threat – which disappears once we enter the realm of pre-emption as it has been formulated by the key figures of the Bush administration. This means that the relations of futurity and presence, which determined the previous logics, are dismantled in the logic of pre-emption. In pre-emption the threats we are facing are neither present ones as in deterrence nor are they possible future threats as in the logic of prevention. The threat is, according to the logic of pre-emption, in a sense fluid. It fits neither a determinate present nor a determinate future. It could be everywhere and anywhere at any time. The distinction between present and future simply vanishes when one is dealing with this kind of potentiality. It is with the concept of potentiality that we complete the step from the old Cold War logic, where it was known *that* there was an enemy out there, *who* he was, and *what* he was capable of, to the logic that is relevant in the so-called war on terror.

Of course that should come as no surprise given the arguments that were made above concerning the theory of 'new' terrorism and the concept of potentiality, which was developed from those considerations. But because of the logic we expounded from the theory of 'new' terrorism, we should be able to see how one specific element of the logic of deterrence is carried over into the logic of pre-emption. This element is the demand for absolute certainty. As we saw there is a demand, for example, in the 1 per cent doctrine, that one must be absolutely sure that terrorism does not occur. This means that the war on terror has inherited the demand for absolute certainty dominating the Cold War, while at the same introducing the field of absolute uncertainty, in which this demand is to be met. Thus, the war on terror represents a curious episteme. The point is that in this particular war, it cannot even be known what it is that one does not know about one's enemies. They could be anywhere or nowhere. They could attack today, tomorrow, in a year from now or they could have already attacked yesterday. But at the very same time what is demanded of this situation is that one must make every bit as certain that these enemies will not, or preferably cannot, attack, as one had to during the Cold War. In other words, even though the enemy is understood to reside in complete potentiality it is this potentiality itself we must act against. Thus even though the legal concept of preventive war is considered to be the more radical and problematic one – saying that one is engaging in a preventive war is very much akin to saying that one is an aggressor – whereas the concept of pre-emptive war is much more easily recognized as a concept of legal self-defence, on the ontological level it is the concept of pre-emptive action which is the more radical one. It is in the connection with the curious episteme that corresponds with the notion of pre-emptive action against the potentially catastrophic occurrence – an episteme which demands absolute certainty in a realm of absolute uncertainty – that we find a concept of potentiality which is present, forceful and threatening, while at the same time being completely without empirical actuality. Such a notion of potentiality without actuality can make for a daunting foe indeed. And it was this very potentiality the United States set out to combat in Iraq.

Nothingness at work

Given that we have here extracted the notion potentiality from a particular form of empirical research on terrorism, namely the notion of new terrorism, given that we have shown how the notion of potentiality at stake in this idea is also at work in the politics of the war on terror, given that we have presented a certain degree of scepticism towards this notion and given that we professed an affinity for the form of terrorism studies which positions itself as the critical counterpart to the classical approaches to the subject, the road might seem to be clear from this point on. A more or less classical case of critique of ideology seems be presenting itself at the present stage of the investigations. The road ahead could simply consist in further revealing the emptiness of this notion of potentiality, and in investigating the ideological motives behind presenting such emptiness as if it had genuine reality. We could then go on to line up the consequences that have followed from the policies undertaken, and a familiar form of self-righteous condemnation of the present structures of power would have been achieved.

If we were to follow the road of revealing how potentiality is simply abstract nothingness, then we would be happily on our way to the epistemological fallacy I warned against in the introduction above. Ideology critique in the form of unmasking the emptiness of certain high strung ideological concepts – and what could be more dramatic than the idea of a potential nuclear terrorist attack – has the inherent error of assuming too much about the power of unmasking. As I argued above, the problem with the ideology of terror and the war on terror is not that there is a dirty secret hiding behind the mask of ideology. Indeed, most of us have probably at some point heard one of the amusing yet troubling statistics about the dangers of terrorism – for example, between 1974 and 1994 more people died from bee stings than from terrorist attacks in the United States (Zulaika & Douglass 1996: 6). The point is rather that the ideology of the potentiality of terror still works in spite of the apparent emptiness of the central concepts.

The politics which works on the basis of a pure potentiality is a form of politics, which can continue to function no matter how empty its ground is. The Cheney quote puts the notion to the point: politics of potentiality is not about the reality with which one is confronted. It is about action. It *would* be possible indeed to argue most forcefully that the reality of the 'unknown unknown' is pure empty nothingness. One could argue that there is nothing there, but the ideological postulates presented by certain political interests. But that would not strike the core of the issue at stake here, because the crucial point is not that these policies are based on pure nothingness; the point is rather that they still work. The metaphysical plunge one has to take in relation to the study of the phenomena that have our interest is the realization that *nothingness itself works*.

The argument we must follow should therefore not simply consist in the attempt of showing that this potentiality, which is presented as if it had some actual content, is in fact nothing at all. Instead we should be concerned with this curious form of a nothingness that has a reality of its own. How can something merely possible be said to contain a reality all by itself? What does it mean that nothingness can have a very concrete almost material existence?

Perhaps surprisingly, we can find aid in the theory about *comedy* developed by Alenka Zupančič. In her article 'Comedy and the Uncanny' (Zupančič 2008b: 59ff.), she writes:

> Comedy does a lot of things with nothing. But above all, it likes to point to the irreducible materiality of nothing. Let us look at a very direct example of this, a joke told in a comedy (Ernst Lubitsch's *Ninotchka*), a joke that excellently captures one of the crucial mechanisms of comedy: 'A guy goes into a restaurant and says to the waiter: 'Coffee without cream, please'. The waiter replies: 'I am sorry sir, but we are out of cream. Could it be without milk?' (Zupančič 2008b: 59–60)

As Zupančič argues this joke is no mere case of amusing logico-linguistic peculiarities. Her point is that the joke reveals 'a certain – rather ghostly – materiality of nothing' (Zupančič 2008b: 60). Comical discourse, just like discourse on terrorism, is a way to not only talk about and describe nothingness, but also to invoke it. These forms of discourse make nothingness appear in all its spectral materiality.

To a certain degree the point *that* nothingness works is already a well-known point within critical scholarship on the ideology of the war on terror. One of the central themes of this literature, the notion of the politics of fear, does to a great extent focus on exactly this point that fear as such very often gets hold on us, even though there is no substantial or rational reason for us to be fearful. Fear and anxiety can be a result of nothingness itself. Still, arguing *that* nothingness itself works – since it can make us irrationally fearful – does not bring the point home. It is not enough to simply say nothingness works. We also need to find out how. Nothingness can have quite a range of qualities. It can be powerful, weak, spatial, temporal, open, closed, potent and impotent. As Zupančič indicates, nothingness can take on very concrete material existence. And as her example shows, it is not a given from the outset that the spectral materiality of 'the nothing' should cause only anxiety. Indeed, it could also be comical.

The ways in which nothingness works are the central topics we should pursue in the attempt to investigate the metaphysics of terror. We have already seen how nothingness has an important companion in potentiality. The nothingness which most investigations and actions relating to terrorism revolve around is constantly invoked as a potentiality. The tendency of the general discourse on terrorism in academic and political circles could very well be described as one which invests all its energy in bestowing concrete reality upon something that is mere abstract possibility. Thus our next step should be to give further content to these notions of possibility and potentiality.

Aristotle on potentiality

The place to start an investigation of the notion of potentiality is Aristotle. That is all the more the case since the concept we are here after is not merely one of logical or formal possibility. The potentialities of terrorism are not potentialities in the sense that something is possible, if it is not impossible; we are not dealing here with mere logical possibility. Instead we are dealing with potentialities having a certain kind of force. Let this distinction between possibility and potentiality serve as an important terminological distinction, I take for granted in the following. The possible is to be understood as a category which describes those things, elements, events, etc., which are not logically impossible. The potential on the other hand, is the category for that, which is in some way powerful with regard to its own possibility. Potentiality is not merely a concept of the things that *can* happen; it is a concept of the things that are *capable* of happening.

The crucial ontological claim we are pursuing is that one can conceive of a form of potentiality that is not inherently linked to its own actualization, but where this potentiality nonetheless contains a certain form of potency or force; a potentiality of nothingness as such. One could put the point in the way that what is real does not necessarily have to be actualized. Indeed, thus goes my argument, this reality of nothingness as potential is precisely the potentiality which we are encountering in the phenomenon of terror – it is this kind of potentiality which more than anything has been the target of the war on terror. To be sure, such a notion of potentiality, which could also be described as one that does not see potentiality as ontologically secondary to actuality, would break with most standard accounts of Aristotelianism, such as the one that has been defended among others by Martha Nussbaum and Amartya Sen (Nussbaum & Sen 1993; Nussbaum 2007). Thus, we will be best served to present this standard account in some detail in order to have it as a negative background against which we can proceed.

On this account, to be potential means to be actualizable, but actualization of a potential is something which can take place in several different ways. In book Θ of the *Metaphysics* Aristotle initiates his discussion of the terms by dividing potentialities into passive and active ones (Aristotle 1046a). A thing can potentially have another form or be another thing altogether. In this way wood can be cut to change its shape and in the end become a chair or a table – this is passive potentiality. A thing can also have the active power to change the form of another thing. In this way fire has the ability to burn wood and to turn it into ashes – this is active potentiality.

Aristotle is particularly interested in how such notions of change relate to human beings, and his discussion thereof shall bring us a few steps further. Human beings possess both active and passive potentialities. A child for instance possesses mostly passive potentialities. It first of all has the passive potentiality of being able to learn. Through education a child can be formed into something that it is not yet; it could for instance be taught carpentry. Prior to such education a child already has some potentiality for learning carpentry. Given a knife and a piece of wood most children will be able to cut the wood into some new form. Rough as it is, such forming still does not amount to carpentry, but by having such a basic ability to deal with knives and wood the child is potentially a fully capable carpenter.

Whether they are found in wood or in fire or in a child such forms of active and passive potentiality all share one crucial characteristic. The common factor in all of these forms of potentiality is the fact that once they have become actualized the original potentiality disappears. For example, when a piece of wood has been burned there is no longer any potentiality to be burned in what has by then been turned into ashes. More importantly the child's potentiality to learn can be understood as lacking of knowledge, which disappears once this potentiality becomes actualized. Once the child has learned how to do carpentry it would be wrong to say that it potentially could learn how to do carpentry. This potentiality has been replaced by something else.

At this point Aristotle introduces a second kind of potentiality. This is the kind of potentiality that is found in a fully educated carpenter. An educated carpenter has fully actualized his potentiality to learn carpentry, but this fully actualized potential is in itself yet another potentiality. This second potentiality is the carpenter's ability to form wood in a skilful manner – his ability to do carpentry.

It is this second form of potentiality, which Aristotle defends in his discussion with the Megarians in chapter three of book Θ of the *Metaphysics* (Aristotle

1045b). According to the Megarians there is 'no power apart from its operation' (Aristotle 1046b). If one were to accept such an idea, one would have to argue that a carpenter would only be a carpenter in so far as he actually is doing carpentry – his being-a-carpenter would disappear as soon he stopped working with wood. Aristotle argues against such thought that it makes it impossible to understand what it means to have acquired a capacity, because if a carpenter only knows how to be a carpenter when he is actively forming wood, and loses this knowledge when he stops, how can he suddenly regain it, when he later on wishes to continue his work (Aristotle 1047a)? Clearly that would be impossible if we do not accept that potentiality of the second order is something that a person acquires, and is both able to actualize and refrain from actualizing, as long as he is in the possession of that potentiality. This second form of potentiality is therefore to Aristotle a form of potentiality which does not disappear when it is actualized; it survives its own becoming actualized so to speak.

A capacity is a potential a thing or person or situation has, when it is able to actualize its potentiality without losing that potentiality itself. Aristotle's argument against the Megarians seems to at least prove this much. There are potentialities which do not simply disappear, even though they are not actualized. Still, on this account of Aristotelianism the notion of second potentiality does not fundamentally alter the ontological hierarchy between potentiality and actualization. To Aristotle there are no potentialities without a prior or higher actuality. Thus there can be no potential fires if there is no actual wood. And there are no potential carpenters, if there are no actual children. Furthermore, the notion of second potentiality or of a capacity is a notion of potentiality, where potentiality is being understood through its relation to its own actualization. To have a capacity exactly means to be able to *actually* do the thing one is capable of. If a young bashful man with no skill in carpentry were to say 'I can make a beautiful chair' it would in a certain sense be true. He could indeed make a beautiful chair, if he were to take the time to learn the necessary skills. But in the important sense it would of course false, precisely because he does not yet have the capacity to make a chair. He is precisely not *actually capable* of doing so.

In this way the standard account of Aristotelian thought brings about a crucial difference between mere logical possibility and actual capacities – a distinction which certainly is an important one in its own right. It is this distinction which has led people like Amatya Sen and Martha Nussbaum to formulate a neo-Aristotelian 'capabilities approach' in the social sciences. The idea of this 'capabilities approach' is to focus on the capabilities a person has in order to assess his or her 'ability to achieve various valuable functionings as a part of living' (Nussbaum & Sen 1993: 30). This should be seen as a countermove to more common approaches within the social sciences that focus for instance on utility, opulence, negative freedom and other concepts that are more easily reduced to formalisms. A good example is found in the study of constitutional law, where Nussbaum argues that rights formally guaranteed by the constitution are worthless, if they are not also actualizable in the concrete life of the people living under that constitution (Nussbaum 2007: 6–7). In this way Nussbaum's Aristotelianism precisely targets the idea that to have a capacity means to *actually* be able to do something. A capacity is an actualized state one is in, where one can actualize a certain potential.

This means that this standard account of Aristotelian thought serves very well as a *negative* background against which the crucial point relating to potentiality, which we are here after, can be made. The potentialities, we are interested in here, are the exact opposite of these more traditional Aristotelian ones. Our interest lies with the potentiality of in-actuality (of nothingness) rather than with the actuality of a potentiality.

The potentiality of a non-dancing dancer

A good way of making the point about the potentiality of nothingness clear would be to take a different example than the carpenter discussed above. I believe that we can fruitfully take up the example of a dancer instead. It has often been said that everybody can dance. In an important sense this is absolutely true. Moving around to music is something that almost all human beings are capable of, and no matter how hopeless it may look to others, when some of us engage in this activity, it is nonetheless clear that we are in some way dancing. What separates trained and skilful dancers from the rest of us is rather their ability to *not* dance. When a skilful dancer is not dancing he can do so in a way which makes abundantly clear that he would be really good at it, if he were to dance. A skilled dancer can *not-dance* in a way, which no-one, who is not trained to dance, will ever be capable of. In this way the dancer who is not-dancing provides a vivid example of the potentiality of the 'not-'.

In an Aristotelian line of thought, this notion of a dancer who is not-dancing will probably be dismissed as an example of the potentiality of nothingness. Instead, it would be argued that it is the thing that the dancer is actually doing – that he *actually* is holding his body in *this* particular way – that enables us to see that he is really a dancer. It might be said that he is *actually* being extremely graceful in his way of walking or standing around, and that it is the actuality of this grace, we are seeing. That would merely be to miss the crucial point about the example, however, because to see that he is actually standing in this particular way, means precisely to not see that he is not-dancing. If we insist on the Aristotelian line of thought, when we see a dancer who is not-dancing, then we simply see someone standing or sitting or taking a walk. But the point is that we *can* in fact see the capacity to *dance* in the absence of actual dancing. It is of course true that when we see a skilful dancer not-dancing we see someone, for example walking gracefully, standing around with a particular composure or holding his arms in a certain way. One could probably make an Aristotelian argument that everything we see in a dancer who is not dancing can be described in such terms of actuality, and that once we had given a complete description of such actualities there would be nothing more to add. Against this view my point is simply that there *really is* nothing more to add. The nothing more which should be added is the not-dancing that is really going on while the dancer is actually walking gracefully (and doing lots of other things). One can describe the actualities of a non-dancing dancer in great detail, but in order to get the point about what it is, we can see in a non-dancing dancer, we must add the minimal negative trait of not-dancing.

But the point here is of course not to argue about dancers. The point is to argue about terror. As we saw above, a great deal of recent research on terrorism investigates the things that could happen, the potential dangers that are lurking 'out there'. I have spent a considerable amount of text trying to show the exaggerated nature of the imagined threats, and furthermore on showing how such exaggeration can have very concrete political effects. Nevertheless, there is a crucial point to the nature of terrorism which should not deceive us, no matter how wrong the catastrophic projections may seem: Terrorism *is* essentially about potentiality. Whatever actual terrorist attacks occur, no matter how spectacular they may be, it is always the promise of the next attack, which is crucial. When terrorism works it is not because of the actual attacks that already happened, nor is it because of the probability of certain future attacks. Terrorism rather works when every train and every airplane and every public gathering is experienced as a potential terrorist attack, which is *not-occurring*.

The importance of the insight which I hope to achieve with this example of a not-dancing dancer cannot be overstated. As we will see, much of what follows in our investigation of the political psychology, the political cosmology and the political theology of terror will be interpreted along the lines of this example or some consequence that is drawn from it. In this way the idea that there is a potent nothingness in not-dancing dancers and in terrorism forms the core of the political ontology of terrorism, I am unfolding here.

This point also projects the task for the remainder of this part of the investigations. It should first of all be clear that the Aristotelian framework in which actuality is always of a higher ontological order than potentiality must be surpassed. But this framework is no mere Aristotelian oddity. Indeed, is can be said to be a dominant theme in most ontological investigations. For better or worse, ontological investigations have the general tendency towards asking the question of which things are actually real (i.e. objects, processes, subatomic particles, dark matter, the Higgs boson, the soul, the cosmos, God). Asking the ontological question in this way means to ask it under the heading of actuality. The ontological question becomes: which things are *actually* 'out there'? One can of course have a meaningful concept of possibilities and potentialities within such a framework, but these concepts would always have to be subsumable to an overarching concept of actuality. Potentialities would necessarily be understood as potential *actualities*. Indeed, is not so-called modern modal logic formulated around the idea of possible actualities (i.e. possible worlds)? Thus the first step in the ontological revolution, we are looking for here, would consist in pointing out a notion of potentiality, which is not subsumable to any concept of actuality. It is such a concept of potentiality I have tried to illustrate with the dancer who is not-dancing. This means that the task at hand must consist in searching for the best and most detailed way of describing the curious ontological figure of potentiality as non-actualization.

In doing so I will discuss two authors who have keen eyes for forms of potentiality: Agamben and Schelling. Agamben's view on the matter is intriguing, as he formulates his ideas of potentiality with specific reference to the Aristotelian texts on the matter. He conducts in other words a non-Aristotelian reading of Aristotle. In this way Agamben's work functions very well to open up a space of ontological investigation that goes beyond the valorization of actuality. But perhaps because of his adherence to Aristotle, his view on the matter can in some respects seem limited. We will use it as a lever with which we can open up a gap to another scene of ontological thinking, but once we get to this other scene I argue that the Schellingian dialectic of potencies offers us some more refined conceptual tool to carry out our investigation.

Agamben's peculiar Aristotelianism

Agamben's way of interpreting Aristotle takes the second notion of potentiality as a capacity as its starting point. His interest is a potentiality that is 'carried over' as potentiality in being actualized. But from there he leaves the standard interpretation behind and instead goes on to search for a concept of 'potentiality as such' that as we will see below is central to his political thought. Potentiality as such is a potentiality which relates only to potentiality itself; it is a potentiality which is not a potential actualization; in the end therefore, this form of potentiality is understood as impotentiality. As a result of this Agamben emphatically denies that Aristotle places actuality at a more fundamental ontological level than potentiality, something which seems to bring him in flagrant contradiction with most standard readings of Aristotle as well as the texts themselves. In Metaphysics Θ Aristotle writes 'It is evident that actuality is prior to potentiality. And I mean prior not only to the definite power which is said to be the source of change in something else or in some other aspect of the same thing, but to any source of motion or of rest generally' (Aristotle 1049b).

Aristotle does in fact leave room for one specific kind of priority to potentiality over actuality: that of a particular kind of temporality. It is however a very restricted form of priority and it is immediately subsumed to a higher priority of actuality. The wooden table, at which I am writing these pages, could not have become an actual wooden table, if it had not been a potential table first. In this sense the potentiality for something to come into being must necessarily precede the actual coming into being of that thing. Thus there is a kind of temporal priority of potentiality over actuality. However, this prior potentiality itself, must immediately be subsumed to an actuality, because no matter how one conceives of the potential table, before it comes into actual being, it is only possible by being actual in some form or other – if there are no actual trees then there are no possible wooden chairs. Thus even where Aristotle admits that potentiality can have some priority with regard to actualization, he immediately retracts and argues that this form of priority is only thinkable under the assumption that this prior potentiality is again subsumed to a higher order of actuality (Aristotle 1049b). And thus actuality remains prior to potentiality in all relevant aspects.

In short, what Agamben does in his reading of Aristotle is to turn upside down the entire ontological hierarchy taken for granted by most forms of Aristotelianism. Nevertheless, Agamben insists on finding what he is looking for within the Aristotelian corpus. It should thus be no surprise that he is rather selective in his choice of passages from Aristotle's work, and it is hard not to think that it would be impossible to uphold the reading Agamben is conducting, if one were to engage with the entirety of texts that are available, although Agamben claims that this is certainly possible – indeed, he claims his reading of these few select passages, which we to be fair should grant are very important, calls for a reconsideration of all of Aristotle's philosophical work (Agamben 1999: 183). While this project may seem overstated – to my mind it is, not because of the concept of potentiality Agamben seeks to develop, but because of his insistence upon finding it in the Aristotelian corpus – this should not discredit the work he is doing. The engagement with the history of philosophy should never be reduced to simply an exercise in reconstructing the thoughts of a great philosophical mind that is long dead and gone. Any honest engagement with the history of philosophy must contain some element of violence conducted against the philosophers one is discussing – at least in so far as it is an engagement which purports to also have relevance for its own time.

The limited number of passages which Agamben discusses does mean that it will be an easier task for us to evaluate his arguments. Agamben puts special emphasis on three passages from Metaphysics Θ.[10] First of all: 'Impotentiality is a privation contrary to potentiality. Thus all potentiality is impotentiality of the same and with respect to the same' (Aristotle 1047a quoted in Agamben 1999: 183, 2004:45), and 'What is potential is capable of not being in actuality. What is potential can both be and not be, for the same is potential both to be and not to be' (Aristotle 1050b quoted in Agamben 2004: 45, 2005a: 183). Agamben claims that in these two passages Aristotle himself is going beyond the standard conceived notion of Aristotelian capacity. His claim is that for Aristotle 'All potentiality is impotentiality of the same and with respect to the same' does not merely mean that to have a capacity is to *also* have a specific capacity of not actualizing one's capacity. His claim is rather that potentiality *essentially* is impotentiality. The point is that one only finds the full force of a capacity in its ability to not come into actuality; it is not simply that potentiality means that which can both become actualized and not become actualized, it is rather that the ultimate truth of potentiality is im-potentiality.

This idea can in fact be expressed quite nicely in the terms of the argument, we saw Aristotle present against the Megarians above. If we can only make sense of the capacity for carpentry by accepting that it does not disappear, when the carpenter is not engaged in carpentry, then it must be the case that what characterizes this capacity more than anything else is found where it is not actualized. What is crucial about the capacity for carpentry is something that must remain un-actualized – it is im-potentiality. This Agambendian understanding of the Aristotelian argument against the Megarians does come quite close to the notion of potentiality we found in the not-dancing dancer above. The potentiality of the carpenter in the Aristotelian argument is argued by Agamben to consist essentially in his im-potentiality, and the potentiality of the dancer in my idea of a dancer not-dancing is equally focused upon the crucial form of potentiality that is alive only in some form of negativity.

The crucial difference between the two is that the capacity in Agamben's Aristotelian argument does not need to have some clear or visible expression; the carpenter retains his capacity for carpentry while inactive regardless whether or how he is actually walking, talking, eating or sleeping for that matter. There is no way to tell a carpenter who is not doing carpentry from, for example a cook who is not cooking. A carpenter who is not doing carpentry, while sitting in a chair, would look more or less the same as a cook, who is not cooking, while sitting in a chair. The point about the not-dancing dancer on the other hand is that here we *can* in fact see the minimal reality of not-dancing. There is a negativity in the not-dancing dancer which can be experienced as a reality – a very minimal one, but a reality nonetheless.

The central issue for these notions of impotentiality and potentiality not-to is thus how they stand in relation to actuality. Agamben is quite aware of this. The crucial manoeuvre of his reading of Aristotle lies precisely in the way he gives an answer to the question: how does potentiality at all retain any relation to actuality, if it essentially is im-potentiality? If potentiality is ultimately impotentiality, meaning that its essence consists in not coming into actuality, in what sense can potentiality then at all be said to have a relation to actualization? It is in answering this question that Agamben points to a third passage from Metaphysics Θ. It goes: 'A thing is said to be potential if, when the act of which it is said to be potential is realized, there will be nothing impotential' (Aristotle 1047a quoted in: Agamben 1999: 183, 2004: 45). The importance these lines hold for Agamben's interpretation of Aristotle is evident from his characterization of them: 'The answer Aristotle gives to this question [i.e. the question of the relation of impotentiality to actualisation] is contained in two lines that, in their brevity, constitute an extraordinary testament to Aristotle's genius. In the philosophical tradition, however, Aristotle's statement has gone almost entirely unnoticed' (Agamben 1999: 183). That these lines have gone unnoticed is due to the fact that they are mostly interpreted quite differently from the way Agamben sees them. Generally, they are simply understood to render a tautological statement saying: 'Potentiality is that from which there results no impossibility when it is actualised'. This way of understanding the sentences is also very clear in many, if not most, translations of the text (e.g. Aristotle 1933: 1047a, 1960: 1047a; Aristoteles 1995: 1047a).

Agamben's point is instead that the final clause of Aristotle's statement – that is, 'there will be nothing impotential' – specifies a way in which potentiality, understood as essentially impotentiality, can actualize itself. In *Homo Sacer* he writes, 'What is potential can pass into actuality only at the point at which it sets aside its own potential not to be (its adynamia). To set im-potentiality aside is not to destroy it but, on the contrary, to fulfil it, to turn potentiality back upon itself in order to give itself to itself' (Agamben 2004: 46). In setting aside impotentiality, potentiality can become actualized, but this is not simply a cancellation of impotentiality, it is rather a way of carrying impotentiality over into actualization. What Agamben means by 'setting aside' should here be understood in terms of the Paulinian *katargein*, in which he sees a horizontal suspension, not a vertical negation. 'Katargeo is a compound of argeo, which in turn derives from the adjective argos, meaning "inoperative, not-at-work (a-ergos), inactive"' (Agamben 2005b: 95). For Agamben the Paulinian katargein is the notion of a weak messianic force. According to Agamben it does not enforce a suppression of the law; it rather means that the law is set aside and rendered inoperative. Katargein is a form of setting free, but instead of a strong negation it offers a weaker suspension. In a similar way impotentiality is here set aside; it is left to itself or given to itself. Impotentiality is made to remain what it is, while potentiality turns into actuality. But precisely because impotentiality in this way is merely suspended, it is not destroyed. It is still there, in a sense, ready to be activated once the actuality needs a break. (Or the carpenter does!)

In this way Agamben's reading of Aristotle places actualization and potentiality on the same horizontal level. Pure potentiality, potentiality as such, is understood as impotentiality, as that which is never actualized. But this pure potentiality can be suspended and set aside in order for potentiality to become actualized. And conversely actuality can be suspended and set aside without being destroyed, for example when the carpenter takes a break from his work, but does not lose his skills in carpentry as a result. His actuality as carpenter is in this case precisely suspended rather than negated. Thus, neither potentiality nor actuality is superior to the other. Each is placed at the same ontological level. In the end he argues 'At the limit, pure potentiality and pure actuality are indistinguishable' (Agamben 2004: 47). It is by following this idea of a zone of indistinction between actuality and potentiality that Agamben establishes the link between ontology and his notion of sovereignty – a point to which we will return, when we discuss political theology below.

What Agamben does, is to introduce a notion of potentiality quite different from the notion of potentiality found in more traditional readings of Aristotle. The notion of a capacity discussed by people like Nussbaum and Sen put focus on the idea that in order to be a genuine capacity, a capacity must be actualizable. Agamben turns the table on this view by finding in the Aristotelian corpus the idea that the essence of potentiality is impotentiality. This is an idea which seems much better suited to describe the kind of potentiality, we have identified above in various forms of discourse about terrorism and in the politics of the war on terror, namely the potentiality of nothingness. There is, however, still some ground to be covered. As I argued above, the notion of a potentiality of nothingness inherent in our politics of terror can be understood in analogy to the dancer who is not-dancing. And I further indicated that Agamben's reading of Aristotle, albeit highly innovative, does not fully capture the notion of potentiality, we are looking for. It is at this point that I believe we can helpfully change perspective and take up the Schellingian notion of potency.

The two and the three

While Agamben's introduction of a potentiality that is essentially impotentiality could seem to suit our present purpose, it does suffer from a deficit I touched upon above. Having now seen how the Paulinian concept of *katargein* is what at bottom defines this notion of potentiality as impotentiality, we are in a better position to identify the problem. What Agamben highlights is a *potentiality which is not at work*. His notion of potentiality finds its best expression in being inactive, but this inactivity is neither a negativity nor a nothingness; it is rather a suspension, a setting aside. What we are looking for is something quite different. Rather than a potentiality that is not at work, we are looking for an *in-activity which is at work*. The not-dancing dancer we discussed above is precisely at work in not-dancing. Instead of leaving an activity in inactivity he activates a nothingness – and of course it is a similar kind of structure we are looking for in terms of terrorism.

The problem with Aristotelianism, which is not fundamentally challenged even in the Agambendian interpretation of it, is in the end not simply a problem of Aristotelianism. In fact this problem is found in a doxa so seemingly self-explanatory that it in general will be accepted without question by most strands of thought. The doxa can be described in the following way: given a present potentiality there are exactly two mutually exclusive outcomes: either potentiality is actualized, or it is not (Aristotle 1050b). In the Aristotelian line of thinking, given a potential chair in the form of an actual tree in the woods there are two possible futures: either the tree is made into an actual chair, or it is not. In the latter case it could be left to stand, or it could be used for other things, but with regard to the potentiality for the tree to become a chair, all that matters very little. It is this binary principle and its hold on the relation between potentiality and actualization which we should take care to dismantle. And because Agamben's interpretation of the Aristotelian notion of potentiality precisely identifies a potentiality which is not at work, this binary principle is not fundamentally challenged.

What we should do is to look for a third possibility. Apart from the possibility that a potentiality becomes actualized and the contrary possibility that it does not become actualized, there is the possibility that a potentiality can become realized as not becoming actualized. In the very process of not turning into actuality potentiality can be made real.

This way of adding a third element to the story of potentiality is very closely linked to the notion of dialectics pointed out in the introduction above – identity is the identity of identity and difference. At that time I argued that this notion of identity is at work in the philosophical notion of the two. The idea that identity itself is the identity of identity and difference should not be seen as the consolidating synthesis which overcomes all difference, but rather as the notion that in all identity there is an inherent split. The one is not a stable thing, but rather always at odds with itself.

In the present context of potentiality and actualization this dialectical notion of the two is immediately transposed onto a notion of the three. The dialectical notion of the two is not the idea that a thing in being identical with itself could at a certain point become something different; it is precisely not captured simply in the Aristotelian notion of potentiality and actualization. Instead this dialectical notion of the two is the notion that whatever a thing is, it is always also something more. A thing is excessive in terms of being what it is. We find the expression of this excess in terms of potentiality by saying that given any potentiality there is always three possible outcomes. A potentiality can become actualized, it can remain unactualized and it can realize its potentiality by not-actualizing it. This reality of the non-actualization is precisely the point of excess in everything; it is the inherent difference at the heart of every identity.

Nothingness is never simply lack (of being, presence, etc). It is always also that which is excessive. Nothingness as such is precisely that which is too much. This is a point which Agamben comes close to making himself. In so far as he is putting focus on the idea that potentiality is fundamentally im-potentiality, he is also very close to pointing out how nothingness itself can have a potentiality, and indeed even a reality of its own as distinguished from actualization – an excessive reality as it were. But he seems to stop short. Precisely because the operative term in the interpretation of the functioning of the impotentiality that is at the heart of every potentiality is the notion of *katargein*, therefore he precludes the possibility of a genuine dialectical account of nothingness-at-work.

In this regard it is most striking that when he does entertain the notion of (Hegelian) dialectics, he does so by invoking the link between the Hegelian notion of *Aufhebung*, and the Paulinian *katargein*. 'How does Luther translate this Pauline verb, whether in Romans 3:31 or wherever else the verb occurs in the Letters? Luther uses *Aufheben* – the very word that harbours the double meaning of abolishing and conserving (*aufbewahren* and *aufhören lassen*) used by Hegel as a foundation for his dialectic' (Agamben 2005b: 99). What Agamben does to the Hegelian dialectic is therefore in a way to soften the blow of negativity, to the point where it becomes very similar to his account of Aristotelianism, we saw above. And again the result is the same. Where dialectics on my account at its most basic level operates with a notion of 'a nothingness at work', the notion of katargein pursued by Agamben precisely is a notion of 'a something not at work'.

The reason why Agamben is so hesitant towards the notion of a dialectic, which entails a more vertical notion of negativity, could perhaps be resulting from his ambition to resist the juridification of thought. In the words of some recent commentators he specifically wishes to resist 'reducing it to judgements about this and that, a weighing of pros and cons, a problem-solving technique' (Murray & Zartaloudis 2009: 208). When Agamben thus can be said to open up a space of ontological thought which sets aside the dominating understanding of being as actuality, it would, in his view, be to go too far to begin to simply describe what goes on in this field using our ordinary juridified language. And one could quite possibly worry that something like that would be the danger entailed in taking on the Schellingian dialectic of potency at this point, since this introduction precisely is done with the intent of finding concepts to adequately describe what goes on in the field where potentiality is at work without being actualized. I believe this is a risk, we must accept, but I hope to show that the Schellingian dialectic at work here does not simply end up a sterile calculus or a weighing of pros and cons.

Schellingian potency

This minimal cut, which separates a thing from its non-actualized being something else, is not simply something which is everywhere at work in the same way. It is a minimal negative difference which can be more or less apparent. The more ambitious claim of the philosophers, such as Hegel or Schelling, who sought to give a dialectical account of reality, is that there is a certain structure to the way in which such minimal negative difference makes its appearance. In Schellingian thought this structure is precisely described in terms of *potency*.

As we recall, Schelling develops his dialectic of potencies through three stages that follow upon each other. We will also recall that a crucial point for Schelling is the idea that the first stage is one of contraction. If we understand Schelling's dialectic as a description of the stages of creation, then the initial move is one that goes from bland indifferent nothingness to aggressive and destructive nothingness. Only against the background of such contraction is it possible for there to be an expansive force. But this expansive force is itself again only a step along to the way to successful creation. Taken merely in itself, it is in a sense too much. It is excessive. The moment where creation is fulfilled, the moment of spirit, is only achieved with the third potency that emerges once the concretive forces are able to hold the excessive expansion in check.

The important point about this tripartite structure is the fact that Schelling's dialectic of potencies can provide a more detailed description of the ontological structure of the not-dancing dancer I introduced above. The dancer who is not dancing corresponds perfectly to the third stage in Schelling's dialectic, the moment of balance where expansion is held in check by contraction. To see why, one can compare the third stage of balance with the second stage of expansion in relation to this dancer.

Imagine a dancer who tried to convince someone that he was truly a dancer. This sceptical someone would then say: 'If you are such a great dancer, then show me'. And the dancer would reply by starting to dance. He would do all the things he had been taught by his instructor in order to prove that he was truly a dancer. In a very precise sense his sceptical counterpart would in that case be justified in saying: 'Well, that looks great, but I am not really convinced that you are doing something that could not be done by somebody not trained in the way that you say you are'. The only viable response our dancer would have, would then be to dance some more. And in response to this the sceptic would simply repeat, what he had already said. One can easily imagine how desperation would soon set in for our poor dancer. In fact, the more he would try to prove that he is really a dancer by dancing, the more ridiculous he would seem. Aware, as he would probably be, of the awkwardness of the situation, he would soon start to lose control of his technique. Steps, that he on any other day would have been able to do with ease, would suddenly feel impossible to do right. In short, the more our unfortunate dancer tries to fully be a dancer by dancing, the less a dancer he is. In this sense the actualization of a potential can be very excessive.

One can overdo the actualization of a potential. One can be excessively actualized. This is no mere fancy idea of some German thinker of the nineteenth century. Indeed, most of the reactions taken by governments across the world in the wake of 9/11 could very well be described as excessive actualization. The one thing, governments were incapable of at the beginning of the twenty-first century, was exactly their own im-potentiality. The dominating tendency was the call to action. 'We must do something!' was the rallying cry. And then things were done.

But one can also overdo contraction. In the case of our dancer it is again possible to describe how. Imagine that the dancer, who is being asked to prove himself a dancer, simply refuses. (Confronted with a sceptic of the sort that we imagined above, he would surely have every reason to. Is it possible to imagine anything more obnoxious than the demand 'Show me that you are truly X'?) If the sceptic persisted ('If you won't show us, why should we believe you?') the dancer would quite likely only harden his stance and simply say 'No I will not. I don't owe you anything'. It is not hard to imagine how the mood of this kind of conversation would quickly turn sour. The dancer would perhaps cross his arms over his chest, and generally look annoyed. The sceptic on the other hand, if our dancer were unlucky enough, would continue with his demands ('Why won't you show us?' 'It's nothing to be embarrassed about!'). And the scene could go on. It should be clear that the dancer in this case precisely does not prove himself to be a dancer by not dancing. He would be in a mode of pure contraction in the Schellingian sense. Angrily, he would be holding everything back. Rather than not-dancing he would in so many words simply not be dancing.

From these considerations it should be clear that there can be no *guarantee* that the dancer will be able to convince anyone that he is a dancer by not-dancing. In the end there can be no proof in such matters. If confronted with a truly obnoxious sceptic, that is, a sceptic of the kind that certain philosophers take great pride in rejecting – the juridified sceptic if you will – the dancer would be better served to produce a diploma from a dance academy. The point is that the kind of enactment of inactivity we are finding in the dancer not-dancing requires a certain kind of recognition on our part.

One could imagine the desperate dancer being saved from the obnoxious sceptic by a third intervening party, who would say: 'Of course he is a dancer. Just look at the way he is sitting on that chair!' But that is more or less all there is to be said about this case here. The kind of 'proof' that shall guarantee that such and such is really the case, when we under controlled circumstances perceive that such and such seems to be the case, will be of no interest to these investigations. What we are looking for when we are investigating the 'other side' of reality, that is reality in the various forms of en-actment and in-actment of potentialities, are not the sort of grounded proofs one can expect when one is dealing in actualized beings. Instead, we are trying to change the focus upon reality ever so slightly. The wager of the investigations is that only in this way can we truly begin to understand the metaphysics of our own time, that is the metaphysics of terror.

What the Schellingian dialectic serves to do for us in this regard is to provide an overall framework, and more than anything the right way of looking at the concepts of potentiality and actualization. Actions, events and ultimately history itself does not move unproblematically and smoothly from that which is merely possible to the point where it is either actualized or not. Instead, we should take an approach, in which we are aware that there are twists and turns and gaps and traps, but also sometimes miraculous successes, on the road from potentiality to actualization. The times are out of joint, as Shakespeare once put it rather succinctly. The aim of the present investigations could very well be said to be to investigate what this out-of-jointedness amounts to.

The language of terror – Desperation and impudent propaganda

At this point in our investigations we have achieved several things. We have taken a look at relevant literature on terror, and we have found an abundance of potentialities invoked in it. We have also seen how this potentiality is far from being politically innocent. And we have developed a concept of potentiality which will serve us in further investigating the metaphysics at work in this field. What we should do before we close the book on the political ontology of terror is to return in a sense to the place we started. Namely with the language of terror we saw Ashis Nandy give a most vivid description of.

In this regard it should be noted that we have not yet given any definition of terror. Instead we have simply taken for granted that when scholars and politicians speak using the words terror and terrorism, they are indeed invoking the thing we are interested in here. In the introduction it was claimed that terror should be understood as a kind of excess, not as excessive violence in any way, but rather as an excess in relation to language. We have already seen to some extent how this excess relates to the concept of potentiality, but we are still lacking a more clear-cut understanding of how the concepts of potentiality and excess relate to the notion of terrorism. The method for solving this task is again metaphysics in the form of *last philosophy*. We will take a look at how definitions of terror and terrorism have been given, and most importantly we will look at some of the more potent emotional investments, that seem to go along with these definitions. From there we will be able to develop an account of how terror is to be understood as meaningfulness-as-excess.

Right from the beginning when one enters the field of terrorism research one gets the feeling that something fuzzy is going on with the very object of study in the field and the way it is defined. We have already encountered Schmid's famous study *Political Terrorism*, which enumerated no less than 109 distinctly different definitions of terror (Schmid & Jongman 1988: 5). From that number alone and the seemingly never-ending definitional debates, it could almost seem as if it is impossible to know what terrorism is – in the look of things that I am offering here, this is not entirely false. This means that when it comes to the question of definition, scholars are ultimately forced to simply make a choice – a choice that will tend to have crucial political implications. Therefore the task for us cannot be to try to form a synthesis of definitions for future research, but instead to investigate what it is about terrorism that makes it impossible to define in a way that is universally acceptable. It is with this purpose in mind that we eventually will characterize terrorism as an excess. We will set out by taking a look at two very telling attempts to define the concept.

There are those, who deliberately try to remove all traces of the excessive meaning of terrorism, when they define it. For instance one could try to argue that terrorism is merely a strategy and nothing more. This can be said to serve both a scientific and a moral or political purpose. It serves a scientific one since this excess seems difficult to handle within a normal scientific framework. It serves a moral or political purpose, because the excessive nature of terrorism is the very thing which gives it its inflated political force. At least if one should wish to limit the political consequences of the 'war on terror' a deflation of the notion itself would seem to be a good place to start. One very good example of deflation by definition is found in Jeffrey Bale's *The Black Terrorist International* (Bale 1994). He defines terrorism as 'nothing more than a violent technique of manipulation' He explains: 'Whether or not one sympathizes with a given perpetrator's underlying motives, every individual who commits an act of violence which is specifically designed to influence or manipulate a wider audience is, strictly speaking, a terrorist. Period' (Bale 1994: 33).

The point here is to notice the desperation of the scholar, who is putting this kind of emphasis on an attempted definition. 'Period!' Bale seems painfully aware that no matter how much he insists upon the point that terrorism should be viewed as a strategy and nothing more, the world will not listen. Writing, as he does, a few years prior to 9/11 one can only imagine that his desperation must have grown since then. The question we should be asking ourselves when we read such definitions, is of course: what is it about the concept of terrorism that causes this kind of desperation? Wherein lies the magic that forces research, which in Bale's case is otherwise quite coldblooded, neutral, and perhaps to a certain point sterile, to reveal such desperate emotions?

Before we go on to discuss those questions let us take up another example of a definition, which reveals a similar point, even though its intent is very different. I have already mentioned that Benjamin Netanyahu figures among the 109 definitions that Schmid enlisted to discuss what a proper definition might look like. The definition is from a book with the telling title *Terrorism. How the West Can Win*, and it goes: 'Terrorism is the deliberate and systematic murder, maiming, and menacing of the innocent to inspire fear for political ends' (Netanyahu 1986: 9). Such a definition is clearly the antithesis to the idea that what defines a 'terrorist' in the end is the result of a contingent political struggle. The first sentences of the introduction to Netanyahu's book confirm this point: 'To win the war against terrorism, free societies must first know what they are fighting. This is why this book begins with what has been regarded as the most elusive but indispensible starting point – a definition of terrorism. It rejects absolutely the notion that "One man's terrorist is another man's freedom fighter" ' (Netanyahu 1986: 3). It would be almost too easy to prove that exactly by insisting on these kinds of sweeping formulations, and exactly by flat out denying that there might be any doubt as to what might constitute a terrorist in contrast to a freedom fighter, Netanyahu's book is precisely confirming the point it tries so emphatically to deny. The clue is given already in the subtitle 'How the West Can Win'. Anyone not finding himself geographically, morally, politically or otherwise part of the 'West' is likely to think that whatever such a book defines as terroristic, might very well look more like a freedom fighter.

What we should notice here, however, is a different and somewhat simpler point. There is a certain kind of poetry to Netanyahu's definition. It is short and to the point, and it is clearly intended to be that. Most of the book is short and to the point. The point regarding Netanyahu's definition is that even though it seems to follow trajectory of brevity quite nicely, it nevertheless contains three almost synonymous terms to describe the actions of a terrorist and it even takes care to use alliteration: 'murder, maiming and menacing'. It would certainly have been more precise to say something like 'the use of deadly and/or mutilating violence or threatening to use deadly and/or mutilating violence', but something crucial would then be lost. What would get lost is the *eloquence* of the definition. 'Murder, maiming and menacing' would have a nice ring to it, if one were to use it in a speech.

The point is that both definitions – Bale's and Netanyahu's – indicate the excessive nature of the concepts of terror and terrorism. Bale seems to struggle mightily against this excess; Netanyahu on the other hand seems to revel in it. As we have already learned from the discussion of Nandy above, there is no necessary link between excessive forms of violence and the words terror and terrorism. Quite the contrary in fact: The violence itself of a terrorist act is, it would seem, lacking in comparison to the excessive meaning that comes with the words themselves. But this excess cannot simply be captured in any kind of definitional move. It does not suffice to single out specific agents, motives, victims or the like. Whatever one does with the concept of terror in terms of defining it along these terms, it would seem that something extra appears in the very act of saying 'terror'. It is said, and immediately something additional has been added, but not something that can be captured as a particular something. My suggestion is that this particular something is better understood as a potent nothingness. When I am calling terror meaningfulness-as-excess it is because the word itself seems to invoke the nothingness-at-work which we have found to be fundamental to terror above.

One thing that both of the mentioned definitions have in common is the strange fact that they seem meant for speech rather than text. The desperate 'Period' of Bale's definition seems perfectly suited for being shouted loudly while banging the table. Likewise the 'murder, maiming and menacing' from Netanyahu's definition seems perfectly suited for being said a grand political rally with thousands of listeners cheering. To prefigure an important point that will follow below this should be taken as an indication that language use about terrorism is inherently linked to the *voice*. To see why we will need to first take a look at some classic positions in the science of language.

From Saussure to Guillaume

It should be clear we are in need of an extraordinary theory of language to get hold of these issues. Given the specific theme we are dealing with, the potentiality of nothingness, I believe we can learn a great deal from the work of the French linguist Gustave Guillaume, who took up linguistics as it was developed by Ferdinand de Saussure, and gave it an Aristotelian twist. The interest Guillaume has for us lies therefore in the way he introduced the distinction between potentiality and actualization to the science of language. As we will see however, Guillaime's edifice remains too restrictive for our purposes. What we should do is to introduce a notion of *voice*, which has recently been subjected to an illuminating investigation by the Slovenian psychoanalytic philosopher Mladen Dolar in *A Voice and Nothing More* (Dolar 2006). It is by forming an understanding of language that helps us see the potentiality of the blind spot in language, namely the voice, that we will be able to characterize 'terrorism' as a linguistic excess. We will begin by introducing briefly a few central linguistic ideas.

It is a well-known dogma of the science of language that a genuine breakthrough was accomplished with Saussure's *Course in General Linguistics* (Saussure 1959). We shall not go into depth with Saussure's ideas here, but merely consider the famous distinction between *langue* and *parole*. The distinction between langue and parole is the distinction between language as a system (langue) and in actual usage (parole). A crucial lesson, which has been taken from the teachings of Saussure by the subsequent linguistic structuralism, is the idea that the study of language should focus merely upon the side of langue. Language is primarily a system of differences, and the specific way in which those differences are utilized in particular speech-acts is in the end an arbitrary matter. The sign itself is arbitrary. As Saussure insists, language is not a nomenclature. There is no necessary connection between the sound image (signifiant), and concept it signifies (signifié). A typical way of making this point consists of considering how one would teach a person who is unfamiliar with colour-concepts the meaning of the word 'brown'. If one were to do this by showing him a number of brown objects one after another, and telling him that they were all brown, one would probably not get very far. How would he be able to distinguish a brown object from one that is coloured somewhere in the spectrum between red and brown, or black and brown? How would he be able to distinguish between brown and tan? The only way to teach a person the meaning of the concept 'brown' is to teach him the whole system of colour-terms, and to enable him to make distinctions between terms (Culler 1976: 25). Crudely put this is the general idea behind Saussure's attempt at understanding language (langue) as a system of differences.

In a simplified way of putting things, it could be said that if structuralism took this lesson of language being a system of differences to heart, and hence set out to investigate langue, then one could say that the event of post-structuralism meant the return of interest in the phenomenon of parole. To a certain extend this meant giving up upon the idea of being able to give a fully objective synchronous description of language as a system (langue). Instead, a central focus became the investigation of how concepts are *articulated*.[11] The point of post-structuralism was in other words that the specific way in which certain concepts are articulated as belonging together effectively constructs their conceptual meaning. The ultimate structure of the system of language thereby fell apart, not because it was contended that there is after all some special essence to the sign, but instead because the very act of naming itself was thought to have a crucial importance for the meaning of the name.

By introducing this very simplified story, we can characterize the tendencies of terrorism research with regard to their linguistic ambition. The proponents of classical terrorism studies are acting as good structuralists, when they try to pin down the precise meaning of the term 'terrorist', for instance by distinguishing it from other forms of violence, war and crime. This precisely is what Bale is attempting by calling terrorism 'A violent technique of manipulation'. Conversely, the proponents of critical terrorism studies act like good post-structuralists by focussing on how the very act of giving someone, something or some event the name 'terrorist' can redefine the linguistic field in which we are politically and socially operating. This was what we saw Nandy investigate with an eye to the discreet charms of Indian terrorism above. While each of these agendas could therefore be said to occupy very solid positions in relation to established linguistic theories, we must nevertheless insist that both are missing something crucial. What is missing is an eye for the excess.

The crucial thing here is to avoid the conflation of the notion of the excess with a certain post-structuralist notion of articulation. This is not to deny that post-structuralism has a point. Naming something is not merely a neutral move within language, as we saw Nandy unfold it with great clarity above. Still, we should not too hastily accept the explanatory power of the notion of articulation. If post-structuralism has a point in the claim that language does not function smoothly as an objective system of differences, then it could perhaps be said that the notion of articulation itself describes a functioning of language that is 'too smooth'. Is it not exactly the case about articulation, in the way it is conceived by the post-structuralist inflection in terrorism studies, that it indeed works like perfect machinery? If certain groups are identified with terrorism through discourse, the assumption often seems to be that this precisely is causing us to associate the group with terrorism. If linguistic practices were really contingent and subject to change, if our sociolinguistic space was really un-sutured, as certain post-structuralists like to claim, it should be expected that the assigning of signifiers such as 'terrorism' from time to time goes wrong – that it sometimes misfires. But the assumption in many critical analyses about the use of the concept terror often seems to be that language about terror works like clockwork – not as a descriptive tool, but rather as a tool for political power.

In order to gain a better view of this problem, we can find great assistance in the work of Gustave Guillaume. Guillaume was one of the many linguists who followed in the steps of Saussure's breakthrough. But as we shall see, he did go some length to accommodate the theoretical point about articulation, which was brought to the table by post-structuralism. He took up the distinction between langue and parole, but gave it an important twist. Guillaume chose to distinguish between *langue* and *discours* (translated as tongue and discourse), rather than langue and parole, in order to mark a crucial difference between his own views and those of Saussure. Where Saussure made the distinction between langue and parole in order to be able to focus exclusively on langue and set parole aside as something arbitrary and uninteresting for the science of language, Guillaume conceived of the relation between tongue and discourse by utilizing the Aristotelian concepts of potentiality and actualization. Guillaume still agreed with Saussure that the important and interesting side of language would have to be the side of tongue (langue), but he also argued that the side of discourse could not be considered merely accidental. Tongue was still to be considered language as system, and it was still to be the central focus of linguistics. But this system should be understood as a *potentiality*, which could become *actualized* in discourse.

The parallel between potentiality and tongue on one hand and actualization and discourse on the other is not the only part of Guillaume's work which should interest us here. At a lecture in 1948 he argued that many of the facts which we once felt assured of regarding language would have to be considered invalid. The separation of time and space had been discovered to not be universal (Guillaume 1984: 53). The article is far from a universal phenomenon – indeed it was a very late occurrence in the history of grammar (Guillaume 1984: 123). Nevertheless, Guillaume still thinks that one can point out a few universal facts about language. First of all, all language contains a universalizing tendency (an expanding movement), and a particularizing tendency (a contractive movement) (Guillaume 1984: 53).

In other words the two key components of Guillaume's theory of language are surprisingly similar to the operations we have become acquainted with in Schelling's dialectic. Just like Schelling, Guillaume deals in the relation between the Aristotelian concepts of potentiality and actualization, and just like Schelling he uses concepts of contraction and expansion (in the French original the terms are 'en direction de l'étroit et du large' (Guillaume 1973: 97)). Still, there is a crucial Schellingian point that precisely is not captured by Guillaume's theory, as we will come to see.

Guillaume binds what he terms tongue and discourse together in such a way that the system of language and the act of saying something are not qualitatively different parts of language, but rather two poles of one and the same process. At one end there is the system of that which can be said, and at the other end there is the act of saying something, which is determined by that very system. But these two belong together. In order to describe how, Guillaume introduces

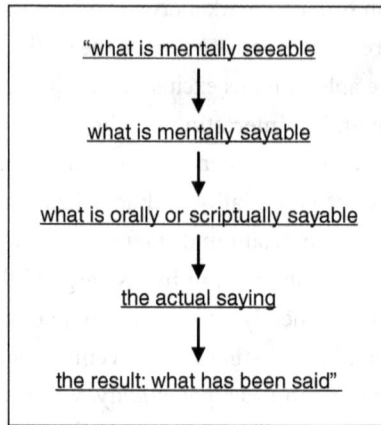

Figure 1.1 Guillaume on the relation between tongue and discourse.
Source: Guillaume (1984: 19).

a certain hierarchy, which precisely draws upon the contracting and expanding movements of thought (Figure 1.1).

For Guillaume this hierarchy describes a process which goes from the utmost potential and wide that the human mind is capable of conceiving, to the utmost actual and narrow. In order to go from 'what is mentally seeable' to 'what is mentally sayable' we impose certain structural restrictions – not everything that can be seen by the mind can also be said. 'What is orally or scripturally sayable' imposes a further narrowing upon 'what is mentally sayable', and so on.

In other words according to such a hierarchy, the relation between potentiality and actualization would be one of wide to narrow. The more potential, the wider; the more actual, the narrower. That is not the whole story though. It would be the whole story, if the act of speaking only worked as the enactment of a specific meaning which simply had to be chosen from a greater set of possible meanings. In that case articulation would simply be the presentation of fully constituted potential meanings. If that were the case, the post-structuralist notion that the very act of saying in itself can help construct the meaning of what is being said, would be lost. Guillaume accommodates the point by introducing a distinction between *expression* and *expressiveness*. He argues

> The established system which language – the act of language – resorts to is tongue. In cases where, for any reason, this established system is lacking, the act of language – insofar as the lack is felt – resorts to means of its own on the spur of the moment. (Guillaume 1984: 84)

In other words the point Guillaume is making is that tongue, the system of language, is incomplete. There are things that human beings sometimes would like to say, for which there is no codified expression. In such cases the act of language, the act of speaking, will have to resort to its own inventiveness, for which Guillaume uses the technical term expressiveness. 'Those demands [upon language] that are met by tongue make up what we call *expression*. Those demands that are not met by tongue, and which the language act must therefore meet, through suppletion, using its own improvised means, make up *expressiveness*' (Guillaume 1984: 85).

Guillaume uses the examples of utterances such as 'Silence!', and 'Curtain!' (Guillaume 1984: 86) to illustrate what he means by this notion of expressiveness. The point is that if one takes the expressiveness out of the utterances 'Silence!' or 'Curtain!' they stop conveying actualized meaning. Expressiveness marks a contrast to the hierarchy presented above, where the actualization side of language is a contracting or narrowing movement. In expressiveness we have a way of creating new meaning through the very act of speaking. It *expands* the potential usage of a sign. In the examples of 'Silence!' and 'Curtain!' expressiveness generates a whole meaningful sentence out of a single word that otherwise does not constitute a well-formed expression. In this way Guillaume integrates some form of articulation in the sense I alluded to above into his overall theory of language. There is, however, a crucial restriction upon the scope of expressiveness. Guillaume produces a very simple relation between expression and expressiveness 'Expression + expressiveness = 1' (Guillaume 1984: 85). In this way Guillaume sees expressiveness as a function of language which fills out the white areas on the map of codified language.

This picture can be applied very nicely to the schools of terrorism research we have been dealing with. Classical scholars will tend to put emphasis on the expression side of language. Critical scholars on the other hand will focus on the expressiveness side of language.

The excessive potentiality of language

Having characterized the linguistic views that are inherent in the more traditional approaches to terrorism research, we are now in a better position to pinpoint the elements that are missing. What we should take care to do, is to introduce the lessons we have learned about potentiality and actualization from the discussions above. If we are to be able to analyse correctly the various discourses on 'terror', then we need to construe a theory of a linguistic element equivalent to the dancer who is not-dancing. As we recall, the dancer who is not-dancing was said to exhibit a kind of excessive potentiality from the viewpoint of Aristotelian ontology. It is a similar excessive feature of language, which we must try to point out in order to see how 'terror' can be understood as a linguistic excess.

The notion of a linguistic excess fits very poorly with the picture we have just laid out by introducing the work of Guillaume. If we accept the formula Guillaume lays out (expression + expressiveness = 1), then there is absolutely no room for an excessive potentiality. The idea Guillaume seeks to formulate has to do with the *relation* between expression and expressiveness. The point is that if there is a white spot on the map of expression, then expressiveness must take over in order for meaning to be successfully delivered. But the consequence of the formula is the point that meaning always must amount to *one*. In this sense there can be no gaps in meaning. Meaning is always delivered. There is neither too much nor too little. It always adds up. Guillaume makes this point clear when he argues 'The relation between sign and significate: a vast subject. It is a relation of suitability. *A law: the suitability will never be excessive*' (Guillaume 1984: 72, italics mine). Consider also: 'Zero meaning cannot be "applied" to anything' (Guillaume 1984: 81). Guillaume would in other words seem to be aware of the possibility that one could imagine excessive meaning and zero meaning, only he emphatically denies it. It is exactly at this point that we must depart from Guillaume's theory.

The suggestion I am making about the signifier 'terror' is that by using this concept in discourse one is effectively applying zero meaning. That does not, however, mean that one is simply uttering nonsense – quite the contrary! The application of zero meaning is precisely what is entailed in saying the excessive. *The excess of language is found in the application of zero meaning.* This might seem as a contradiction in terms. On one hand it seems to be claimed that 'terror' produces 'too much' meaning, since we are talking about an excess, and on the other hand it seems to be the claim that 'terror' produces 'too little' meaning, since we are talking about zero meaning. The point is that the two fit together. Exactly by producing zero meaning, one is effectively doing something excessive. One is making sense beyond the sense that can be rendered within the confines of what is possible within the Guillaumean schema of expression and expressiveness. Zero meaning is, when it is expressed, an extra meaning, something more than the standard meaning, which Guillaume marks with a '1' in his formula. If we should complete the Guillaumean schema, while taking this point about the excessive nothingness into account, it would therefore have to look like this: 'expression + expressiveness = 1 + 0'.

The zero does not add anything to the expression. And it does not add anything to the expressiveness of the utterance. It merely adds something extra, a ghostly substance, an excessive zero. It is this zero, which is not 'something', as it does not make 'some sense', but which nevertheless is not mere 'nothing', which we should understand to be the excessive meaning that is invoked by the signifier 'terror'.

In the light of the points we have made above regarding the concept of potentiality we should be able to pinpoint where this excessive sense might be found. The interesting point about Guillaume's formula is the fact that it describes the relation between two different forms for language to become *actualized*. It describes two different ways in which we can *actually* say something. In expression we are actualizing one specific potential meaning, which can be rendered by picking out and combining symbols that have already been subjected to the structure of the mentally sayable in tongue (the potentiality of language in terms of langue). In expressiveness on the other hand we are creating new meanings through the very *act* of saying them. The point is that *both* expression and expressiveness are forms of actualization. But what does not receive any attention in such a view of the matter is the possibility of not-saying something in a way that is analogous to the way we argued above that a dancer can be not-dancing. My argument is that when we use the signifier 'terror' in discourse *we are actively not-saying something* in a very similar way. When we are not-saying something we are marking out an empty spot in language, where something could have been clearly said, but was not.

This precisely is what characterizes the signifier 'terror'. In a way it marks a spot where language begins to malfunction. The point this analysis raises against both classical and critical studies of terror, is that both of them assume too much, when they investigate the possible meanings of 'terror'. They assume too much when they assume that terror can be made to work just like any other signifier in political or scientific discourse. But this is a point which can be rectified by paying attention to the excessive nothingness of language.

The excess and the voice

At this point we have reached the first goal of our investigation of the excess of language. We have constructed a theory in terms of which we can begin to make sense of it. Nevertheless, there is still a lot of work to do. First of all there is a problem, which relates to the comparison between the excess of language and the not-dancing dancer. This should be clear from the following consideration.

What we saw in the discussion of the dancer who does not dance, was a way to *work with and control* a potentiality by not actualizing it. But in the case of someone using the signifiers 'terror' or 'terrorism' in discourse, something else seems to be going on. The dancer who does not dance does not take himself to be dancing. The speaker who says 'terror' does however take himself to be saying something. However, if I am correct in the analysis of how the signifier 'terror' works, then he is wrong in this particular case. This in turn means that there is a stark difference between the dancer who is not-dancing and the speaker who is not-speaking, as he is trying to speak about terrorism. Perhaps the best way to describe what happens to us when we speak about terrorism is that language itself reveals us to be expressing mere in-expressiveness. In discourse on terrorism language works behind our backs so to speak.

It is this problem of language not functioning 'properly', which critical scholars of terrorism could be said to be in danger of overlooking when they identify the discourse on terror as a special kind of language use, which exercises power and control. The problem with Nandy's otherwise very convincing analyses above is, in other words, his idea of a 'universal language of the modern nation-state' (Nandy 1995: 23). My argument is that this language might not be properly described as a fully functional language after all. The things that are said in this language could perhaps be said to make both much less and much more sense, than is realized by its speakers and analysts alike.

In order to render this idea more clearly, we shall have to look for another example than the dancer who is not-dancing. I propose that we instead imagine an intimate concert at a small venue. It could be with a group of jazz musicians or a singer-songwriter. At many such concerts one will find that the audience is quite intoxicated. And at some of them there will be one member of the audience, who is just a little *too* intoxicated. While not likely to become directly violent, such a person will often shout just a little too loud at the wrong moment during a gentle passage, or he will insistently shout for some old song, which everyone else knows the artist is probably not going to play. This will make both the audience and the artist feel quite uncomfortable.

What is it about this person? Why is he so annoying that quite often he will find himself taken aside by the security personnel at the venue of the concert? An obvious answer would be that his *voice* basically is too loud. While compelling this answer is too simple. The problem for this kind of person is not simply that he shouts louder than the rest of us. In fact he is doing the very same thing we are, only in a slightly different way. Just like us, he is shouting 'Oh yeah!',

'WUUUUH!' or 'We want more!' – but he somehow gets it wrong. For instance when the singer has just finished a melancholic song by letting the final note ring out, and is still holding her breath for one final second of silence while the entire audience is captured in joyful suspense, such a person will begin to shout just a moment too soon. He shouts the very same thing that the rest of us will be shouting just a moment later, and still he will have ruined something beautiful. It is thus not simply that his voice is too loud, but rather his lack of control of his voice, which is the problem. His voice has an uncanny way of appearing where it should not.

A recent work by Mladen Dolar entitled *A Voice and Nothing More* (Dolar 2006) should help us to further insights here. Dolar begins his book with a joke:

> In the middle of a battle there is a company of Italian soldiers in the trenches, and an Italian commander who issues the command 'Soldiers, Attack!' He cries out in a loud and clear voice to make himself heard in the midst of the tumult, but nothing happens, nobody moves. So the commander gets angry and shouts louder: 'Soldiers, Attack!' Still nobody moves. And since in jokes things have to happen three times for something to stir, he yells even louder: 'Soldiers, attack!' At which point there is a response, a tiny voice rising from the trenches, saying appreciatively 'Che bella voce!' 'What a beautiful voice!' (Dolar 2006: 3)

As Dolar notices this is more than simply a proto-racist joke about national stereotypes (i.e. about Italians as cowardly opera lovers). It also describes a case of failed interpellation (Dolar 2006: 3). The command to attack is not simply rejected; the soldiers do not say 'no we will not!' Instead the command is not received as a bearer of meaning. It is exactly at this point of failed communication, where language so to speak breaks down, that the voice appears. The soldiers hear the voice and *therefore* they cannot hear the intended meaning. Is it not the very same thing that characterizes our drunkard at the concert? The intended meaning of what he is shouting is exactly the same as the intended meaning the rest of us are expressing; only he is not able to express it, without calling attention to the very thing in his utterance, which distorts that intended meaning. He stumbles over his own voice so to speak.

Taking this point to the end should make it clearer why it is necessary to go beyond Guillaume's formula (Expression + Expressiveness = 1) and add an extra excessive element. Adding the '+0' to the right side of the equation (i.e. Expression + Expressiveness = 1 + 0), does nothing to alter the balance between expression and expressiveness, wherever meaning is *adequately* rendered.

Wherever language is spoken and understood, there must be a balance between language as a codified system and language which invents the meanings that are not yet fully codified. But when the voice appears to disrupt the very rendering of meaning, then we need an extra element. Only this element itself is not adding any new meanings in the form of codification or invention. It only adds zero. We can thus make another adjustment to Guillaume's formula: 'Expression + Expressiveness = 1 + Voice'. When the voice becomes too present the delicate balance between expression and expressiveness is dismantled, and consequentially meaning starts to disappear.

The relation between voice and language is far from straightforward. It is clear that the moment the voice is too present is the moment where meaningful language is dismantled. But conversely, if the voice is completely absent, we stop being able to speak. Without voice there can be no language. This claim in itself opens a wide range of issues which I cannot cover in full here. But it should be clear that voice is something other than simply the physical phenomenon which gives sound to our verbal discourse. Instead it should be considered as that in the utterance, which is the very instance of 'here someone is saying something'. The voice is precisely that which makes it clear for us that we are hearing something more than mere physical sound. To put this succinctly the voice is that which calls us and announces that an act of language is taking place.

There is thus a strange duality in the relation between voice and language. On one hand the voice is the very element, which announces that 'here language is spoken'. To be able to speak, to have language, means in this sense to have a voice. But on the other hand this element, which announces that language is spoken, cannot be too present in discourse, if language is going to work. If the element which announces to us *that* language is being used is all we can hear, then we have no opportunity to hear *what* is actually being said.

The point that we should take from our analysis of the example of the drunkard at the concert is thus that he embodies the lack of control over the very thing which is the condition for the possibility of speech. The potential to speak is the voice. The enactment of the potential to speak is the enactment of the voice. But such enactment is precisely something which makes speech impossible. The voice is in other words a condition for the possibility of meaningful language that must be excluded from language, in order for it to flourish. Only by not paying attention to this condition for our potentiality for speaking in the first place, are we able to actualize this potentiality.

What we encounter at this point is nothing other than the Schellingian (un) ground. The Schellingian ground is that which founds the system by being excluded from it. We can thus make one final adjustment to Guillaume's formula: 'Expression + Expressiveness = 1 + ground'. The problem for the drunkard at the concert could therefore be said to be that he is so close to the foundation of language that he is unable to speak.

This short introduction of the theme of the voice, and the special inflection this theme has been given in our example of the drunkard, should enable us to see what is going on in various types of discourse on 'terrorism'. The point is that discourse on terrorism should be seen as analogous to the discourse of the drunkard at the concert. On the content side of things everything seems to be normal. The drunkard is shouting all the right things, such as 'WUUUH', 'YEAH!' and 'We want more', or he might even be whistling. But his discourse is nevertheless slightly off, precisely because it continually calls attention to the element of the voice. The drunkard is in other words caught up in his own potentiality for speaking. His problem is that he more or less unwillingly announces 'here someone could have been making sense' again and again. It is his own capacity to speak, his capacity to be heard, that is his voice, which is getting in the way of his attempts to make sense.

If we recall now the point that was made above with regard to the nature of terrorism, then the parallel between the discourse of the drunkard and the discourse on terrorism comes into clear view. What concern us about terrorism are never the actual attacks that have already happened, but rather the potential future ones. Whatever the potential future attacks might turn out to actually be, they will in virtue of becoming actualized prove themselves to not really be *it*. In this way terrorism is that, which is not-yet. It is not *this*. It is always and forever the potential next one. What we do, when we speak of terrorism, is therefore precisely to announce a potentiality. This is the crucial point. Discourse on terrorism makes an intonation of a special form of potentiality. Not a potentiality, which could at some point become actualized, because once it is actualized it will no longer be *it*, but instead a potentiality, which continually makes itself real as mere potentiality. Discourse on terrorism is a discourse which purports to speak about something, about things that have happened, for example attacks, planned attacks and attacks that were prevented, but what is announced behind the back of the speaker, as he speaks about these actual occurrences, is the potentiality of terrorism.

Just as it is the case with the discourse of the drunkard, there is a content side to discourse on terrorism, which looks just like any other use of language.

The drunkard is cheering. The ones who speak about terrorism are talking about attacks, threats, motives, etc. But in both cases there is an extra excessive element of potentiality, which on one hand neither adds nor subtracts anything to or from that which is said, and which on the other hand disturbs the entire discourse, and puts it into a different light. The drunkard is calling attention to the potentiality of the voice. The ones who speak about terrorism are calling attention to the potentiality of terror. They continually announce: *It* could really happen. Precisely because discourse on terrorism continually invokes this potentiality, which never becomes fully real, for this reason 'terror' can be said to be meaningfulness-as-excess.

In this way those who speak about terrorism, as they are desperately trying to make sense, instead end up not-saying something, in the very same way that a dancer can be not-dancing, only with the important difference that the speakers who are speaking about 'terrorism' generally are unaware that this is what is going on. This is the point which is often missed by structuralists and post-structuralists alike. It should be clear why it is a problem for the structuralist who seeks to pinpoint the exact meaning of 'terrorism' by distinguishing it from what it is not, but this is just as much of a problem for the post-structuralist, who seeks to understand how the articulation of the word 'terrorist' can shape our collective political imaginaries. If 'terror' and 'terrorism' work in the way I have described here it can hardly be expected that they can be made to simply fit a certain kind of power-discourse – that is, the discourse of securitization and never-ending fear. While it can certainly be argued that this discourse has had some effect in what could now very well be termed the decade of terror, it should, in the light of the current point about the excessive meaningfulness of terror, be expected that something extra, excessive even, was going on as George W. Bush and Dick Cheney and others were telling us to be afraid – something extra which precisely did not simply fit smoothly into the fabrication of an environment of fear.

As we move beyond the discussion of the political ontology of terror, we will precisely focus on this aspect of our contemporary political situation. Therefore the first move in the particular metaphysics to be unfolded next will be an investigation into the political psychology of terror.

Part Two

Metaphysica Specialis

The Political Psychology of Terror

Having at this point arrived at a method for our investigations (metaphysics as last philosophy) and a specific concept for the (non)phenomenon we are investigating (the potentiality of nothingness at work in our politics of terror) we are now in a position where we can focus on the particular fields of metaphysics. Beginning with psychology in this regard only seems natural. And after all, is not the whole question about terror a question of psychology? Whether rational or irrational, realistic or unrealistic, do we not all in general accept the notion that terrorism creates fear? While it would certainly seem that we do, the purpose of the present chapter will to a great extent consist in trying to show that fear, after all, is not at the core of the issue of terror. First of all it will be argued that there is a philosophical distinction between fear and anxiety which is very much relevant with regard to the issue at hand, but that is not all. Far more than modalities of fear and anxiety, what we are confronted with in the psychology of terror are modalities of boredom. At least that is the point to be argued. What we are facing in the world of terror, and what we are fighting with the war on terror, is in the end not even a nothingness, which continues to emerge and haunt us, but rather a nothingness which emerged from the beginning as an answer to boredom and which, ten years later, slowly but surely is sinking back into boredom again.

To put the point in the form of anecdote, consider the situation of global politics in the final years of the twentieth century, just prior to the 9/11 attacks. In a purely occidental view of the matter there probably never was a time in history when international politics were more boring. The EU had certainly worked to make European politics increasingly uninteresting and boring ever since the first treaties in 1958. And with the fall of the Berlin wall, on the European 9/11 (9th November 1989), it would seem that occidental powers for the first time in history lacked genuine rivalry. It was the end of history as Francis Fukuyama famously put it, and what could possibly be more boring than that? Indeed, an overlooked part of Fukuyama's argument regarding the end of history is found in the very last passage of the article published in *The National Interest* under the title 'The End of History?'

The end of history will be a very sad time. The struggle for recognition, the willingness to risk one's life for a purely abstract goal, the worldwide ideological struggle that called forth daring, courage, imagination, and idealism, will be replaced by economic calculation, the endless solving of technical problems, environmental concerns, and the satisfaction of sophisticated consumer demands. In the post-historical period there will be neither art nor philosophy, just the perpetual caretaking of the museum of human history. I can feel in myself, and see in others around me, a powerful nostalgia for the time when history existed. Such nostalgia, in fact, will continue to fuel competition and conflict even in the post-historical world for some time to come. Even though I recognize its inevitability, I have the most ambivalent feelings for the civilization that has been created in Europe since 1945, with its north Atlantic and Asian offshoots. *Perhaps this very prospect of centuries of boredom at the end of history will serve to get history started once again.* (Fukuyama 1989)

For all the attention received by Fukuyama's article and the book that followed, *The End of History and the Last Man* (Fukuyama 1992), it was never the predictive power of these last few words that caught the eye of the readers.[1] Fukuyama's argument was generally received as bearing the happy news that liberal democracy was going to conquer the world and freedom and prosperity was thus expected to spread to all corners of the globe. Indeed, one could argue that the 'Happy 90s' following the fall of communism were first and foremost lived in the belief that Fukuyama was right in this precise way. Certainly, there were still problems to be dealt with globally – such as the wars on the Balkans and the genocide in Rwanda – but in the Happy 90s such problems were precisely to be dealt with in way that was unheard of only a few years earlier, namely through humanitarian interventions.[2]

Nevertheless, I think it is with these last few comments that Fukuyama strikes an important point. It is difficult to imagine anything more boring than the situation of global politics just prior to the 9/11 attacks. Fukuyama is quite precise: 'economic calculation, the endless solving of technical problems, environmental concerns, and the satisfaction of consumer demands' – certainly not something to get emotionally excited about. 'Environmental concerns' are perhaps a candidate for something one could today get excited about politically, but in the eye of Fukuyama, at the time of his writing, such concerns were clearly mostly an aestheticized interest of the privileged few, not a theme which could gather massive public support.

What then was the effect of 9/11, if not simply the occasion that made it possible to again become genuinely excited about global politics? Suddenly it was possible again to hate an enemy. Suddenly we had someone out there, who was really out to get us, and whom we could feel justified in pursuing in turn. There was going to be war on TV! And this general re-emergent excitement about politics was not limited to those who really believed in the story about the terrorists, who were out to get us. Those of us, who were sceptical about the whole agenda of the war on terror, with its not-so-veiled neoconservative intent, were equally capable of finding political excitement in the prospects of war. Our enemy even had a name: George W. Bush.

Having mentioned Fukuyama we should of course also mention his supposed intellectual antithesis from the aftermath of the fall of the Berlin Wall: Samuel Huntington. Following 9/11 it was all too easy to draw the conclusion that Fukuyama was thereby proven wrong. The presumption quickly gained ground that the Happy 90s were merely an illusion, or at least an aberration. Before us lay the millennium in which we would have to confront Huntington's *Clash of Civilisations* (Huntington 1996). The crucial point, however, is the lack of a distance between the positions of Fukuyama and Huntington. It was Žižek who first read these two as two sides to the same coin: 'we find the truth when we read them together: *the "clash of civilizations" is "the end of history"*. [. . .] when politics proper is progressively replaced by expert social administration, the only remaining legitimate source of conflicts is cultural (ethnic, religious) tension' (Žižek 2002: 132).

The end of history – the moment where all universal projects have been set aside in favour of administration, economic management and political correct struggles for recognition – is precisely the moment where conflicts can erupt in the form of the most brutal cultural, ethnic and religious forms. Is it not a commonplace fact that the more politics takes the form of expert administration and economic calculation, the more does political discourse tune in on themes of nationalism and racism? Furthermore, what could be a better evidence of the closeness between the end of history and the clash of civilizations than the situation in Iraq ten years after 9/11? The war was initiated in a strange conglomerate of themes that all in various ways fit the politics at the end of history like a glove. First of all it was launched and legitimated with reference to security. Second of all, it was argued by some to be a kind of humanitarian intervention. Third, there was the whole discussion of the UN mandate, and even though the United States never succeeded in achieving a new resolution for going to war, the sheer amount of time and effort that went into the discussion at the UN serves as a vivid example of administered politics, as it is conducted at Fukuyama's end of history. The moment where Fukuyama turns into Huntington is the moment where the endless UN discussions are circumvented by the decision of the United States, along with its coalition, to simply initiate the war. Precisely, against the background of administered politics, where every course of action is debated endlessly, and where all decisions are based on commissions, which debate for even longer than politicians do, rash action can be easily legitimized. And finally, what better example of the clash of civilization do we have than that of post-war Iraq, where numerous ethnic, religious and cultural fractions fight a bloody civil war?

The argument I am making here concerns the (metaphysical) psychological background to this link between Fukuyama's end of history and Huntington's clash of civilizations. This background is found in the closeness of the emotions of boredom and anxiety. In other words: Just as much as the clash of civilizations is just the other side of the coin of the end of history, so too can we argue that the politics of fear and anxiety is simply the other side of the politics of boredom. If 9/11 marked a spark in the politics of fear and anxiety, it did so in a climate that was dominated by an overarching feeling of boredom. And now, some ten years after 9/11, it would seem as if the politics of terror is again tending towards the point where boredom is the name of the game.

A few points should be mentioned in support of this. In a survey reported in the Danish newspaper *Information* (on 19th December 2010) it was concluded that 79 per cent of all Danes believe that Denmark will be struck by a terrorist attack within the 'next few years'. In the same survey it also came out that only 10 per cent of all Danes feel afraid because of the terrorist threat (Ritzau 2010). Even though Danes believe themselves to be potential targets of terrorism, they do not feel particularly afraid.

Likewise, it is interesting to notice what happened in US elections with regard to the issue of terrorism over the last ten years. George W. Bush was elected the first time before the theme of terrorism became a central notion of politics. The issue certainly helped him get re-elected in 2004, but it did not work as a campaigning theme for the Republican Party in the Congress Elections in 2006, where the Democrats gained the majority in both chambers (albeit only narrowly in the Senate). And in the 2008 presidential election economic issues by far distanced those of terrorism and homeland security in terms of importance in the mind of the electorate.[3] It probably was not his positions on terrorism and counterterrorism that got Obama elected in November 2008, but these issues did not stop him from being elected either. Would it not be fair to say that the story of our emotional (dis)engagement with terror over the last decade was one that started in fear and ended in boredom? The crucial point however is found in the linkage between these two emotional (dis)engagements. It is this linkage which we shall now explore.

The politics of fear

In order to achieve a genuine understanding of what goes on at the intersection of terror, fear, anxiety and boredom, we shall have to begin with the notion I will be trying to dismiss. That is the notion of the politics of fear. Our last philosophical investigation into the political psychology of terror sets out with the many varied forms of research within sociology and cultural studies which since 9/11 have sought to understand how fear of terror has been used as a tool to control a population and to legitimize antiterror legislation and wars.

The very idea that fear is an important factor in politics was not, of course, invented as a result of 9/11. Some 15 years before 9/11, Ulrich Beck argued, in *Risk Society: Towards a New Modernity*, that what engenders social transformations is no longer articulated in terms of 'I am hungry', but rather in terms of 'I am afraid' (Beck 1992: 49).[4] And we can certainly go further back than that and find arguments that stress the political importance of fear. Thomas Hobbes famously argued that it is the fear of a violent death, which makes it necessary for men to transcend the state of nature (Hobbes 1997: 70). Similarly, Machiavelli argued that it is better for the prince to be feared than loved, because 'men have less scruple in offending one who is beloved than one who is feared, for love is preserved by the link of obligation which, owing to the baseness of men, is broken at every opportunity for their advantage; but fear preserves you by a dread of punishment which never fails' (Machiavelli 1992: 46).

While the analyses from which we set out in the following are neither Machivellian nor Hobbesian, they nevertheless share the notion that fear can be used as a tool to control and paralyse people (see, e.g. Dillon & Reid 2001; Massumi 2005; Stenson 2005). The point we will be making however is that in order to understand how the political psychology of terror works, we should take care to include the lessons that we learned from the discussion of the political ontology of terror above. As we will come to see the discussion of the politics of fear reveals a central theme which should be familiar to us by now, namely the theme of potentiality. From the very way in which it is argued that the politics of fear works, we will be able to find the concepts of potentiality that in the end will push us beyond the perspective of the politics of fear.

Let us begin the discussion by considering some examples of the ways in which people react as they are confronted with terrorism. When Norwegian Anders Breivik detonated a powerful bomb in the political centre of Oslo, and later on killed 69 persons (mostly children) on the Island Utøya, the immediate, and almost dull, reaction of international media was that this had to be yet another terrorist attack by al-Qaeda or some similar Islamic group. As it turned out that the perpetrator was a Norwegian conservative nationalist the words used about the attacked changed drastically. Almost immediately the commonplace story was that he was a madman. But this notion itself did not help us relate to the events in any way; it was as if it would be impossible to find a proper way of speaking about Breivik. Two different teams of forensic psychiatrists have evaluated Breivik and arrived at completely different conclusions. The first concluded that he was a paranoid schizophrenic and its publication resulted in public outrage. The second, conducted a few months later, concluded that he was as normal as the next man, and it too resulted in public outrage. This makes clear the predicament we are faced with. As long as terrorism is conducted by a well-defined enemy, we are comfortable condemning it, but when it is done by someone, who looks a bit too much like ourselves, and who perceives himself to be a warrior in the fight against the terrorist enemies, we have been used to condemning, things get complicated. Breivik is an interesting figure to the collective consciousness of a Western society, because the very existence of such an extreme serves to make it impossible to simply follow the standard rules of distinction between us and them, inside and outside, friend and enemy. Such deterioration of ordinary lines of orientation is often associated with feelings of anxiety.

This is a point to which we will return below, but it is interesting to note that something similar can be read out of the blog entries written by survivors of Utøya. I will focus on one specific account of the events that was written by Prableen Kaur on the day of the attacks after she was rescued. Kaur's heart-breaking description is worth reading for several reasons. First of all because she gives a very tangible description of the fear she felt, when her summer camp was turned into a nightmare, but second of all because her description seems to fluctuate very tellingly between two very different emotional attitudes, on the one hand she recollects the sheer panic she felt as she was attacked, and on the other hand her description often turns into a quite factual report of the things she did to escape: First of all she tells of how she pretended to be dead, as Breivik approached her and a group of others, which he killed, and of how long she lay motionless among corpses. Second of all she tells of how she considered trying to swim to the boats that were gathering away from shore to help the ones who escaped. Deciding to swim, she deliberated whether or not she should take her jacket off, whether or not she should keep her mobile phone. As she swam her arms started aching, and she tried to swim on her back, but started sinking, so she turned around again and swam normally. She tells us how she screamed and cried and prayed.

Having read the entirety of Kaur post, which is genuinely horrifying, and which contains quite a few descriptions of sheer fear and panic, it can certainly seem quite odd to claim, that boredom is the name of the game in relation to terror. By making this claim I am of course not denying that Kaur and the others on Utøya were afraid. The point is not to argue that there is no fear in relation to terrorist attacks. There certainly is. The point is instead that the fear would seem to appear in moments other than the ones one would perhaps immediately expect. One passage is telling in this regard. Kaur describes how, after she had played dead while Breivik were shooting people around her, she lay 'for at least an hour' on the ground. Then 'It was completely quiet. I carefully turned my head to see, if I could see any survivors. I saw bodies. I saw blood. Fear' (Kaur 2011). In other words, as the killer approached and starts shooting, Kaur makes a decision and acts accordingly – she plays dead. But after he has disappeared and she begins to orientate herself, fear sets in.

Two things should be mentioned in this regard. First of all, it should be clear that certainty is what separates these experiences from each other. As she is directly confronted with the terrorist, there is no question about what she is confronted with, but after he has left, uncertainty can set in again. Is he about to return? Will I end up like the ones lying dead around me? Second of all, her descriptions make it quite clear that as long as she was acting, or planning action, she was precisely not concerned with being afraid. Her very factual descriptions of what she did to escape are precisely not descriptions of someone who is panicking. Fear is what sets in the middle ground between the absolute certainty of the presence of the murderer, and the certainty she created for herself by acting and deciding to act. When there was uncertainty about what she should do and what she could do, when there was uncertainty concerning the whereabouts of the attacker and about who he was, those were the times when fear and panic took hold.

A similar point can be drawn from a different case of people being under attack. In her mammoth work *Fear: A Cultural History*, Joana Bourke reconstructs the experiences of the people of Great Briton before the Second World War: '[I]t was usual for people to find the anticipation of danger much more frightening than actual disaster. This was a common experience for civilians in wartime Britain, where people reported that their terrifying nightmares of future military conflict vanished with the declaration of war in 1939' (Bourke 2006: 229). About the raids themselves she concludes. 'Undeniably, *waiting* for air raids was emotionally wearing. When they came there was almost a sense of relief' (Bourke 2006: 229–30).

This general tendency found its most extreme case in point at the Bethnal Green disaster on 3 March 1943. The alarm sounded a quarter past eight in the morning and some ten minutes later 1,500 people were gathered in Bethnal Green Underground station – one of the largest bomb shelters in London. At 8.27 an Anti-Aircraft Artillery battery close by fired a series of rockets. This caused a large-scale panic among the people who had not yet reached safety. Bourke describes what happened next. 'Tragically, terrified people reached the steps of the underground shelter at the same time. A woman and her baby stumbled on the steps. Within a few seconds hundreds of panic-stricken people had fallen on top of one another' (Bourke 2006: 233). A total of 173 men, women and children were crushed to death immediately.

One could find many reasons to explain why things unfolded in such a catastrophic way. As Bourke explains the Britons were at the time becoming increasingly aware of the British air-raids over Berlin, and as a result they feared German retaliation. Furthermore, the fact that there was only one entrance to the shelter and that it consisted of a large staircase with no handrails at the centre probably also contributed. But crucially the nearest bomb had fallen more than two miles away. Indeed, it was the panic itself that had killed people.

One of the more promising analysts of the politics of fear at work in the war on terror is Brian Massumi. From a strict Deleuzeian standpoint he argues that fear is not a feeling that is caused in us by an external effect, rather it is something that emerges and *affects* us from our own movements and (e)motions. By introducing fear in this way, Massumi is doing something with the concept that is quite distinct from the way Bourke herself describes it. She argues that fear is an emotion which has a determinate object in order to distinguish it from anxiety (see, e.g. Bourke 2006: 189–92). When I am fearful, I'm scared because of . . . (Islamists, George W. Bush, Men, Women, Traffic, etc.). Massumi argues in a different way. In 'Fear (The Spectrum Said)' (Massumi 2005) he refers to William James: 'As William James famously argued, fear strikes the body and compels it to action before it registers consciously. When it registers, it is as a realization growing from the bodily action already under way: *we don't run because we feel afraid, we feel afraid because we run*' (Massumi 2005: 36). In the end the question 'what causes fear?' serves to misconstrue the understanding of what fear is. The description given by James, though it is catchy, should be immediately specified. If fear arises affectively – that is out of bodily movements and connections – it is not irrelevant which kind of motion, we are talking about. As we saw in the case of Kaur above, one can find a safeguard from fear by running or, as it was the case for her, swimming. One the other hand, running while thinking one is being bombed can certainly cause panic, and crucially the stress of waiting for an attack can often be more frightening than an actual attack, as we saw in the cases from the British being bombed during the Second World War. As Massumi argues, it is the vagueness and indeterminacy of the situation itself that affects us. Fear is something that takes hold on us when we are put in an uncertain position of stress and alert; it is much less dependent upon a confrontation with something truly threatening.

While Massumi's assumption that fear is an affect rather than an effect could seem to lend a helpful hand in interpreting the cases we have presented above, his genuine interest is not the question of how people react in certain situations. It is rather aimed at the ways in which people's fears can be utilized as an instrument of control.

Here, the policies of the Bush administration offered plenty of initiatives that could be interpreted in just that way. Perhaps none were more telling than the Homeland Security Advisory System introduced by the Department of Homeland Security in March 2002. This was the system that introduced the colour coding of the threat from terrorism: Red for Severe, Orange for High, Yellow for Elevated, Blue for Guarded and Green for Low.

Two things should be noted about this system. First of all it came without an expiration date; there was no natural end to the times in which the threat from terrorism needed to be reported with these kinds of information systems. Massumi's point is that we should take literally the fact that the war on terror at times was described by the Bush administration as the 'long war' in order to make it clear that this would be an almost never-ending struggle (Massumi 2007: 25). Second of all, and most importantly, *there is no colour for safe on the scale.* 'Insecurity, the spectrum says, is the new normal' (Massumi

2005: 31). For Massumi, this constitutes a crucial point about the way of life produced by the policies of the war on terror. The normal state of life is one of constant suspicion, constant alertness and awareness. Never let down your guard, never stop thinking about all the terrible things that could happen, never stop being afraid.

The system has since then been taken out of order (on 27 April 2011 by the Obama administration), but at the moment we should not use that fact to take anything away from Massumi's analysis (we will reconsider this fact and the replacement system below), since at the time of his writing, the system was indeed without an expiration date. Furthermore, throughout its existence the system always hovered in the upper echelon of Red, Orange and Yellow. It was never at the level of Blue or Green.

There were many other examples. Among the more striking we find the campaign by the LA Police Department called iWatch, and the US Federal Government website ready.gov. Ready.gov was launched soon after the 9/11 attack to teach the population to be ready for the next terrorist attack. It delivered everything one could expect in terms of false choices 'we can either be afraid or we can be ready', and borderline self-parody, as Mark Andrejevic observed: 'the image of man standing in the path of nuclear radiation with a timer pointing to him ("minimize time spent exposed") borders on self-parody: the twenty-first century version of "duck and cover" ' (Andrejevic 2006: 451). iWatch on the other hand was a system planned by the LA Police Department in order to gather information about potential terrorists on the ground by engaging ordinary citizens in what is euphemistically termed 'Suspicious Activity Reporting' (McNamara 2009). In the commercial that ran as the system was launched, we are confronted with the faces of numerous people of all ages and skin colour telling us how iWatch is a system for reporting suspicious behaviour. 'So if you see, hear or smell something suspicious, report it', the faces tell us, 'Let law enforcement determine if it's a threat, and let the experts decide', and it concludes 'I watch, I report, I keep us safe'. As the video goes on, the faces speaking to us move closer and closer to the point where they are almost bursting through the screen – then they retract and are put at a certain distance, only to come closer once again, thus creating an utmost uncanny effect. In this pulsing movement back and forth the faces keep telling us about how the watching of the suspicious behaviour of others is really a friendly and neighbourly activity that is for the best of us all, while at the same time it effectively indicates that there really is a most severe, bloodthirsty and barbaric force looking to destroy everyone and especially our families and children, right beneath the surface of our otherwise calm and peaceful daily lives.

One could go on endlessly about these and similar examples, but I will spare the readership. In retrospect the mechanisms involved are so painfully obvious that it almost seems embarrassing to expose them through analysis. Nevertheless: by being constantly confronted with systems that are supposed to help us feel safe and ensue our safety, we are constantly reminded that there really is an extreme potential danger lurking around every corner; by being recommended to keep watch over suspicious behaviour in our communities and neighbourhoods, we are effectively learning that these are suspicious environments. In this way I could go on with the unmasking of the ideology of terror. Our present purpose, however, is of a different kind. What we should take care to do is rather to link the political ontology of terror expounded above to the analysis of fear of terrorism and to the measures taken by governments to remind us, it would seem, that we should remain fearful of terrorism.

Ontic fear versus ontological anxiety

As mentioned Brian Massumi's analysis is an interesting one for our considerations. His focus is on the way potentiality and potential threats, or better yet virtual threats, affect us. But precisely by working from a Deleuzian point of view, he is at odds with the perspective, we are working with here. The general idea of the analysis Massumi presents of the Homeland Security Advisory System is that potentiality is at work at the bottom of politics of fear. In 'Potential Politics and the Primacy of Pre-emption' (Massumi 2007) he further pursues this idea and argues in a way similar to what I have done above, that there is a connection between the politics of the war against terror and the ontology of potentiality. He too finds that the paradigmatic ontological statement about the war on terror was Rumsfeld's argument about the unknown unknown. The point in the war on terror is not that there are actual terrorists out there trying to kill us all, but rather that there is a field of potential terror waiting to happen. The analysis Massumi makes of the Homeland Security Advisory System – an analysis which, as I have indicated, could very easily be expanded to cover numerous other examples – goes to say that this potentiality precisely works as a tool for governmental control of the emotional response of the population.

The difference between Massumi's analysis and mine lies in our understanding of the concept of potentiality, and as a result in how we see the emotional responses to the war on terror. Massumi's point is that the war on terror fosters an as of yet unseen level of generalized fear. Where the cold war produced an arms race, which gave us a distinct feeling that the world might end any day in a nuclear war, it also functioned with a certain level of certainty that the eschatological moment would never actually come about. If the MAD doctrine worked, then we would not need to be afraid. But in the war on terror this point is inverted according to Massumi, not because the threat is any greater – it is not – but because it is less specific. The very fact that we are being told that we are fighting something that we do not even know that we do not know anything about, means that it could be anything anywhere all the time. Because of this, the political psychology of the war on terror is never-ending fear according to Massumi.

Concerning the latter point about potentiality a Heideggarian question forces itself upon us. It is quite simple: Given that Massumi's analysis targets the indeterminacy of the unknown unknown threats and the related ontological concept of potentiality, why not simply make use of the most helpful dichotomy, discussed by Heidegger and others, between anxiety and fear? Indeed, it almost seems as if Massumi insists upon *not* using the concept of anxiety, even if it could seem like an obvious way to go.[5]

The distinction between anxiety and fear is tangent to the crucial Heideggarian distinction between the ontic and the ontological. This is of course the distinction between beings and the being of beings – between objects and the mode of their existence. When we are fearful, we are able to say what it is that causes our fears (e.g. Jihadists, George W. Bush, Jews, Danes, Ducks, TV Show hosts, Monsters under the bed or the tingling sensation at the back of my head). That is precisely what we are not able to do when we are struck with anxiety. When we are caught in the mood of anxiety, we have the feeling that something somehow is terribly wrong, but we cannot say exactly what it is. It is anything, everything and nothing at all at the same time. Anxiety reveals *nothingness*, as Heidegger puts it *What is Metaphysics?*, and in doing so it reflects us back upon our fundamental being-in-the-world (Heidegger 1998: 35). Thus anxiety reveals a fundamental ontological truth whereas fear merely works at the ontic surface of beings.

Significantly for our purposes, the Heideggarian view of anxiety posits it in relation to potentiality, where fear relates to actuality. This is a point which follows quite nicely from the distinction between ontic fear and ontological anxiety. Because fear relates to intentional objects, we are always therefore able to point out some *actuality* which makes us fearful. Conversely, because there can be given no corresponding intentional object of anxiety, therefore it is merely the realization that the possible (whatever it is) is really possible which is revealed in that mood. In this way the notion of anxiety does seem to fit the logic Massumi analyses in relation to the politics of fear – so why not simply use the term? The answer lies with Massumi's Deleuzianism.

While Deleuze does praise Heidegger's ontological difference at the very beginning of *Difference and Repetition* (Deleuze 1994: xvii), it should be clear that they do not understand the concept of difference in quite the same way. In ontological difference Heidegger finds *the* difference, Western metaphysics has been guilty of forgetting, because of its tendency towards conceptualizing being (Sein) as an entity (Seiendes). Deleuze contrarily aims at a notion of difference which does not allow for *one* overarching difference. This is what is entailed in his notion of a plane of immanence. Whatever the one difference might be suggested to be, the two differing terms would have to immediately be (re)inscribed in the same plane. Thus, if Heidegger's claim is that being should never be thought as an existing thing – that there must be a fundamental difference between being and beings – Deleuze's counterclaim would be that this difference would have to take place in a plane of immanence. Immanence must be thought as immanent to itself, if it is to make sense at all. And for this precise reason Massumi, being the strict Deleuzian that he is, would find it very troubling to introduce any kind of distinction which would introduce an ontological difference that would not fall back on a field of immanence. The distinction between fear and anxiety, with its close relation to the Heideggarian ontological difference, would seem to be a candidate for just this kind of hidden transcendence.

Heidegger argues that Anxiety is a mood which provides a more privileged point of departure for investigating the meaning of being, than fear does. Anxiety is more profound. It is deeper in a sense. This is far from coincidental. There is a kind of hierarchy which is clearly an important theme in Heidegger's thought. Again and again in *Being and Time*, Heidegger is forcing the issue of being more radical in the sense of going deeper at the roots of thought. He searches for the more *original* hermeneutic situation, from which the being of beings would be able to appear for Dasein (Heidegger 1983: 199–201, 1993: 232–3, 1998: 33–4). The lectures on *The Fundamental Concepts of Metaphysics: World – Finitude – Solitude* (Heidegger 1983) are equally telling in this regard. Here Heidegger is clearly aware of the trap contained in the project of searching for originality. When he announces the project of finding an adequate mood for the interpretation of our current being in the world, he specifically states that he is on the search for *a* fundamental mood, and that there are several (Heidegger 1983: 89). One cannot objectively determine *the* fundamental mood. To do so would be a way of doing violence to the project of thinking from within finitude; it would be to postulate an a priori concept in which the original meaning of being would already be anticipated. But still, the entire trajectory of his analysis of the mood he chooses to analyse, namely boredom, has the form of going-deeper-towards-the-one (see e.g., Heidegger 1983: 200). And once he has found the profound and deep meaning of boredom this sense of boredom is meant to be used in the unfolding of *the* fundamental concepts of metaphysics: world, finitude, solitude. As Heidegger argues with the aid of Novalis at the very outset of the lectures, philosophy is really homesickness – a longing towards finding home, a oneness with and in the world (Heidegger 1983: 7).

It is this very notion of the depth of human existence, which would be problematic from Massumi's Deleuzian perspective, because it would seem to sneak in a hidden transcendence in the very midst of immanent human finite existence. Heidegger attempts to accomplish on one hand a first philosophy, as he seeks the most fundamental and original meaning of being, and on the other hand he does this from the site of finitude. It is in, or at, or around, Dasein, in the sense of the concrete human existence that is spread out between birth and death, that the one original truth about being is revealed. His original move consists in positing the very site of epistemological limitations, the human existence with all its flaws, errors, antinomies and inconsistencies, as the site where the truth of being comes to the fore. But while his rejection of onto-theo-logical metaphysics precisely is the rejection of an overarching infinitely valid system of concepts, which secondarily can be applied to finite things, this rejection does not save him from belonging to the very tradition he himself is criticizing. Precisely because of the tendency towards always seeking the one meaning of being, therefore his fundamental ontology easily comes to look like an onto-theo-logy itself. It is certainly a *finite* onto-theo-logy, but it is an onto-theo-logy nonetheless.

The problem of onto-theo-logy, the problem of the hidden transcendence in the midst of a philosophical programme of immanence, is in Deleuze's universe condensed in the notion of the body without organs, which on the one hand describes the virtual dimension of the body and on the other, more important in our case, describes the virtual dimension of reality in general. In *Anti-Oedipus* Deleuze and Guattari write: 'To anyone who asks: "Do you believe in God?" we should reply in strictly Kantian or Schreberian terms "Of course, but only as the master of the disjunctive syllogism, or as its a priori principle (God defined as the Omnitudo realitatis from which all secondary realities are derived by a process of division)" (Deleuze & Guattari 2004a: 14). The body without organs is the notion they use for this God, who is the very opposite of God. The body without organs is the virtual space in which all real flows take place. But the crucial point of the body without organs is that it cannot remain a mere abstract potentiality, a theoretical concept of totality, from which everything can be derived by virtue of division. It cannot be understood as the ontological being of all ontic beings. It is not simply the transcendental condition of all immanent reality and change. On the contrary, the body without organs is itself to be encountered in this very realm of reality that it is the ultimate medium of. The crucial example of this folding of the virtual space back onto a real one is found in the notion of capital. 'Capital is undoubtedly the body without organs of the capitalist, or rather of the capitalist being. But as such it is not only the fluid and petrified substance of money, for it will give to the sterility of money the form where money produces money' (Deleuze & Guattari 2004a: 11). Capital is not simply money in the sense of a common medium of exchange, because it can itself become an object of trade. And in the trading of money with money, more money is produced – a point which we have experienced both the excesses and the pitfalls of in the financial and debt crises that dominate much of the global political agenda ten years after 9/11. Because of this ability of capital to at once be the utmost medium of capitalist exchange and at the very same time an object of exchange, therefore it serves as a perfect example of the notion of the body without organs.

In the present context the notion of capital is not simply a good example however. Massumi's Deleuzian perspective has the significance of capitalism front and centre. It is not simply the functioning of power in one state among the many states in the world that is of interest to him; his specific interest is the United States as the site of military domination and global capitalism. This point should clarify the problems inherent for Massumi in accepting a Heideggarian distinction between fear and anxiety. If we accept the notion that fear is bound to the ontic surface of human existence whereas anxiety taps into the ontological depths, then we might find ourselves in the situation where what is really at stake in the war on terror is something far more metaphysically fundamental than what goes on in the contingent ontic horizon of the war on terror itself. Indeed, if the fear we are confronting in the war on terror, is really anxiety, does it then not simply relate to an ontological condition of being human in general?

And if that is the case, does it not make irrelevant any criticism of ontic political measures such as the Homeland Security Advisory System? Precisely because of such questions, the very notion of anxiety as something which cannot be (re) inscribed at the level of ontic fear, must be dismissed in Massumi's Deleuzian perspective.

Where Massumi's interest lies the with political and social consequences of present political and military strategies, and thus at the level of what Heidegger would dismiss as merely ontic, Heidegger instead searches for the ontological foundations of what it means to be human regardless, in the end, of such surface phenomena as the war on terror. To make a caricature of a Heideggarian reversal one could ask: what is the ontic catastrophe of the war on terror, compared with the ontological catastrophe of man in his modern state of having forgotten being? Asking in such a way Heidegger would, in Massumi's perspective, be lost in antiquated and (more problematically) uncritical metaphysics. As Heidegger went on the search for the original meaning of being, he was blinded to the very real political issues of his own time (we need no reminder of just how naïve Heidegger was in this regard), and accordingly we would, in the light of Massumi's position, commit the very same mistake if we were to introduce the Heideggarian notions in a contemporary analysis of politics. Conversely, Heidegger could, in our imaginary conversation, return the favour and call Massumi's infatuation with the comings and goings of the ontic history of the world the result of the forgetting of being (*seinsvergessenheit*) that is characteristic of the history of metaphysics, he set out to destroy. To both of them, therefore, metaphysics would be like the name given to the worst theoretical position imaginable.

My aim in the present investigations is to do precisely what is thus forbidden: metaphysics. But since this is a metaphysics that is to be seen as our own time captured in thoughts, this imaginary conflict between Massumi and Heidegger puts a crucial question to the point: In which sense can ontological reflections upon being, potentiality and reality remain relevant for the specific contemporary historical situation in which we are placed? This is of course a reformulation of the question I have already posed in the introduction, where I argued for the Schellingian road we have followed so far. In a way the current imagined debate between Heidegger and Massumi repeats this original metaphilosophical question at the level of political psychology. How do we navigate the difficult path of asking ontological questions about the fundamental structure of being, while at the same time insisting upon the relevance of ontic reality? The danger of the Heideggarian conclusion for Massumi's project, and for mine, is clearly discernible. If the anxiety can ultimately be identified as something which originates in the fundamental structure of our existence as such, then all the contingent historical matters relating to the end of the Cold War and the so-called war on terror are more or less insignificant. That again would make political critique and critical theory moot. But Massumi's insistence upon a Deleuzian plane of immanence does not offer any way out for us as it is both strictly anti-metaphysical and anti-dialectical.

The Schellingian third

Fortunately, we have a third option. That is the Schellingian perspective we are working with here. In Massumi's terms the politics of the war on terror, the notion of unending fear and the notion of potentiality fit each other perfectly. Potentiality here is not a dialectical term, but rather a notion of vagueness and uncertainty. In the politics of potentiality we are put on constant alert and in stressful awareness of . . . that which we do not yet know that we do not know what is. In Heidegger's conceptual universe we find a notion of anxiety which is tied very closely to the notions of potentiality and nothingness, we are presenting here. Indeed, the Schellingian concepts we presented above would seem to fit the Heideggarian notion of anxiety like a glove. Yet Heidegger's penchant for seeking the one fundamental meaning of being, does present a problem as was just argued. The trick of the Schellingian perspective will thus have to be to reject both the strict Heideggarian interpretation of anxiety, while at the same time rejecting the anti-dialectical perspective of Massumi's Deleuzianism.

The Schellingian concept of potentiality has a tripartite structure, as we have seen. Given any notion of potentiality, there are, in the Schellingian perspective, always three different possible outcomes. A potentiality can become actualized. It can remain a mere potentiality. Or it can become realized as un-actualized, in the way we saw it in the shape of a not-dancing dancer. In this perspective it is the third option that is being denied by Massumi. To put the point crudely the Deleuzian thought focuses on becoming; it seeks out the state of phenomena in their being-not-yet-fully-formed. It is in this way Massumi conceptualizes fear. The notion of potentiality he presents is one of vagueness; it is one that highlights an uncertainty regarding whether we are dealing with an actuality or a mere potentiality. But what we do not find is the notion of a realization of potentiality as un-actualized; he does not admit of a potentiality of nothingness. In a way

Massumi thus remains on a par with Agamben. The vagueness of the situation, the potentiality in the form of being-not-yet-fully-formed likens Agamben's notion of potentiality as impotentiality. What we find in Massumi's analysis of fear is precisely a threat that is working by remaining 'a something not at work' whereas the figure, we should be searching for, is that of 'a nothingness at work'.

This hesitation towards a third term of dialectics again goes all the way back to Deleuze himself. Deleuze's stated ambition of thinking difference and repetition together is to avoid the categories of identity and negation. The classic dialectical terms of negativity, nothingness and being were to be subsided for the terms difference and repetition, conceived in such a way that one could precisely avoid being caught up in the metaphysics of the one. As soon as one admits the terms of negativity and nothingness, it would seem, one is right back with the traditional metaphysical notions of identity and oneness.

Interestingly enough Deleuze finds an ally in Schelling in the struggle against Hegelian dialectics, which of course is the main enemy. He writes for instance in *Difference and Repetition* 'The most important aspect of Schelling's philosophy is his consideration of powers. How unjust, in this respect, is Hegel's critical remark about the black cows! Of these two philosophers, it is Schelling who brings difference out of the night of the Identical, and with finer more varied and more terrifying flashes of lightning than those of contradiction: with *progressivity*' (Deleuze 1994: 240). It should be clear that I do not accept Deleuze's account of either Hegel or Schelling. While I agree that Schelling's philosophy is centred in the notion of potency, the crucial point is that it is a potency of nothingness. In other words the Schelling I am defending here would probably look a little too much like Hegel in the eyes of Deleuze. But against Deleuze it should be held that this condemns neither Hegel nor Schelling to reiterating a philosophy of the one, as I argued in the introduction above. Indeed, it could seem that the fundamental idea of German Idealism, as I presented it above, namely the idea of an ontology of the split-into-two, is the very thing Deleuze flat out denies: 'There has only ever been one ontological proposition: being is univocal' (Deleuze 1994: 44). Would it not be fair to say that it is this insistence that ontology can only be a thinking of the one which makes him blind to possibility that dialectics could be something other than a technique of reiterating oneness?

Instead of insisting that dialectics must be condemned to reinstate the all-engulfing one, we should follow the path of Schelling's potencies as excess and lack, which in terms of precision has a distinct advantage over Massumi's notion of potentiality as indeterminacy. That an indeterminate danger looms, simply means that anything is possible. An unspecified threat indicates that something dreadful is bound to happen, but *what* is going to happen remains open. The field of what could happen is simply the field of the possible. Everything is possible. Even the things that we do not know that we do not know anything about are possible. But in a crucial sense that has *always* been the case. It is always the case that the field of what could happen is radically open. As one walks down the street it is always possible that one could be hit with the proverbial brick in the head. The point about the war on terror and the invoking of the Rumsfeldian unknown unknown, is that here the *potency* of potentiality changes. In Schellingian terms what happens to potentiality in the war on terror is that it becomes excessively potent.

Now suddenly everything that potentially could happen is interpreted in analogy to the dancer who is not-dancing. A plane going from A to B is a terrorist attack, which is not-happening, a railway station during rush-hour is the site for a catastrophe that constantly is not-occurring. What Massumi must end up characterizing rather vaguely as indeterminate potentiality, we can now describe in a more precise way as excessively *potent* potentiality.

Interestingly Kierkegaard made a very similar point when he argued that anxiety is the 'possibility of the possible' (Kierkegaard, SKS IV, 348). Anxiety relates to the very force inherent in the potential, not specifically to the content of the possible – be it determinate or indeterminate. It is these more detailed dialectical structures of the concept of potentiality which I find to be lacking in Massumi's analysis.

And it is precisely because of the Schellingian dialectic of the potency of potentiality that we can find a workable distinction between fear and anxiety, which does not commit us to the kind of uncritical existentialist dismissal of ontic political history that at the very least is a possible outcome of the Heideggarian metaphysics of finitude. The concept of potentiality we are working with here is not a concept of the depths of human existence. It has been construed by investigating the political reality of the war on terror. Thus the anxiety that relates to the potent potentiality we are dealing with is a surface phenomenon much like fear.

The uncanny

The best way of seeing the difference between the Schellingian and the Heideggarian concept of anxiety is to focus on the concept of the uncanny, to which it is closely linked. Heidegger makes that much clear both in the lecture

What is Metaphysics? (Heidegger 1998: 34) and in *Being and Time* (Heidegger 1993: 188). In both cases he underlines the point that the uncanny (das Un-heimliche) means the un-homely. The feeling of anxiety is to Heidegger the feeling of not being at home in the world. In anxiety we feel the utmost form of alienation. 'The Being-In arrives at the existential mode of Not-at-Home. Speaking of the uncanny means nothing else' (Heidegger 1993: 189).

I will argue Heidegger is wrong in this claim. Heidegger could have usefully concerned himself with the discussion given to the concept by his Austrian contemporary Sigmund Freud. That would have led him back to Schelling, to whom Freud directly refers in giving his definition of the uncanny: 'Everything is uncanny that ought to have remained secret and hidden, but which has come to the fore' (Schelling, SW XII, 649; Freud 1987).[6] The Freudian/Schellingian understanding of the uncanny focuses on the fact that 'heimlich' not only means homely, but also secret or hidden.[7] The uncanny is that which ought to have remained secret and hidden, but which nevertheless emerges. The significance of this idea can be seen by interrogating Schelling's use of the concept in his interpretation of Homeric mythology.

Homer represents a pivotal point in the history of mythology for Schelling. His point is that here, for the first time, one finds a pure and unabashed polytheism. While all mythology is understood as polytheism by Schelling, the ones that preceded Homer were really to be understood as serial monotheisms. It was not until Homer that each singular God (Apollo, Hera, Zeus, etc.) was fully and wholly a God (Schelling, SW XII, 650). In the prior forms of mythology Schelling found that no matter what allegorical forms, and no matter what shapes the Gods took, they were always a shape of one and the same principle. The principle which dominated the earlier forms of mythology according to Schelling, was the principle of ground as contraction, which we have discussed in detail above (Schelling, SW XII, 649). The serial monotheism is the 'false' monotheism where the contraction of God, his envious and egoistic tendency, remains the highest principle. That was the structure of all pre-Homeric, but not really polytheistic, polytheisms. Schelling's point with regard to the success of Homer's mythology is in other words that here, finally, the principle of ground is defeated and placed in its proper setting in the eternal past. The ground is posited as the first moment in creation, and exactly by being posited as the first it is also posited as that which is secondarily overcome. The point now is that this entails a certain forgetting of the principle of the ground in Homer (Schelling, SW XII, 648). It is precisely because of this forgetting of the envious destructive one that Homeric mythology can emerge as a true mythology of the many.

Of course Freud would have been drawn to such an interpretation of Homer. One could very well argue that Schelling's reading of Homer points out a mythological unconscious – indeed perhaps the emergence of the unconscious in the history of mythology. It is only *after* the contracting principle is banished back into the eternal past in Homeric mythology that it is possible for it to re-emerge as that, which *should have remained hidden* but which re-emerges again and again. The creation of the uncanny as that which should have remained hidden, but which comes to the fore, is precisely made possible by the Homeric forgetting of the ground. It is only when it has been effectively forgotten, after it has been placed in the eternal past, that the ground is able to uncover its hiddenness and emerge as truly uncanny. In this way the Schellingian uncanny is on a par with the Freudian unconscious, as that which emerges from the eternal past where it has been posited.

By taking up Freud and the famous concept of the unconscious, we should take great care to specify its meaning – if there ever was a concept which has been hopelessly misconstrued over the course of its intellectual history, surely it was the Freudian unconscious. I believe Eric Santner is very precise when he gives the following description: 'Freud's crucial breakthrough, the feature that distinguishes his conception of the unconscious from all previous attempts to think this "other scene", is, as Jacques Lacan has often emphasized, that unconscious mental activity has something mechanical, something machinelike about it' (Santner 2001: 28). The point, which Santner takes great care to expound in *The Psychotheology of Everyday Life* (Santner 2001), is that this mechanical machinelike feature of the unconscious has nothing to do with biological or, what would be the version in vogue today, neuro-scientific reductionism. The Freudian unconscious is a machinelike feature of human spiritual activity as such. The unconscious is that which appears as the lack of freedom in the midst of the sphere of human freedom. But this should not be mistaken for the idea that the unconscious is another scene of hidden reasons or causes which pull the strings of my actions behind my back. In a sense it is much less than that. There is not some meaningful content to the unconscious; it does not harbour secret, or more true, desires, that is, that I secretly want to kill my father and sleep with my mother. That the unconscious has a mechanic or machinelike way of functioning goes to say that it does not contain fully fledged meanings of this sort. The unconscious does not want this or that, it does not signify anything specific; it merely wants without an object of desire; it merely signifies without a signified.

Kierkegaard makes a similar point in his analysis of anxiety, which he develops in a reading of Genesis 3. When God forbade Adam to eat from the tree of knowledge of good and evil, Adam surely could not have understood this prohibition. If he had, he would already have known about good and evil, but he had not yet eaten from the tree, and thus he did not. Therefore the prohibition must have made little sense to him. But for Kierkegaard it is precisely this prohibition, which does not really make sense that creates the feeling of anxiety (Kierkegaard, SKS IV, 350). The incomprehensible prohibition makes him painfully aware that he could . . . He is not quite sure what it is that he could, but the very tangible sense of potentiality arises.

Of course Heidegger was right to point out that the meaning of the concept of the uncanny has to do with not feeling at home in the world. The problem lies with his idea that the uncanny means unhomeliness *and nothing else.* The problem is again that Heidegger insists on the search for the one original meaning of being. The analysis of the mood of anxiety is exactly used in order to uncover the meaning of Dasein as being-unto-death. Anxiety uncovers our being placed in a fundamental relation to our own death, and the consequential solution for the early Heidegger is that human existence has the all-important task of embracing this finite existence in a resolute manner: 'F r e i h e i t z u m T o d e' (Heidegger 1993: 266, Heidegger's emphasis).

What is argued in the Schellingian/Freudian line of thought is precisely the opposite. There is no freedom in the depths of human existence. Instead there is something far more banal. The depths of human existence are a stuttering, a repetitious contraction, a nothing appearing in the midst of nothingness. The uncanny is accordingly that which happens when this 'depth' is revealed in all its flatness. It is that which takes place when meaning is cut up, involuntarily held back. The uncanny is a speech impediment of spirit.

The uncanny and terror

Finally, we can bring these insights into the concepts of anxiety and the uncanny to bear on the analysis of the politics of fear. The very easy mistake one often commits in any investigation of the politics of fear is to suppose a much too straightforward causal link between policy measures, such as the Homeland Security Advisory System or the NSS-2002, and the environment of political fear that they create. Too often it is implicitly assumed that if people are being told that there is reason to be afraid, then they will become afraid, simply because they have been told so (in these not very veiled ways). As if the telling and the meanings produced by telling possessed a kind of magical quality, which made people afraid. The crucial analytic point I am making with the introduction of the notion of terrorism as a linguistic excess and the Schellingian interpretation of anxiety and the uncanny consists precisely in challenging this kind of simplicity. The problem is that it in one sense is too 'spiritualistic' and in another sense not 'spiritualistic' enough. It operates with a causality that is generated by meanings, by spirit if you will, but it lacks an understanding of the speech impediment of spirit.

Massumi is certainly not the only one who is guilty of this kind of negligence. A very general tendency in literature critical of the politics of the war on terror during the Bush years could more or less be characterized as Bush-bashing. To this author there certainly is nothing wrong with a little Bush-bashing, but becoming caught up in the condemnation of what a particular government is and does, can lead to blindness towards the truly problematic issues at hand. Characteristically, Massumi wrote about the Homeland Security Advisory System:

> In the aftermath of 9/11, the public's fearfulness had tended to swing out of control in response to dramatic, but maddeningly vague, government warnings of an impending follow-up attack. The [Homeland Security] alert system was designed to modulate that fear. It could raise it a pitch, then lower it before it became too intense, or even worse, before habituation dampened response. Timing was everything. Less fear itself than fear fatigue became an issue of public concern. Affective modulation of the populace was now an official, central function of an increasingly time-sensitive government. (Massumi 2005: 32)

This is no coincidental way of arguing. While there certainly is something to be criticized about the way governments across the world reacted to 9/11, the problem with this way of arguing is that it seems to assume that these governments *know what they themselves are saying and doing*. One could likely assume that there was an intention to affectively modulate the populace as Massumi claims, but one assumes too much about the techniques invented with this purpose, if one thinks that they successfully accomplish this intent. To put the point in linguistic terms the problem is that by arguing in this way, one implicitly or explicitly accepts the Guillaumian formula: expression + expressiveness = 1. When Massumi argues that the Homeland Security Advisory System *can be used* in such and such ways, then he is precisely assuming that the meaning of the intent behind the system can be successfully expressed though some kind of combination of expression and expressiveness – without speech impediments as it were. What is missing is the reconfiguration I have given to Guillaume's formula above: expression + expressiveness = 1 + 0. This is generally the problem with much of the critical literature on the war on terror (and if we extend the scope a little bit I would wager that the same counts for much critical literature on the functioning of power as such). *There is too little focus on the function of zero meaning.*

The notion of the uncanny that we have dug out using Freud and Schelling should exactly be taken to relate to the added element: '+0'. The uncanny is precisely the work of this zero. It does not, as Heidegger thought, reveal something crucial about the *meaning* of human existence or being as such. There is no full meaning to this element. Instead, our investigation has put us in close relation to Louis Althusser's idea of interpellation, as it is expounded in his *Ideology and Ideological State Apparatuses (Notes towards an Investigation)* (Althusser 2008: 48). The call which affects us is pure empty form of the call, the mere 'Hey, you there!' made famous by Althusser's policeman. In the Althussarian analysis, ideology does not primordially tell us what we should do, it merely tells us that we should pay attention and be alert to its calling. In an analogous way the uncanny is speaking to us as a mere poking, as the emergence of an address, which we recognize to be directed at us, but which we cannot explicate in terms of its intent or meaning. In this way the uncanny is precisely about the excessive element of meaning which has no meaning as such.

Take the Homeland Security Terrorism Alert system: The mere content of the utterances from this alert system are fairly innocuous. Does it really make a difference if the threat from terrorism is 'severe' or 'high'? Can one tangibly feel the difference between the two in terms of how afraid one is to walk in public places? In the end such differences are minimal at most. But every time the system itself is brought about and talked about by public officials, every time the level of the threat is changed (regardless whether it is up or down), the very acts of speaking about the system or of announcing the change serve to reiterate an almost tautological statement that the terrorist threat is threatening – just like Althusser's policeman says nothing but the tautological 'you are you'. These acts produce the spectre of the nothingness, which never ceases not to happen.

If the politics of fear can be said to have gained force following the 9/11 terrorist attacks, then it is precisely because of this excess-meaning itself. It is this excess-meaning which is produced everywhere and all the time, as public discourse motions on and on about the terrorist threat.

Boredom

The crucial problem with the lack of attention paid to the speech impediment of spirit in the analysis of the politics of fear is that the importance of boredom is all too easily missed. Quite often the discourse on terrorism and the potential dangers of the world we live, does not serve to produce fear. Quite often it would even be wrong to say that it creates a mood of anxiety. Quite often the constant reiteration of potential threats lurking everywhere all the time can simply be boring.

Consider the fate of the much maligned Homeland Security Advisory System. On 27 April 2011 the system was finally taken out of order. This event was as unceremonious as the instalment was spectacular. In order to know that it took place one would have to have had a somewhat fetishized relation to the system (yours truly is probably guilty of this). The system had long been hidden deeper and deeper into the Homepage of the Department of Homeland Security. But even more telling is the system that was put in its place: the National Terrorism Advisory System. Under this system alerts will only be issued when there is credible evidence of an actual threat – when there are threats they will be announced either as elevated or as imminent. At other times the system will simply announce 'The Secretary of Homeland Security has not issued an elevated or imminent alert at this time' and that is the current state of the system (Department of Homeland Security 2011). One can hardly find a clearer way for a government to say 'Nothing to see here. Move on.' What is interesting in this regard is the fact that from 13 August 2006 until it was replaced by the NTAS in 2011, the Homeland Security Advisory System was constantly at Orange – the second highest level on the scale. Is this not a clear sign that whatever energy there might have been in the concept of terrorism is now gone? We go directly and unceremoniously from a state in which terrorism is described as a constant high threat to 'nothing to see here'. In this way the previously so serious and terrifying threat of terrorism slowly but surely has become uninteresting and boring.

Arguing in this way forces a certain return of Heidegger upon us. Having argued the intricacies of fear, anxiety and the uncanny in detail in order to make a point about the way in which one should analyse our current political emotional climate, and having discussed and in the end dismissed much of the Heideggarian take on the concepts of anxiety and the uncanny, we are now in a position to harvest an important fruit of this analysis by taking the step that will link the emotions of boredom and anxiety, and suddenly we find ourselves deeply involved with Heidegger yet again! This is so, because Heidegger more than anyone has made an important mark on the philosophical interpretation of the concept of boredom. In Heidegger's hidden masterpiece *The Fundamental Concepts of Metaphysics – World, Finitude, Solitude* (Heidegger 1983), one finds almost 150 pages devoted to the analysis of this mood. As a short summary of Heidegger's view on boredom will show, we are confronted with a crucial formation of the potency of potentiality in boredom, which will help us see the curious link between anxiety and boredom.

Heidegger argues that there are two 'structural moments' in the mood of boredom. These are being-held-in-suspense ('Hingehaltenheit') and being-left-empty ('Leergelassenheit') (Heidegger 1983: 130). When we are bored, nothing really seems to be able to give meaningful content to our lives. That is the element of being-left-empty. But boredom is not only something which leaves us empty. In a sense we are forced into the state of being-left-empty. When we are truly bored, there is just no escaping it. Everything we do to escape boredom, various forms of pastime (Zeitvertreib), just seems to pull us further in. That is the element of being-held-in-suspense. Heidegger presents a phenomenology of boredom, which has three stages of increasing profoundness (yet another Heideggarian search for depth) according to the way in which being-held-in-suspense and being-left-empty are functioning. These stages are called 'Becoming bored by . . .' ('Gelangweiltwerden von . . .' (Heidegger 1983: 117–59)), 'Being bored at . . .' ('Sichlangweilen bei . . .' (Heidegger 1983: 160–98)) and 'it is boring for one' ('es ist einem langweilig' (Heidegger 1983: 199–238)).

'Becoming bored by something' is the first and most superficial stage analysed by Heidegger. It pretty much relates to what we mean, when we say of some particular thing that it is boring. Heidegger's example is a desolate railway station. When we through some unfortunate circumstance are stuck waiting for a train for several hours in a part of the country with which we are completely unfamiliar, we are very much at the risk of being bored. In this instance it is the particular railway station that is boring us. When we are bored by something, then that, which is boring, is some particular and clearly identifiable thing.

In the second stage of boredom this determinacy of the boring thing begins to dissolve. Heidegger's example here is an evening party, which as such does not seem to be any sort of boring thing. There are plenty of interesting conversations, the food is wonderful and one cannot find anything disagreeable about the music that is being played. And nevertheless, once one returns home, one cannot shake the feeling of having been immensely bored. There was nothing there which was boring, and yet one had a clear sense of boredom. Heidegger's point is that it is the whole situation as such which is boring.

In the third stage of boredom, 'it is boring for one', which Heidegger calls the most profound (tief) kind of boredom, the indeterminacy of what shows itself as boring is taken to the very limit. Symptomatically Heidegger also finds it very difficult to describe a definite situation, in which profound boredom shows itself. In *The Fundamental Concepts of Metaphysics* the only mention of something concrete goes as follows:

> To mention a possible, but completely contingent occasion for profound boredom, which perhaps will be familiar to some of us, only without our having noticed that we were caught in it: 'it is boring for one' to walk through the streets of a large city on a Sunday afternoon. (Heidegger 1983: 204)

Compared to the rich and colourful analyses of the railway station and the dinner party, this surely is not a lot to go by. But it seems to follow from the radical indeterminacy of profound boredom that it is almost impossible to give an analysis of something, which gives occasion to it. The point for Heidegger is that profound boredom, much like anxiety, is rooted in human existence as such. It is at the very core of our being-in-the-world, of our relating to beings in their totality. In profound boredom, we find that the totality of existing things is left fallow to us (Brachliegen). We experience a profound sense of lack, of the world simply being there, without rendering any kind of meaning. However, exactly because profound boredom enables us to experience the world as being completely devoid of meaning, in this way, it is also what can reveal to us that the world *could have had* a profound or deep-felt meaning.

Heidegger's point is that in the first two stages of boredom 'Becoming bored by . . .', 'Being bored at . . .', we are never put in a situation, where we have no possibility of escaping boredom. In fact, each of these forms of boredom is characterized by the ways in which we are able to (try to) escape being bored.

Concrete possibilities emerge everywhere. At the railway station, we look at the clock, we walk back and forth, we look at the timetable, we look at the clock again, we count the trees along the road, we try to read, we look at the clock and so on. All of these things present themselves as concrete ways in which we might escape our boredom. And likewise with regard to the dinner party, we have the arrangement of an entire evening with eating, conversing and listening – all with the purpose of escaping boredom.

In profound boredom all such concrete possibilities disappear. Heidegger's point in the analysis of profound boredom is that because all these concrete possibilities disappear, profound boredom reveals 'the originary *possibilitization*' (*die ursprüngliche* Ermöglichung) that characterizes human existence (Heidegger 1983: 215–16). Profound boredom reveals human existence as freedom – much in the same way as anxiety does according to Kierkegaard. This is also the point where Heidegger reveals himself to be a philosopher of homesickness (Heidegger 1983: 7). His aim with the analysis of boredom is precisely to find the kind of deep boredom, where it becomes impossible to get preoccupied with beings, and instead find a home with being as such. His relentless critique of the times in which we live ('Unseres heutigen Daseins' (Heidegger 1983: 89)) is thus that we are not able to be *bored enough*, we constantly flee our profound boredom into the more ontic spheres, where we try to kill time with various forms of entertainment (looking at the clock, counting the trees, speaking to the other guests at the dinner party, etc.).

Boredom and the war on terror

Our interest in this analysis is of course that boredom and anxiety thereby reveal very similar structures. Just like anxiety, boredom is concerned with potentiality, that is, with potentialities that are not potentialities for this or that concrete actualization, but rather with potentiality as such. In terms of content the moods of anxiety and boredom are exactly the same. Both are ways in which we experience nothingness.

What was learned about the understanding of anxiety in the above discussion was that it relates to the *potent* potentiality of nothingness. In anxiety we experience the potentiality of the nothing as excessively potent. The potential that things *can* . . . forces itself upon us in its very form of being potential. In boredom exactly the opposite is the case: here again we are confronted with nothingness, but instead of forcing itself upon us, it lies fallow. In boredom the myriad of potentialities that are open to human existence do not become impossible. Instead they lack force; they present themselves as unworthy of attention. To put the point as clearly as possible: they become *impotent*. In terms of the Schellingian dialectic the excessive potency of the potentiality of anxiety contracts back into the lacking potency of the potentiality of boredom.

In a final consideration of this predicament, it will be helpful to remind ourselves of a crucial point that was made by Kierkegaard with regard to anxiety. 'Anxiety is a sympathetic antipathy and an antipathetic sympathy' (Kierkegaard, SKS IV, 348). There is always an element of enjoyment in anxiety. Kierkegaard claims a certain 'sweetness' for anxiety. As we recall Kierkegaard makes the point that the initial prohibition to eat from the tree of knowledge must have been completely enigmatic. It only gives rise to the awareness of potentiality as such – it makes Adam aware that he can . . . 'What it is that he is capable of, thereof he has no idea; [. . .]. Only the possibility of being able is present as a higher form of ignorance, a higher expression of anxiety, because it in a higher sense both is and is not, because he in a higher sense loves it and flees it' (Kierkegaard, SKS IV, 350). Anxiety pokes us without revealing. It merely makes us aware of the potency of potentiality. In this way it gives rise to that uncanny feeling, but it also provides us with lure and excitement.

It is precisely this element of enjoyment that disappears, when the potent potentialities of terrorism slide into impotent potentialities. Terrorism continues to be potential, and (at least according to the Danish survey mentioned above) we may even regard it as a likely occurrence (even though we have no idea what this occurrence might be), but this potentiality no longer provides the excitement of anxiety. In this way the former potent potentialities slide into impotent potentialities. My argument regarding the emotional development of life during the war on terror is that this is what has happened. The incessant repeating of the threat from the unknown unknown slowly but surely began to lack potency and became boring and impotent.

In the second part of *Either Or* Kierkegaard's pseudonym author, Assessor Wilhelm, provides a striking analysis of Nero, which cuts to the heart of the issue here. Emperor Nero was for all relevant purposes on top of the world. Indeed, in many ways his empire simply was the world. There was nothing which could threaten his position. He could do as he pleased in every conceivable way. Unsurprisingly, Nero was extremely bored. The Assessor recollects how his young enjoyment-seeking friend[8] has often praised Nero: 'You once said with your usual temerity that one should not blame Nero for letting Rome burn in order to have some idea of the fire of Troja, but one should ask oneself if he really possessed the arts necessary for him to enjoy it' (Kierkegaard, SKS III, 179). The predicament of Nero is that he is so bored that he has lost the capacity to enjoy. Precisely because enjoyment is the only thing that is on his mind, therefore he cannot escape his boredom. Nero engages the entire court in finding satisfaction. 'All the knowledge in the world is set the task of finding new pleasures for him' (Kierkegaard, SKS III, 181). But to no avail. His boredom cannot be dispelled.

The result is, according to Wilhelm, that Nero's 'spirit contracts in him like a dark cloud, its anger hovers over his soul, and it turns into an anxiety, which does not even disappear in the moment of pleasure' (Kierkegaard, SKS III, 181). In this way Nero's boredom so very easily turns into a deep anxiety. The slightest change is enough to make the entire world of the emperor crumble. 'Look, that is the reason why his eye is so dark, that no-one dares look into it, his gaze so like a flash that it creates anxiety, because behind the eye the soul is shrouded in darkness. Such a gaze is often called an imperial gaze, and the whole world trembles before it, and yet his innermost essence is anxiety. A child that looks at him in a different way than he is accustomed to for a mere moment can terrify him, it is as if this human being owned him' (Kierkegaard, SKS III, 181). No wonder then that Nero in the end set the world ablaze.

It is not difficult to see the parallel between the acute characteristic Kierkegaard provides of the predicament of Nero and the global political situation of the West following the fall of the Berlin Wall as it is described by Fukuyama. Precisely because the West found itself in the situation where history had practically ended, therefore the dominant political sentiment was that of boredom. And it is exactly in the mood of boredom that we, so Kierkegaard, are susceptible to be stricken with anxiety at the slightest disturbance. A child looks at us differently. A nothingness takes place in the midst of nothingness, and suddenly all hell breaks loose. Thus we set the world ablaze and guard our every step, until we are slowly but surely calmed, and bored, again.

The Political Cosmology of Terror

By now we have gained quite a lot of ground in our investigations. We have worked out a method for capturing our own time in thoughts by revitalizing of the ultimate academic *faux pas* of the twentieth century: metaphysics. This has required a reformulation of metaphysics as last philosophy (rather than first). Furthermore, we have put this method to use in the investigation of the political ontology and the political psychology of terror above.

The present chapter sets out to investigate the political cosmology of terror. As such it sets out to discuss a theme which is less likely to make intuitive sense to the reader. Whereas anyone who has been even remotely sapient for the first decade of the twenty-first century will certainly be able to ascribe some general meaning to the notion of a political psychology of terror, it is far less likely that the political cosmology of terror is going to make immediate sense.

Where the political psychology set out to investigate the emotional aspects of living in a time of terror, the political cosmology aims at a description of the world in which these emotions are lived out. Crucial in this regard is the question of the relation between the state and its wars, which precisely might not be the state's to have after all. In so many words we are in the political cosmology of terror taking up the specific theme of what war means in the so-called war on terror. An investigation of this theme turns specifically cosmological once we seek out the spatial and temporal structures that are at work in this war. How is time structured in the political world where terror is the central problem? How is space? And how do the two relate to each other? These are the questions that will keep us occupied for the remainder of the present chapter.

Cosmological investigations of this kind have a lot to learn from architecture, first of all because architecture, as we will come to see, is the discipline of structuring space and time, and second of all because architecture has a distinct and increasingly important relation to war. As Thomas Hilberth argues in *Prolegomena zu einer Architectur der Sicherheit*, 'The origin of architecture is found in anxiety' (Hilberth 2007: 7). What do we do when we are anxious?

We seek shelter. And if we can find no shelter, we try to build one. We build, construct and order space; we create worlds.

Carl Schmitt famously argued in the *Nomos of the Earth* that the appropriation of land is the original act of creating law, the founding gesture of imposing an order (Schmitt 2003: 44). Building a house, erecting a fence, making a home and subsequently forming an alliance with other homes (in cities and in states) are ways in which we seek to assert our ability to control. It may be because of the wild animals in the forest, it may be because of other human beings, it may even be because we do not trust ourselves, but building, fencing and walling are crucial ways in which human beings attempt to control their world – and not only in terms of spatiality, but certainly also with regard to time. We try to achieve what in Schmitt's catholic vocabulary would be the *katechon*, the suspension of the end of time, the *eschaton* (Schmitt 2003: 59); we build walls in the hope that what is on the inside may live forever.

An example from the history of architecture will help to clarify this point. Himeji-Jo in Hyogo prefecture in Japan will be our case in point. It was first built by Norima Akamatsu, the lord of the land, in 1333. Since then it has been rebuilt and expanded several times until 1608, when the complex that is currently standing was finished under Terumasa Ikeda, son-in-law to the ruling shogun Ieyasu Tokugawa.

The castle is strategically positioned at a hilltop overlooking the surrounding Harima Plains near the inland sea coastline (Coaldrake 1996: 120). This position alone effectively served to control the surroundings and to secure the land. To attack the area where control was asserted from Himeji Castle (Jo means castle in Japanese) without conquering the castle itself would be to submit oneself to a constant threat of ambushed from the castle, and capturing Himeji Castle was at the time of its construction rightly considered impossible (Hilberth 2007: 72). That was not only due to its elevated position but also and crucially because of its architectural ingenuity. The central castle is only accessible through a circular path around the entire complex that takes any visitor or would-be attacker through several gates, along steep walls and around many 180 degree turns and corners. William Coaldrake points out that 'The defensive plan required all who entered the castle grounds to travel almost three times further than the direct distance between the outer entrance gateway and the keep complex' (Coaldrake 1996: 125).

Himeji Castle is a perfect example of architecture-in-war giving shape to both time and space. It served to effectively centre space around itself, as the point of departure for ruling the land. And its defensive system more than anything relied upon being able to *protract time.* The most precise way of describing the problem for the enemies seeking to attack the castle would be to say that it would necessarily take too long: too long for supplies to last, too long for the defenders to be surprised, too long for the attackers to survive. The parallel to the concrete wars on terrorism in Iraq and Afghanistan should be quite clear. The various insurgencies in both Iraq and Afghanistan have and have had one specific weapon that will forever be more powerful than the hitherto most devastating military force known to man – the US Armed Forces – namely patience. No matter how many 'surges' the United States would engage in either war, the delinquents on the other side could always rest assured that the American troops and their allies would eventually have to leave. The inability to accept casualties, the unpopularity of the Bush administration (and later on the unpopularity of the Obama administration whose main and perhaps only real 'winners' have been the efforts to end the wars), the unpopularity of the wars themselves and certainly also the massive costs in combination with the economic situation in general all combine to function as the Himeji-Jo of the Iraqi and Afghani insurgencies. There is no real telling at this time what will eventually happen once the United States finally withdraws its personnel from Iraq and Afghanistan, but one can rest assured that certain forces in those societies will claim it as a victory for their course once they do.

But let us remain with the real Himeji Castle a little while longer. By building an imposing structure at a strategically important point of the landscape the Japanese masters of the castle Himeji effectively took control over a piece of land. They restructured the way in which human beings would be moving through space, and they took control over the time in which they did so. In this way Himeji Castle serves to illustrate Schmitt's point from the *Nomos of the Earth* very well. By taking control of land human beings are able to establish structures of control in a more general sense. Himeji Castle made it possible to create structures of power, order, hierarchy, stability and law.

In the scope of the present investigations the right way to describe this ambition of Himeji Castle would be to say that it was built to keep war outside. Much in line with the task of the Hobbesian sovereign, the ambition of the castle is to make sure that war does not engulf society. The way in which Himeji Castle achieves this goal is of course by being a formidable instrument of war. In this way it is not only the insurgencies on the ground in Iraq and Afghanistan that have something in common with the castle; it shares a most important logic with the nuclear arsenals of the Cold War, namely deterrence.

In the hands of a state the machine of war generally serves to keep war on the outside, but that is not all. War is not merely the thing we wall out; it is not merely the thing against which we build our worlds inside our walls; war is also something through which we directly shape those worlds. This is a point which we should credit Brian Massumi for making quite clear in relation to the war on terror. In 'Potential Politics and the Primacy of Preemption' he precisely argues that the real effect of pre-emptive attacks never was to dismantle or intercept threats, before they could have a chance to become truly threatening, but rather the exact opposite. The effect of acting pre-emptively is to create an actual enemy out of one that was hiding in mere potentiality. Massumi refers to this as going kinetic (Massumi 2007: 18). In military jargon going kinetic simply means to shoot things; and in certain ways that can be considered as a viable option exactly in the situation where the enemy is hiding in potentiality – where he could be anywhere and everywhere all at the same time – because the moment you start to shoot, it is highly likely that somebody is going to shoot back. Et voila! You will have effectively created an actual enemy out of a potential one.

No wonder then that Donald Rumsfeld was called 'The Architect' by George W. Bush. War can certainly be world-creating, even if it is also a destroyer of worlds. Let us be more specific here. On one hand war is the reason for erecting a stable structure of state, with a monopoly on the use of force. Here war is the threat *against which* a world is constructed. On the other hand we have the direct link where a state is creating a war in order to create a world. Here war is the thing *through which* a world is constructed. While it thus seems clear that war plays a crucial role in the construction of our contemporary world – one could even go along with Heraclitus and claim war as the father of all things – it is also clear that this point in itself is in need of further investigation and clarification.

This then is the field in which the cosmological questions should be answered in the present context of last philosophical investigations. We must start out by looking at the history and reality of warfare, and work our way from there, by extracting the notions of world, control, space and time that emerge from those discussions and investigations.

The four generations of modern warfare

One very influential theory in current debates about (the history of) military strategy is the theory of fourth generation warfare that was first discussed by

American military historian William S. Lind together with several officers from the US armed forces in the article 'The Changing Face of War: Into the Fourth Generation' (Lind et al. 1989).

Lind's theory is part of a greater trend in studies on military strategy, in which it is argued that war is evolving and that accordingly the soldier and the military theorist should reconfigure the way they think about wars. These authors have been met with rather outspoken criticism from certain areas within the military strategic and academic communities. A good example is Colin Gray, who in 'Irregular Warfare. One Nature. Many Characters' (Gray 2007) has argued that the very notion that war changes nature is flawed; war has always been about forcibly submitting the will of the other to your own, as Clausewitz put it, and according to Gray that is not about to change. Others, such as Antulio Echevarria (see, e.g. Echevarria 2005), have argued that Lind's theory of the development of the history of warfare is severely lacking in historical detail – pointing out for instance that Guerrilla warfare, which to Lind would count as a form of fourth generation warfare, has been used since the beginning of modern warfare. While there may be some truth to both of these criticisms, it does not take anything away from the point that Lind's theory does give some very broad categories that can be used as ideal types to gauge a general historical development, which, lacking in nuance as it may be, still provides us with some crucial points.

As Lind's argument goes, modern war has a history which can be divided into four more or less distinct generations. What drives the changes from generation to generation can be attributed to both technological developments and social and political change, but the crucial and interesting point for us is the effects these changes have had upon the cosmology, the time and the space, of war. In their own ways each of the generations harboured very specific notions of what the theatre of war might be – they each constructed time and space in radically different manners.

First generation warfare was the form of war that was conducted roughly in the time from the Peace of Westphalia until the middle of the nineteenth century. It was conducted with frontloaded smoothbore muskets, frontloaded smoothbore cannons, and cavalry. The preferred tactic of first generation warfare was that of file and column, which on one hand ensured a higher firing rate as the troops to the rear could reload while those at the frontline were firing, and on the other hand kept soldiers together in tight formations, thereby reducing the risk that they would run off as 'an 18th-century soldier's main objective was to desert' (Lind 2004: 12).

These kinds of tactics produced much of the culture of order still so characteristic of the military institution. The military uniform, the graduations of rank and the clear distinction between civilian and soldiers were all products of this era, where the distinction between war and peace in general was clear. War took place in well-defined areas; it was encapsulated. In first generation warfare the time and the space of war were constructed along principles of continuity and linearity. The key components to winning a battle consisted in being able to hold the line, and to keep strict order among the troops – and conversely to break the lines of the enemy and create chaos among his soldiers.

With the rise of nationalism, the nineteenth century suddenly saw 'soldiers who actually wanted to fight' (Lind 2004: 12; see also Hammes 1994: 35). Thus it became possible to extend the lines of battle, without having to fear that unwatched soldiers would run off. Second generation warfare took hold as a result of this and certain developments in military technology: the rifled barrel, the breechloader and most importantly: reliable indirect fire. Heavy indirect artillery fire became the key to success on the battlefield of second generation warfare. The motto was 'The Artillery conquers, the infantry occupies' (Lind et al. 1989: 23). A classic example of this kind of military thinking was found in the French Maginot line built at the German border in the interwar period.

Second generation warfare brought a new kind of order to the battlefield. Where first generation warfare consisted in manoeuvring units of men back and forth and around a battlefield, second generation warfare was concerned with orchestrating firepower. Locating the weak part of the enemy defences, and bombarding it, or predicting the movement of the opponent and directing fire in anticipation, were keys to success in the second generation. In terms of the construction of time and space, we find that a lot is carried over from the first generation: first and foremost, the principle of linearity. Holding one's own lines, and breaching the lines of the other, were still the central goals of both tactics and strategy in second generation warfare. But in second generation the lines were greatly extended to sometimes cover the entire border between warring nations.

It is the assumption, implicit or explicit, about linearity, which becomes discarded with the advent of third generation warfare. Rather than closing with and overpowering the enemy lines the objective of third generation warfare is to bypass him, and to collapse his position from within. Thus the key element to third generation warfare is *manoeuvre*. According to Lind this is more or less a German invention (Lind et al. 1989: 23; Lind 2004: 13). German tactics of the latter part of the First World War and the early parts of the Second stand as the most clear-cut and well-known example of third generation warfare in action. Famously, the blitzkrieg manoeuvre at the outset of the Second World War took the invading German armies around the Maginot Line into the Benelux countries and through the Ardennes Forest, thereby rendering the massive French frontline fortifications irrelevant.

Two revolutions happened with the switch from second to third generation warfare. First of all: 'In the blitzkrieg, the basis of the operational art shifted from place [. . .] to time' (Lind et al. 1989: 23). Rather than seeking to control space, third generation warfare dealt with temporal displacement. When attacking one could try to manoeuvre around the opponents strongholds as the Germans did in the Ardennes. In third generation defence, the objective would turn around. Instead of trying to keep the opposing armies outside, one could let them advance too far, thus forcing them to stretch the lines bearing information and supply to the front. In this view third generation attack is about increasing tempo; third generation defence is about temporal protraction.

The other point which Lind stresses about third generation warfare is that control as such became less of a value. The disappearing of linearity in the third generation was not merely in terms of the lines on the battlefield, it was also achieved (ideally at least) internally in the very command structure of the military. Thus Lind writes of the German military training 'German junior officers routinely received problems that could only be solved by disobeying orders' (Lind 2004: 13). Second generation warfare relied heavily upon orchestration – reconnaissance units had to be at the right place and at the right time, attacks had to be undertaken in just the right moment (after a heavy barrage by aircraft or artillery), etc. – and thus relied on the central command units being the ones who would do the tactical and operational thinking. Initiative, when taken at the lower parts of the military hierarchy, could be outright disastrous. In third generation warfare on the other hand 'Mistakes were tolerated as long as they came from too much initiative rather than too little' (Lind 2004: 13). This relates to an important overall point, which both Lind and his critics are quick to track back to the German strategic classic *On War* by Carl von Clausewitz (Clausewitz 2008). War is a realm of contingency and chance. According to Clausewitz's 'wondrous trinity' war is also always also about enmity and politics, but it is the specific task of the military institution to deal with the elements of contingency and chance (Clausewitz 2008: 40–6).[1] According to Lind third generation warfare was the first time in modern history that states, rather than trying to impose order on chaos, instead attempted to draw benefit from the unruly character of war.

Finally, we have the fourth generation of war. In 'The Changing Face of War: Into the Fourth Generation' (Lind et al. 1989), Lind and his co-authors imagined two different ways in which the fourth generation could play out. One that would rely heavily on technology and one that would rely on the development of new ideas. Since then Lind has strongly criticized the idea of a new technological revolution and instead insisted upon the necessity of recognizing that what the early article described as the idea-driven fourth generation is taking place before our eyes, that is, in the wars in Iraq and Afghanistan and of course on 9/11 itself (Lind 2001: 72). The two trajectories should be clear however, as they follow the developments of the three first generations quite nicely as they have been presented above.

In the technological trajectory war develops with technological ingenuity. First generation warfare was conducted with frontloaded smoothbore weapons, second generation was conducted with breechloaders, rifled weapons and indirect artillery, and third generation was conducted with manoeuvrable weapons, tanks, etc. The next viable step in this trajectory would then likely be the use of GPS-satellites, information technology, smart weapons, etc. In other words the Revolution of Military Affairs as imagined by Rumsfeld and others of a similar mind-set (see Rumsfeld 2002b).

In the idea-driven trajectory war develops according to the ways in which space and time is constructed in each of the generations. First generation warfare was conducted with lines and columns, second generation was conducted with extended lines that often stretched the entire border between warring states (again the Maginot Line is a prime example) and third generation made a qualitative leap by switching focus from a spatial plane to a temporal one. Following this line of thought it should be no surprise that the fourth generation in the idea-driven trajectory takes *terrorism* as its model (Lind et al. 1989: 25). Terrorism takes the development from spatially stable conduction of war (first generation) over temporally fluid warfare (third generation) to yet another level of contingency or instability. Third generation warfare attempted to assert control by engaging in contingency, but it still sought to assert some kind of control; in third generation warfare manoeuvre was key to success, but the movement involved was still heavily reliant upon being able to move quickly from A to B. Conversely, the terrorist is in a sense freed from any spatial and temporal constraints. No matter how innovative its commanders were, the invading German army still had to move through the Ardennes forest in order to get around the Maginot Line. The terrorist on the other hand is potentially everywhere all the time. This point is of course very much in tune with the things we have argued above. The terrorist is to the theatre of war what the non-dancing dancer is to the theatre of dance. If terrorism is really effective it is because the in-activity of terror is taking place everywhere. This means that the battlefield is no longer in any way a confined space. All of society is included in fourth generation warfare.

Terrorism is, of course, a far too politically flavoured and tactically narrow concept to fully capture the entire scope of fourth generation warfare. Guerrilla warfare would probably be a more covering term, but the crucial point is that fourth generation warfare is more naturally fought by sub-state actors. Fourth generation warfare is asymmetric warfare. It is the kind of warfare which the weaker party to a conflict will generally be forced to undertake. This means hit and run tactics; it means to never confront the enemy head on; it means to annoy him rather than to destroy him. First and foremost, it means to try to win a moral victory rather than a military one. If the global perception of the war is that it consists in an unfair fight between a global superpower and independent, poorly armed resistance forces, then it does not matter if the resistance takes ten times as many casualties as the occupation. In fact taking more casualties than your opponent, will often be an advantage in fourth generation war – especially if it happens in a way that provides gory pictures for the global press. Fourth generation warfare is more a struggle for legitimacy than it is a struggle for power.

Lind argues that because of the tradition of hierarchy, order and linearity it was difficult for state militaries to complete the transition from second to third generation warfare, which required not only technological advances that allowed for manoeuvre warfare, but also a new form of military thinking, that is, embracing the contingencies of war. But the appearance of fourth generation warfare means that these problems are brought to a whole new level, since the space for manoeuvring no longer simply is the land and sea of traditional warfare, but also and more importantly that of the global perception of the war. The war in Vietnam was probably the first time the US military experienced the problems for state militaries in fighting fourth generation wars, but according to Lind, the wars in Afghanistan and Iraq are proving that they have not learned to do it yet (Lind 2001: 72, 2004: 15).

The problem states are facing regarding legitimacy in asymmetric warfare is not so much the use of force, according to Lind. At this point his argument becomes borderline schizophrenic. He argues on one hand that within 48 hours of 9/11, the United States should have wiped 'Afghanistan off the map, using nuclear weapons' (Lind 2001: 72). On the other hand, Lind's crucial point regarding state militaries in fourth generation conflicts is that they must seek de-escalation of conflict at all levels. His suggestion is that military forces in fourth generation wars should act much more like police officers than like traditional soldiers. Rather than living in fortified compounds they should live among the general population, instead of always being in full uniform, with loaded weapons and helmets with visors, the soldiers should look more forthcoming, they should preferably speak the language of the local population and most importantly they should only use force as a last resort.

There is a method to the madness, however, as it is not even the *excessive* use of force which causes the stronger party in an asymmetrical war to loose legitimacy, if we are to believe Lind – it is *time*. He provides an example. On 2 February 1982 Hafez El-Assad, dictator of Syria, sent in the army against Hama, because of credible rumours – but rumours nonetheless – that the Muslim Brotherhood were gathering in the city with plans to overthrow the Baath party government. A few days later most of the city had been destroyed and between 10,000 and 25,000 people killed. Syria was vilified in global media for the actions, but the events were over so quickly that there was not enough time for any serious global outrage to be mounted (Lind 2009: 52–3). Lind credits Martin van Creveld for presenting a compelling analogy to describe the issue. If an adult hits a child in the street, few will take notice, almost no matter how hard the blow is. But if an adult subjects a child to a prolonged beating, someone will eventually intervene and the adult will find himself in jail (Lind 2009: 54).

The tendency of a state in a fourth generation war will precisely be to find some middle ground between a complete, but swift, overreaction, and on the other hand a completely downscaled police operation. It will tend to engage in a prolonged operation with a sustained use of force. In the war in Vietnam and later on in the wars in Afghanistan and Iraq, the US military and its allies have found themselves precisely in the position of an adult subjecting a child to a prolonged public beating.

The potent war and the actualized state

The sheer schizophrenia of Lind's suggestions, that is, either a nuclear overreaction or the invasion of the friendly neighbourhood cop, does not simply make clear the radicalism of his thinking; it also reveals an abyssal rift between the institutions that have the task of fighting wars and the wars they are supposed to fight in the fourth generation of modern warfare. The fact alone that the US military would have the ability to even consider *both* options, would probably mean that the latter option is impossible. The invasion by the American friendly neighbourhood cop inevitably carries the message 'We seriously considered killing you all in a nuclear holocaust, but now we are here to help'. If fourth generation warfare is about winning the moral battle, winning the hearts and minds or winning the peace, as Lind argues again and again, then such an initial message alone could easily mean that the war is over before it began.

Indeed, it seems as if there is something more fundamental going on in the discussion of fourth generation wars. It seems as if it is completely impossible for the state to handle the kind of enemy that is both everywhere and nowhere all the time. It is at this point we should begin to draw our cosmological conclusions: there is an ontological difference between the world of the state and the world of war. The enemy the state is facing in fourth generation warfare is of a different ontological order than the state itself. No matter how much the state attempts to go kinetic and thereby to force the pure potentiality it is fighting to take the shape of an actual enemy, the pure potentiality of the terrorist remains. In the end one could say that the state is too actualized to be able to struggle with potentiality.

These notions of the actualized state versus the potential terrorist should be examined in greater detail. When it is said that the terrorist – the primary protagonist of fourth generation wars – is nowhere and everywhere all the time, it should be understood in terms of the notion of potentiality that we have discussed for great parts of the present investigations. The threat from terrorism is not an actual threat standing at the gates. It rather takes that shape of a potent potentiality of nothingness. Terrorism threatens in the way that it makes every train and every airplane a terrorist attack that is not-happening, in the same way as the dancer, who is not-dancing. Terrorism works in the way that it constantly says: 'This place is the place of non-occurrence, this moment is the moment of not-happening.' Terrorism is nothingness taking place.

The problem for the state that is trying to combat terrorism of this sort becomes evident, if we take our model of the state-form, that is, Himeji Castle, into consideration. How would Himeji Castle serve to combat terrorism? It is clear that it simply could not. Its defensive systems consist in the ability to force any outside attacker to abide by the spatial rules it lays out. The 'outside' attacker would have to travel three times the distance from the entrance to the main building through various sharp corners and gates that make for perfect defensive positions. But when there is no *actual* enemy 'out there', those defensive systems would have no effect at all. Indeed, the only thing that no wall can keep out is nothingness itself. Thus if the master of Himeji Castle were to have found himself in a war on terror, he would effectively have had to live with the fact that every walk *he himself* would make, around the many corners and through the many gates of his home, would be a non-occurring terrorist attack. Suddenly every dinner would not-poisonous, every advisor a treachery not-happening. He would be completely safe from outside attacks, a master of the universe in his own right, but nevertheless he would constantly feel exposed. The psychological situation of such a master is precisely the one we saw Kierkegaard unfold with regard to Nero above. As much as his political world would be one in which he could assert complete dominion and control, he would at the very same time be capable of suddenly feeling exposed. The cosmology which corresponds to Nero's feeling at the same time incredibly bored and taken in with absolute anxiety, is precisely such a world in which one feels absolute *actual* security and at the very same time an inescapable *potential* vulnerability.

The problem for such a master of the world is that the only option he has at his disposal is to answer in some form of actuality. Confronted with the constant threat of the not-poisonous food, and the non-treacherous advisor, he would have no other means of reacting than to throw away his actual food and to execute his actual advisor. Whatever he might do to stop terrorism form not-happening, he would always be grotesquely overreacting. He would – much like Nero – find himself in the need of acting out, but no matter what he were to do, he would inevitably end up looking very much like the adult, who is subjecting a child to a prolonged beating in front of everyone in the streets.

What is happening in the war on terror is that this logic of the state-form is coming into clearer view. It is becoming increasingly apparent how difficult it is for the state to keep that which is not-occurring from not-occurring. To stick with our initial metaphor, the state that goes to war to fight terrorism is ontologically on a par with the dancer who is trying to prove that he is a dancer, by dancing. It will inevitably be excessive in its actualization of its potentialities.

The question is however, if this is really anything particularly new. Is it the case that it is only now at the dawn of the third millennium that the problematic relation between the state and the wars it is attempting to fight reaches this level of incommensurability? As we saw above, Clausewitz himself argued that war as such is the realm of contingency and chance. Could it not be the case then that the difference between the state and the sub-state actors in fourth generation wars is to be understood simply under this heading, instead of giving way to the more radical ontological distinction between the actualized state and the potentiality of war?

While the Clausewitzian stance could perhaps represent the more level-headed alternative, the suggestion here is the symmetrical opposite: It is indeed the case that fourth generation warfare does not bring about something radically new in the relation between wars and states, but that precisely does not mean that 'war is the continuation of [state] politics with other means' (Clausewitz 2008: 44), only with an added element of contingency. Instead, the suggestion here is that war always was the radical opposite of state. In the end the argument is that it is war itself that is of a different ontological order than the state. Our argument is therefore that the war on terror in a way brings out the essence of war. War itself is something which to the state is much more like terrorism, than it is like the state. Indeed, war is anti-state.

To be sure, states can go to war. They can build militaries. They can initiate combat. And when they do there will be a tremendous loss of life. But the point remains. When one state successfully subdues the armed forces of another state to its will, its actions would be more adequately understood as politics. In this sense Clausewitz still has a point – what is normally called war (armed conflict between states) is an extension of politics – only the means are not radically 'other'. War *as such* does not serve as a means for the state. The state has no war machine of its own, as Gilles Deleuze and Feliw Guattari have put it in *A Thousand Plateaus* (Deleuze & Guattari 2004b), it can only appropriate one. It is this rather curious claim that we shall have to explore in order to further our investigation into the political cosmology of terror. As it was the case in the political psychology of terror above, we will in the end transcend this perspective, but the initial point we are making about the potentiality of war is a Deleuzian one.

The smooth space of war and the striated space of state

An interesting fact about *A Thousand Plateaus* is that it has had quite an impact on studies of military strategy. The Deleuzo-Guattarian ideas of *deterritorialization*, *smooth space* and of *speed* have provided quite a few strategists with new ideas, which aim at confronting the problems we have sketched above regarding fourth generation warfare.[2] The fact about their argument that is most often ignored or at least overlooked, however, is that it does not seek primarily to investigate the nature of war. Inspired by Pierre Clastres, the question Deleuze and Guattari ask is far more anthropologically minded: Why do certain societies (i.e. nomads) not form states? Their answer is that one needs specific instruments to prevent states from forming, and that the primary tool which the nomads use to ensure it does not happen is war. The machine of war is the tool with which the nomads resist the emergence of a state.

Interestingly for our cosmological purposes, Deleuze and Guattari conceive of the crucial distinction between war and state in terms of *space*. There is a fundamental difference between the space of war and the space of the state. In order to see clearly the precise meaning of this difference it will be helpful to engage the analogy they invoke about the games of *chess* and *go* – chess representing the spatiality of the state, and go representing that of the war machine.

Chess is played in striated space. This means that the space of chess is thoroughly regulated with regard to the movements of each individual piece. Likewise the pieces of chess are completely determined. 'They have qualities' (Deleuze & Guattari 2004b: 389). A knight is a knight, because it moves in the way that it does. Likewise with the pawn, the queen, the bishop, etc. That chess is played in striated space means that the moving elements of chess have to follow the regulatory lines that are laid out.

Chess is a game of coding spaces. For each of the spaces on the board one can calculate, for example, how many pieces are able to capture it on both sides, or how many moves it will take for a particular piece on the board to arrive at that particular field. An example is shown in Figure 3.1.

With the first move of the game, the white knight at g1 is able move to only two spaces: f3 and h3 (No. 1). With two moves the knight could reach nine further spaces: d2, d4, e1, e5, f2, f4, g5, h2 and h4 (No. 2). But if the knight is moved to h3, then d2, d4, e1, e5, h2 and h4 are suddenly further away, and it only covers g1, f2, f4 and g5 with its next move (No. 3). One could go on endlessly, if one should seek to describe how the moves of each individual piece open new

No.1   No.2   No.3

Figure 3.1 Example of the movement of chess pieces through striated space.

possibilities for further movement and foreclose others, but the crucial point about chess is that such calculation is entirely possible. It is this point that makes chess a game of coding space. The striated space of chess, which makes sure that each piece on the board moves in certain clearly defined way, guarantees that this coding is both possible and calculable.

The way space is organized on the chessboard corresponds very well to the way space is organized by Himeji Castle. The black and white spaces make up a landscape, which conditions all movement. They determine the paths that can be followed and those that cannot, in much the same way as the walls of Himeji Castle determine the paths through which one can reach the central building. Indeed, the whole objective of building a castle such as Himeji could be said to be to keep space ordered like a chess board. Still, there is a crucial difference between the two. Where the space of the chessboard is never threatened by a completely different spatial order, Himeji Castle does not offer the same kind of absolute certainty. The other spatial order, which plays no role in chess, but which continually haunts state structures such as Himeji, is described by Deleuze and Guattari with reference to go.

A go piece is a mere marker – 'a simple arithmetic unit' (Deleuze & Guattari 2004b: 389). Go pieces have no qualities that set them apart from other go pieces. They do not have a nature to govern their movement. Indeed, as Deleuze and Guattari describe it, the go piece can only be spoken of in the third person ' "It" makes a move. "It" could be a man, a woman, a louse, an elephant' (Deleuze & Guattari 2004b: 389). Go pieces do not have internal qualities. The way they function is completely determined by their surroundings, that is, by the positioning of the other pieces on the board. Conversely, the positioning of one go piece is capable of changing the entire ordering of the board. An example is shown in Figure 3.2.

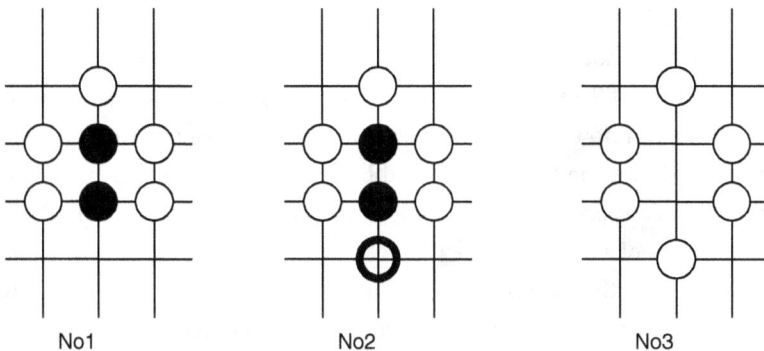

No1   No2   No3

Figure 3.2 Examples of the speed of go pieces in smooth space.

From a given situation (No. 1), white can capture two black pieces by placing a piece at the thick circle (No. 2) whereby white appropriates the territory that used to be occupied by the black pieces (No. 3). The winner of a game of go is the player who possesses the most territory at the end of the game.

The spatial feature which most clearly separates chess from go is the fact that the above move by white could take place anywhere on the board, at any time during the game. Whereas chess pieces are restricted in their movements by their internal rules and the situation on the board, a go piece can potentially be placed anywhere. The space of a chess piece is the space which offers a definitive set of possible future actualities (as described in the example above), whereas the entire space of the go board is a space of potentiality. This is what it means that go is played in smooth space as opposed to the striated space of chess. In go no lines determine movement; one does not have to go through one place to get to the next. Instead, the next place can be any place.

The difference between go and chess is described by Deleuze and Guattari as the difference between what they term *movement* and *speed*. 'Movement designates the relative character of a body considered as "one", and which goes from point to point' (Deleuze & Guattari 2004b: 420). In this way chess pieces 'move'. They go from place to place and by doing so they code and decode space according to the rules of their movement. 'Speed, on the contrary, constitutes the absolute character of a body whose irreducible parts (atoms) occupy or fill a smooth space [. . .], with the possibility of springing up at any point' (Deleuze & Guattari 2004b: 420–1). This is the character of go pieces. They do not move according to a pre-established set of rules. They do not have corridors which they must follow. Indeed, it would be imprecise to say that they move at all. Rather than moving around in space, they constantly reorder, reinterpret and redefine space. Go pieces do not move; they make space reform itself around them. Using a less Deleuzo-Guattarian vocabulary we could say that movement is something one does *in a world*, whereas speed is what *creates worlds*.

The point about the relation between the striated space of state and the smooth space of war can now be seen. Himeji Castle is in a constant struggle to keep space striated. But the space *in which* this struggle takes place cannot itself be another striated space. The castle (and with it any other state formation) would have much less of a problematic existence if that were the case. As a state, it can easily compete with other states for control of striated space. This is a struggle it can both win and lose. But the struggle to keep space striated is not a struggle of control over striated space. It is a struggle which takes place in a different spatial regime altogether, namely smooth space. This struggle is what Deleuze and Guattari call the struggle over de-territorialization and re-territorialization, and it is in this struggle that the state finds itself in direct confrontation with the war machine. This is the invention of the nomads that keeps the state from arising in their societies; it is a machine which first and foremost keeps space smooth. To continue with the descriptions in terms of chess and go, the state is constantly playing a game of go to make space more like a game of chess.

Having said all this, it should be clear that the first three generations of warfare, as they are described by Lind, all take place within the spatial regime of the state. They take place in an ordered environment, where lines can be drawn and where movements take place from point to point, first in the form of files and columns, secondly in the form of the extension of the lines and the clear separation of front and rear and thirdly in the form of the lines followed by the manoeuvring of the fighting forces. The thing about fourth generation warfare is that here movements do not only become more apparent or faster. They become of a different sort altogether. The terrorist precisely does not move. Instead, he threatens everywhere from nowhere. He makes even the most remote and desolate place a potential site of war. In the sense of war that we have been developing here it is only in the fourth generation that 'war' begins to resemble the war machine in the sense of the concept developed by Deleuze and Guattari.

It should be noted that all of this is no mere philosophical speculation. Considerations such as these can have, and have had, very tangible effects in the real world. To see how it plays out in concrete, we should take a look at some of the more advanced military thinking at work in contemporary wars. It is hard in this case to think of a better example than the Israeli Defence Force (IDF).

The IDF

When the IDF in the spring of 2002 attacked the old city centre of Nablus, it faced all the problems state militaries deal with in fourth generation warfare, not least because of the site of the battle (Weizman 2007: 185). The dense city fabric was a death trap in the eyes of the IDF. Every alley could be mined, every window would make a soldier a target, every doorway and every corridor provided the Palestinian resistance (or terrorists if one takes the opposing view) with ample opportunity for ambush. In short, the city was an almost impossible site for the military to wage war. The answer the IDF came up with consisted in a radical reinterpretation and ultimately a reconfiguration of the city's geometry. The IDF made it a rule not to use streets and doors to walk through, and not to use windows to look through. Instead, almost all movement by the IDF soldiers consisted in *walking through walls*. Soldiers dug their way through houses and apartments by blowing holes in walls, floors and ceilings. Eyal Weizman argues that 'Although several thousand Israeli soldiers and hundreds of Palestinian guerrilla fighters were manoeuvring simultaneously in the town, they were saturated within its fabric to a degree that they would have been largely invisible from an aerial perspective at any given moment' (Weizman 2007: 185–6). Thousands of Israeli soldiers made their way through an entire city almost without setting foot in the streets.

The tactics used in Nablus were not a result of coincidental out-of-the-box thinking, but rather part of a conscious effort to revolutionize warfare by the IDF. In this effort the Operational Theory Research Institute (OTRI), led by Shimon Naveh and Dov Tamari, has been key (Weizman 2007: 187). What is interesting about the OTRI's efforts to rethink warfare is that it does not count authors such as Clausewitz and Sun-Tzu as their chief sources of inspiration, nor do they devote most of their time to Creveld or Lind for that matter. Instead, it is critical theory, architectural postmodernism and the works of contemporary artists that top the curriculum. First and foremost, the joint works of Gilles Deleuze and Felix Guattari are said to have aided the IDF in formulating new concepts of effective warfare. The attack in Nablus was coordinated in the attempt to adhere as strictly as possible to a doctrine laid out with constant reference to Deleuze and Guattari's concepts of war machines and state apparatuses, of de-territorialization and re-territorialization, of smooth and striated space. Indeed, if there was a book which co-authored the attack on Nablus it would probably have been *A Thousand Plateaus*.

This small case of a military operation serves quite elegantly to show how the state can appropriate the nomad war machine according to Deleuze and Guattari; here a military institution was able to 'out-guerrilla the guerrilla'. For all relevant purposes the IDF *were not* men of state in their attack on Nablus. On that occasion they were nomad warriors, and they worked to keep space smooth. They reinterpreted and recreated the urban fabric in such a way that *they* potentially could be anywhere at any time. Conversely the Palestinian resistance was caught in its own defensive arrangements. In the case of the attack on Nablus it would be correct to say that here the Palestinian resistance took the role of the state, just like the IDF soldiers were the Nomad warriors. Indeed, for many strategic and tactical purposes the old centre of a Middle Eastern city[3] provided the same architectural defence as Himeji Castle. The striated space of Nablus would have worked to severely protract the movement of the IDF soldiers, had it not been for the fact that they were not moving at all, but rather 'speeding'. And conversely in the smooth space opened up by the IDF the Palestinian resistance precisely fought to re-territorialize space and turn it into a striated space of state, a fight they clearly lost.

The interesting thing about the Palestinian case is the fact that here we have a curious reversal of the roles of the state and the state-less, when the matter is discussed in the terms of Deleuze and Guattari. Here the IDFs very often take the role of nomads, struggling to keep a state from forming. The point however is that *when* they are working as nomads, they are precisely anti-state – as Deleuze and Guattari put it 'The state has no war-machine of its own' (Deleuze & Guattari 2004b: 391). It can only 'borrow' one. The state *can* train nomad warriors, but as warriors they do not function according to the rules of state. Conversely, it would be wrong to say that the Palestinians operate like nomads, just because they do not have a working institutionalized state. They are much better understood as men of state without the state.

The reason why we can say that there is a strict ontological difference between the space of the state and the space of war, *even after we have seen that the IDF has attained the capacity to 'speed' around in the potential space of war*, is thus that when the IDF does so it no longer operates in the register of the state. In other words: the state can from time to time use the nomadic war machine, but only to destroy other states or to prevent them from forming. As a tool for the establishment and confirmation of statehood, the war machine is completely useless. At the level of smooth space, where the state is struggling to make space more controllable and striated, the war machine only works in favour of smoothness. Consequentially, if the state wishes to survive as a state, it can only do so by acting like one. That means to fight against the smooth war to capture and control space and to make it a territory.

Staying with the case of Israel it is worth noticing the 2006 war in Lebanon (between Israel and Hezbollah), which ended in a resounding defeat for the IDF (see, e.g. Inbar 2006; Shield 2007; Biddle & Friedman 2008; Kober 2008). Israel even established an independent commission with the objective of finding out what went wrong (Israel 2006; Winograd et al. 2008).

The conflict began with the kidnapping of two Israeli soldiers by Hezbollah on 12 July 2006. On 13 July, Israel retaliated. The objectives of the IDF were twofold: Free the captured soldiers and strike a decisive blow to the Hezbollah forces in the south of Lebanon (Shield 2007: 4). With regard to this second objective a crucial aim was to disable both Hezbollah's long- and short-range rocket capabilities (Shield 2007: 4; Kober 2008: 3–4). Using its superior air force, the IDF destroyed most of Hezbollah's long-range rocket capacities within 35 minutes (Kober 2008: 4). But after these first 35 minutes of the war, the Israeli Air Force was more or less useless, as it proved incapable of incapacitating Hezbollah's smaller and more manoeuvrable short-range rocket launchers. Thus, throughout the war, Israeli police recorded 3,970 rocket strikes within Israeli borders (Israel 2008). After the initial air strikes, the IDF eventually launched a ground-based offensive, but it proved ineffective in stopping the rockets.[4] As the cease-fire brokered by the United Nations came into effect after a month of fighting, Hezbollah could claim a decisive victory. They had not released the captured soldiers and they still retained many of their rocket capabilities in southern Lebanon.

As many observers, such as Kober and Shield, have argued, the problem for the IDF was that they approached the war with the same strategic outlook they used in Nablus four years earlier. The aim of both land and air attack was to get in, do damage and get out quickly again. Acting like nomad warriors the IDF again tried to be potentially everywhere, without having to commit to actually be all over southern Lebanon. The same observers argue that what was needed to achieve any kind of success in the war in Lebanon was a far more conventional approach. Indeed, even though the Hezbollah in the eyes of many would be considered a semi-sub-state actor, they behaved much more like a regular state army than one would expect. Some guerrilla tactics were used, but in general the Hezbollah forces worked to hold their ground and the lines of battle (Biddle & Friedman 2008) – traditional principles of first and second generation warfare. If the IDF were to have had any success in the campaign, they should have worked as states do towards a territorialization of space.

The crucial point concerning the relation of state and war remains therefore. As long as the Israeli forces attempted to out-guerrilla the guerrilla, they were certainly capable of working to undermine the formation of state structures (both at a tactical and a political level), but they were also completely incapable of doing the work of state against war. Fighting a war as a warrior means not fighting it as state; fighting a war as a man of state means not fighting it as a warrior.

Beyond smoothness

In the perspective of Deleuze and Guattari these kinds of oppositions would have to be analysed in terms of the two very different spatial regimes, we have discussed above. The difference between the striated space of state and the smooth space of war does not simply designate the difference between order and chaos. Instead they designate different regimes of spatiality which permeate all spheres of life. It is not given from the start which actors will be the ones dominating each spatial regime, but it is a given that there are these two regimes and that they will be in constant conflict. It is important to note here that even though Deleuze and Guattari valorize the fluid life of nomads against the sedimentary life in a state, their argument is not that the state represents any kind of fall of man. As far as they are concerned the state has always been around (Deleuze & Guattari 2004b: 397). The important point is merely that the territory of state is conceivable only as an interior against which the exteriority of the nomad war machine must be given.

As mentioned above I believe the theoretical framework of Deleuze and Guattari can only bring us so far. This is the point where we have reached that limit. The thing the Deleuzian outlook seems destined to miss, with its famed insistence upon a thinking completely devoid of negativity, is the thing that separates these two spatial regimes, namely the potentiality of nothingness as such.

The reason why state militaries are finding it very difficult to wage fourth generation war is that here war, to put the point in Hegelian terms, arrives at its notion. And the notional core of war is anti-state. But to describe this antithesis I argue that it is not enough to simply say that war takes place in smooth space and that the state can only exist in striated space, nor is it enough to say that in smooth space war is a process of de-territorialization and state is one of re-territorialization and capture. It is true that we could say that genuine war is that which happens to the state, behind its back, while it believes itself to be waging war. The question is however, if this thing that happens behind the back of the state is merely the fluidity of smooth space.

War is at one and the same time something states engage in on more or less Clausewitzian terms, with enmity, contingency and political aims, *and* something that happens to the state behind its own back in the midst of being engaged in war. The crucial question thus lies with how we are to conceptualize the thing that is taking place in this way. The idea I should like to defend is that the right way of doing so is to see it in analogy to the linguistics of 'terror', where the excess of 'terror' takes place behind the backs of those who seek to speak about it. As we recall, the general formula for this kind of discourse was defined as 'expression + expressiveness = 1 + 0'. In a similar fashion we should be able to give a formula for the dual nature of war by drawing upon the Clausewitzian trinity of war. To Clausewitz the whole of war should be understood in terms of the wondrous trinity, we briefly touched upon above. War encompasses enmity, contingency and politics and nothing more. Given a satisfying description of a war in terms of these three concepts, you will, according to Clausewitz, have a description of the whole of that war. Thus we can construct a Clausewitzian formula of war as 'enmity + contingency + politics = 1'. According to the idea of terror as the potentiality of nothingness taking place, which we have been following throughout these investigations, our formula should instead be 'enmity + contingency + politics = 1 + 0'. The problem with the Deleuzo-Guattarian model, which takes fluidity rather than solidity as its starting point, is that it does not really approach the radical notion of nothingness at stake in this formula. Indeed, after we have taken a look at the case of the Israeli military and the attack on Nablus, would it not be fair to say that even though they achieve a crucial focus on smooth potential space as opposed to striated actual space, this model is still a model which conceives of potentiality as the potentiality to actualize something – namely a new configuration of actual space? Is it not precisely the case that the other side of any de-territorialization is new form of re-territorialization? Undoubtedly it is, since Deleuze and Guattari conceive of the relation of striated space to smooth space as that of interiority to exteriority. 'It is in terms not of independence, but of coexistence and competition in a perpetual field of interaction, that we must conceive of exteriority and interiority, war machines of metamorphosis and state apparatuses of identity, bands and kingdoms, megamachines and empires' (Deleuze & Guattari 2004b: 398).

Accordingly, we could make a Deleuzo-Guattarian formula to supplement the Clausewitzian one 'striated space + smooth space = 1'. The point is of course that for all the talk about potentiality and fluidity, the Deleuzo-Guattarian model still adds up to 1. As we recall from Chapter 2, Deleuze insists that ontologically speaking, we can only say one thing: 1. What I am arguing here is that we can say something else: 1 + 0, and furthermore that it is the '+0' that we are seeing the work of in our contemporary political cosmology – most clearly in the war on terror.

The crucial point about war is that this excessive extra element – the zero element – is not simply nothing at all, but rather nothingness at work. This element is not the contingent realm of unreliable intelligence etc., which makes war a game of contingency and chance in the light of the Clausewitzian military thinker, but it is not simply the smooth space of war either, as it would be conceptualized in the Deleuzo-Guattarian model. Rather, it should be viewed as the minimal negative distance between the striated space of state and the smooth space of war. Our modification of the Deleuzo-Guattarian formula should therefore read: 'striated space + smooth space = 1 + 0'. The '+0' is the minimal distance between the actual space of state and the potential space of war as such. What is taking place in this gap? Precisely nothing! It is not simply the potential space through which actual space can be reconfigured as we saw in the case of the IDF working its way through the city fabric of Nablus. It is rather the nothingness of potentiality as such taking place. The specific historical situation of the war on terror is one in which there is an intense condensation of this nothingness. States are cast into an increasing number of highly expensive wars,[5] because of the relentless non-occurring of terrorist attacks.

In order to see how this nothingness is taking place in terms of political cosmology, we shall have to go beyond the current focus on spatiality and instead take on the issue of temporality.

Time is out of joint

Our time is a time in which the times are out of joint. It is a time in which the ontological foundation of the political world itself becomes more and more of a player in that world. Being, nothingness, potentiality, actuality, reality – these are all concepts which do not merely belong to an esoteric philosophical debate. They play crucial roles in the political reality in which we live. Not in the sense of securing a foundation of sorts in which politics can play itself out, but rather in the sense of increasing instability of order.

We have already seen how space itself is far less controllable than Schmitt and others seem to be hoping. The appropriation of land *can* be an effective way of securing law and order, but it *can* also be made to be completely ineffective. We have seen how smooth space can invert the striated space of the state, but we have also seen how the state can enlist the warriors of smooth space, and we have seen that such enlistment is far from unproblematic for the state itself. Indeed, in order for a particular state to survive it will inevitably have to act like one. But then we have also suggested that it is not enough to conceive of these problems in terms of actual space and potential space, and that we instead should consider the nothingness between these two spatial registers – their intersection if you will.

To see why, we will be well served to consider Himeji Castle once again. Coaldrake writes:

> The cannon, which was instrumental in transforming the European castle into a tightly constructed bastion, was never employed effectively against the Japanese castle due to low levels of casting and gunnery skill available in Japan at the time. [. . .] The combined forces of siege and artillery were never brought to bear fully against the Japanese castle. If they had been, the exuberant, flamboyant forms of castles like Himeji would have been transformed into the smooth-walled, hunched shapes of later European castles. (Coaldrake 1996: 125)

Coaldrake here describes why castles such as Himeji still have the imposing and extravagant aesthetics, which they do, but he also gives a description of what would happen to Himeji, if it were confronted with a sudden technological development, for example, of the sort that took place from first to second generation warfare: It would have to quickly evolve or be completely destroyed. In terms of the Deleuzo-Guattarian concepts of war and space, the very emergence of effective cannons in the territory of Himeji would mean the smoothing of its striated space. It would be an act of de-territorialization – or simply an act of war. The crucial point here is that what is truly problematic about war for the state is not only the smoothness of de-territorialized space; it is also and crucially the sudden transition. As Coaldrake rightly argues Himeji Castle *would* have looked different to us today, if there had been effective cannons available earlier in the history of Japan – but it could also have been ruined. If it had been confronted with effective cannons earlier in its history, then the castle would perhaps have been able to evolve later on, but at the precise time of the confrontation it would have been at a loss. In this way the suddenness of war is impossible to handle for the state.

In other words one could very well say that 'war as such' is that, which takes place in the gaps between the so-called generations of warfare. The historical development of the ways in which the state is waging war is thus best described as the development of ways in which the state responds to the reinvention of the nomad war machine. To the political world that precedes the reinvention of war, such reinvention will almost always be experienced as a form of technological eschatology. The reinvention of the war machine brings with it an inescapable feeling that the end is neigh. In the Cold War it was the nuclear bomb, at the start of the twentieth century it was dynamite and in the hands of the Scythians it was the saddle, the stirrup and the sabre (Deleuze & Guattari 2004b: 445–6). If one takes of broad enough historical view, then the end of the world becomes a frequent occurrence. The point would seem to be that there is a temporal background to the spatial discrepancy between state and war. States can keep space striated through various mechanisms, *but for a certain time only.* Eventually, war will happen and make space smooth.

Here we are confronted with the classic philosophical theme of the *moment* – das Augenblick, Øieblikket – and the crucial question for our political temporality of terror therefore must be: how does the suddenness of war take place?

The catastrophe looms ahead

A few years ago, the US Congress set up a commission to investigate how one should mark as dangerous a container of toxic radioactive waste with a half-life of 10,000 years (Beck 2002). The problem quickly identified by linguists and historians of language was that the longest survivability one could expect for any regime of signs would be 2,000–3,000 years. Ulrich Beck has argued that this serves perfectly to illustrate what his notion of *risk society* means (Beck 2002: 40). The idea of risk society is the notion that our current actions can potentially have catastrophic effects that will have greater longevity, than the language we have available to describe them with. This essentially is the knowledge that our world is doomed to self-destruct. In two articles that were published in the immediate aftermath of 9/11, Beck argued that this event could be said to fit with the line of events that make us aware of these problems of risk such as the threat from global warming, or the ecologic catastrophes in Bhopal and Chernobyl (see Beck 2002, 2003.

The interesting part of the argument about risk is not, however, the predictions that certain actual occurrences could mean the end of the world. Nor is it Beck's belief in a new form of cosmopolitanism uniting humanity in the struggle against such threats. What is crucial about the notion of risk, and the diagnosis of a global society of risk, is the temporality of his thinking about catastrophic events. Choosing as his illustration of the essence of risk society the idea that we are producing risk that have a greater longevity than the language we have available to describe them in, Beck is precisely making an eschatological point. It is a modern eschatology – that is, it is one where the end of the world (as we know it) is brought about by human technology and action rather than divine preconception – but it is eschatology nonetheless. Eschatology precisely is the idea of an end of time. The crucial point now is that this particular way of conceiving the end of time in itself entails a very specific notion of time as such. It sets out from an overall cosmological outlook, which takes the viewpoint of the state for granted. As we saw, the crucial cosmological problem for the state is suddenness. The essence of statehood is continuation – of order, of law, of power – hence the one thing that is completely unacceptable in the eyes of a state is the suddenness of war. The way in which a state deals with the problem of suddenness is precisely captured in Beck's idea of the risk society; the potential break in time is banished into the future.

The Schmittian notion of katechon we briefly touched upon above corresponds to the eschatological tendency of the risk society as it is described by Beck. Both of them subscribe to some notion of the inevitable coming catastrophe and to some idea that this catastrophe must be postponed at all cost. This notion of the katechon and the accompanying eschatology, regardless whether it is in the shape of the coming nuclear catastrophe, the coming terrorist attack or the coming Antichrist, provide a very specific notion of time. They work from a preconceived idea of time as consisting of three parts: Past, Present and Future, and what is absolutely crucial: they conceive of this tripartite structure of time by means of a *spatial* image – a line where we are placed in the present with the past behind us and the future ahead, as shown in Figure 3.3.

Past	Present	Future

Figure 3.3 The spatial image of time.

This is far from an innocent image. Given the investigation into the space of war and the space of the state we have conducted above, it should be clear that time is here subjected to not just any spatial order. Indeed, to think of time in terms of a line means to think of time in terms of *striated* space. The line is perhaps the simplest construction of striated space one can give; here movement is determined according to the strictest rules imaginable. To get from A to C, one must move through B, and there really is nowhere else one can go (Figure 3.4).

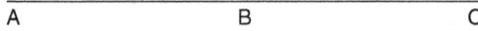

A   B   C

Figure 3.4 The line as striated space.

One cannot have speed, as one moves along a line. One can only move. The point is that the seemingly very commonplace idea that the temporal realm of uncertainty is the future results in a conception of time, which makes a break in time unthinkable. But the whole temporal logic of eschatology and the katechon was built upon the idea that the break in time eventually will come. Thus the very thinking of the state as it tries to combat the coming catastrophe is doomed to collapse. It entails a paradoxical duality of notions of time – on the one hand it conceives of time as a continuous unbroken line, and on the other hand it knows that the break will eventually come. To put the point in the terms of our now very familiar ruler of Himeji Castle: As long as he is able to keep space striated, as long as the war machine is not reinvented, he knows that his rule is secure. But he also knows that at some point in the future the war machine *will* be reinvented, and precisely because his thinking of war is restricted to by a notion of time that is subsumed to the striated notion of space, he cannot make sense of this reinvention.

It would seem that it is precisely such a paradoxical state of denial that is dominating our contemporary political cosmology of terror. The end is neigh, yet it cannot happen. This form of thinking was the dominant theme in the Bush doctrine of the NSS-2002. The looming catastrophe was a given, it was indeed so certain that the only viable counter-strategy had to be to act pre-emptively, as we saw discussed above. The Bush years, of course, are now behind us, but it would be hard to argue that the political cosmology of the war on terror has been effectively dispelled. Pre-emption is not officially on the forefront of the foreign policy of the Obama administration, but this administration did not hesitate, when it was given the opportunity to kill Osama bin Laden in Pakistan on 2 May 2011. And even though jubilant crowds immediately gathered, even though metaphors that it was as if someone won a Super Bowl or a World Cup abounded and even though the financial markets saw an immediate boost, the death of bin Laden does not promise a return to 'normal' either (see, e.g. Berkow 2011; Kollewe & Davis 2011). As shown by the frequency of the use of drone strikes against suspected terrorists, pre-emption is certainly a part of the policies of the Obama administration (Becker & Shane 2012). Thus, the state line of thinking will continue to be to do everything to prevent 'it' from happening, whatever 'it' may turn out to be. Setting aside here the moral and juridical issues in these actions, the crucial problem is that just like the imaginary ruler of Himeji Castle, we discussed above, the only possible cause of action by the states that are confronted with this continual non-occurrence of the potential 'it' is to actually do something: actually start a war, actually assassinate someone, actually engage in extensive surveillance programmes, etc. These are all courses of action that are at one and the same time spectacularly exaggerated and spectacularly impotent. In this way they resemble the dancer who is trying to prove that he is a dancer, by dancing.

The catastrophe has already happened

But the future is not the only crucial aspect of time in political cosmology. Indeed, the past is equally important. With regard to the past we find again that there are two conflicting notions at work in the time of the war on terror. On the one hand the very notion of time inherent in the eschatological view to the future as structured in the image of striated space – that is, as a line – is a way of making all time into the past. The idea of time as a line is a way of turning it into something which does not undergo change, something which in a sense necessarily is what it is and always has been. And this time that forever is going to be what it always was, precisely is what is generally understood to be the past. When the potential breaks in time are continually banished into the future, as it is the case in the political cosmology of terror, the consequence is that one cannot separate oneself from one's own past.

On the other hand we find in this cosmology a very dominating idea that the past is forever behind us. This seemed to be the crucial political call that rang out across the globe in the aftermath of 9/11. 'Nothing will ever be the same!' 'The world is forever changed!' and 'The age of ironi is over!' all seemed to be the order of the day. Most tellingly we saw in the aftermath of 9/11 the fraternization of the great philosophical enemies of the final years of the twentieth century. What better sign of this most spectacular poise of seriousness, claiming that the age of irony is over, could one find than the collaboration of Habermas and Derrida (see Habermas et al. 2003)?

Against these incessant proclamations Žižek was precisely right to counterpoint that on 9/11 nothing really changed at all (Žižek 2002: 46). The so-called wake-up call that chimed out across the globe in a strange form of Beckian solidarity against terrorism should be seen as simply a call to stay asleep – that is, to leave unquestioned the lines of political differentiation implicit in this alleged cosmopolitan order. There is precisely nothing new in the political cosmology post-9/11. Rather, we in the West seemed to solidify our insistence upon our 'way of life' as a direct result of the event.

This captures the paradox inherent in our contemporary political relation to the past. On the one hand our past is thought to entail the paramount event, the radical break which forever changed everything, and on the other hand our sense of time as such is shaped in the image of the forever unchanging past. This is a way of relating to the past that has been captured quite nicely by Schelling in the introduction to the *Ages of the World*. He wrote 'The man who cannot separate himself from himself, who cannot break loose from everything that happens to him and actively oppose it – such a man has no past, or more likely he never emerges from it, but lives in it continually' (Schelling, AotW, 199). Precisely because the event of 9/11 did not in any way help us create distance to ourselves, but rather seemed help us solidify our self-indulgent belief in our own moral, legal and political superiority, therefore we precisely do not have a past and at the same time cannot escape it.

One could argue therefore that the event 9/11 stands as an impossible occurrence that actually took place. As Žižek has argued this temporal paradox takes the shape of a retroactive restructuring. In an article published soon after the 9/11 attacks he draws upon Bergson's reflection on the breakout of the First World War to make the point:

> I never pretended that one can insert reality into the past and thus work backwards in time. However, one can without any doubt insert there the possible, or, rather, at every moment, the possible inserts itself there. Insofar as unpredictable and new reality creates itself, its image reflects itself behind itself in the indefinite past: this new reality finds itself all the time having been possible; but it is only at the precise moment of its actual emergence that it begins to always have been, and this is why I say that its possibility which does not precede its reality, will have preceded it once this reality emerges. (Bergson quoted in Žižek 2003: 140)

The event carries with it its own condition for the possibility of its emergence. Before the event, the event was in a crucial sense impossible. After the event has taken place the event has always been possible. The event itself is what creates its own conditions for possibly emerging. What is crucial, however, is that this retroactive restructuring is posited as having itself taken place in our past. In this way having these events as one's past means precisely to be determined by a mystical inexplicable event of which one cannot fully make sense.

There is of course a crucial difference between the taking place of the First World War and 9/11 – with the former things did in fact epochally change. Nevertheless, the temporal structures are strikingly similar. Just as the First World War in the eyes of Bergson was both impossible before it happened and unavoidable after, so too our relation to 9/11 is one where it was precisely unthinkable before, and after we could think of nothing else. But the difference is important to spell out as well. In 1914 something rather dramatic took place and everything changed. On 9/11 it was rather nothingness that took place with the result that nothing changed. In this way the past that is 9/11 should be seen as the occurrence of an excessive nothingness of the kind we have been investigating throughout these pages. Our past is the '+0'.

There is no time like the present

Having argued this much we can now move closer to an understanding of the work of the '+0' in our contemporary political cosmology. What is at stake in the political temporality of terror is not simply a smooth Deleuzian becoming. It is not simply a process without substance that is at work; it is not simply a vague flow unfathomable in the order of identity and oneness. Rather, it is something quite specific which incessantly does not take place. In this way the Schellingian perspective we are unfolding here is much closer to Lacan than to Deleuze. The Lacanian definition of the real (one of the many) is precisely that which never ceases to not actualize itself. It is the '+0' we have been seeking to understand throughout these investigations.

Temporally speaking we find this nothingness working precisely in the way Schelling described the dialectic of creation as a wavering back and forth between too much and too little, a terrible lack of capacity to make anything definitive come about. In Schelling's genesis of God this lack of decisiveness was eventually overcome by God's becoming contemporary, but in our political cosmology it would seem that we are precisely incapable of finding that moment of contemporaneity. Instead we are continuously wavering back and forth between the nothingness that occurred in our past and the nothingness that looms in our future.

The eschatological way of relating to the future precisely entails an excessive nothingness in the sense that there is a nothingness happening in the future, which retroactively determines our present. The nothingness in this sense precisely is the end of the world, which as of yet is not, but which nevertheless keep insisting in the form of the not-yet in our present. The eschatology of terror is perhaps the most insisting form imaginable in which a future nothingness keeps making itself present in the present.

Likewise the events of 9/11 precisely ended up being the most spectacular non-event imaginable. It was a most powerful way for nothing to happen.[6] To be sure things happened. Planes crashed into building. Lives were lost. Buildings crashed. More lives were lost. But in terms of political cosmology it was not these actual occurrences which took hold. Rather it was nothingness taking place. Nothing took place and as a result nothing changed.

In a recent book *Kantian Deeds* by Danish philosopher Henrik Jøker Bjerre the concluding chapter is entitled 'On the Prohibition of Contemporary Wonders' (Bjerre 2010). The prohibition on contemporary wonders is to Bjerre the ban on any sort of deed which would allow for a radical change of the current state of affairs. Bjerre's book is an extensive plea for the possibility, legitimacy and indeed necessity of genuine deeds of this kind, which he divides into existential deeds that pertain only to the acting subject himself, ethical deeds that pertain to others and political deeds that are universal in the sense that they involve all of mankind. In the present investigations we are merely interested in the latter kind, and their current (im)possibility. The thing that we can learn from our contemporary political cosmology of terror is that here it would not even seem necessary to extend a *ban* on such contemporary wonders. That is so, because here the wavering back and forth, between a nothingness that took place in the past and a nothingness that continually threatens in the future, is precisely serving to make impossible the taking place of nothingness in the present. That there is no time like the present should be taken to mean here that our current political situation post-9/11 is one, where we seem incapable of having a present. In terms of political cosmology we are precisely caught in the past and the future at one and the same time. Indeed, what better way of limiting the break in time from taking place in the present could one imagine than having it continually take place in the future and the past?

The problem here is not that we have been *forbidden* to engage in contemporary wonders. It is rather, I think, that we are finding it increasingly difficult to even imagine what such a contemporary wonder might look like. We always end up, it would seem, imagining the break in time as something which has taken place in the past, and which demands of us a certain kind of 'seriousness,' or as some kind of distant future possibility – regardless whether we see it as radical threat or a radical promise. It is in this way that I argue the problem is a cosmological one – it is precisely a problem of how we can at all think the most important modality of time, namely our own: the contemporary.

That there is no time like the present is thus at first perhaps a depressing conclusion. But perhaps this most depressing and seemingly unavoidable fact that we are incapable of being contemporary should simply be seen as a call to get to work. It is perhaps time that we begin to work towards a reconfiguration of our political cosmology in such a way that we can start to think about a break from the current predicament in the modality of the here and now. In this sense too there is no time like the present.

The Political Theology of Terror

With the introduction of the notion of political theology, we embark on the final part of the road in the present investigations. It is a given that any discussion of political theology must begin by mentioning Carl Schmitt – if not for anything else, then because he coined the term with *Political Theology* (Schmitt 2007b). However, given the structure of the present investigations, the discussion of political theology is put in a somewhat different light than is usually the case. Very often political theology is the name for a discussion of the fundamental principles of politics, statehood, constitutions and law, which accepts the theological trajectory expressed in Schmitt's claim: 'All significant concepts of the modern theory of the state are secularized theological concepts not only because of their historical development [. . .] but also because of their systematic structure, the recognition of which is necessary for a systematic consideration of these concepts' (Schmitt 2007b: 37). In the present investigations, we are interpreting political theology as one of the main disciplines in a reformulation of classic metaphysics. Political theology cannot stand alone. It must be understood in relation to political ontology, political psychology and political cosmology in the ways that we have already dealt with these topics above.

Schmitt's basic intuition in *Political Theology* can be read in the very first sentence: 'Sovereign is he who decides on the exception' (Schmitt 2007b: 5). That is a seemingly simple point: The 'boss', the 'top dog', the 'chief', is the one who gets to decide whether the rules apply or not. Singling out what this is supposed to mean is far from simple, though. Most importantly, the definition hinges on the question of what counts as an exception. Schmitt himself is intentionally vague 'The exception, which is not codified in the existing legal order, can at best be described as a case of extreme peril, a danger to the existence of the state, or the like. But it cannot be circumscribed factually and be made to conform to a preformed law' (Schmitt 2007b: 6). The exception is the thing we cannot know what will be, precisely because it is an exception. It should be noted that in order to achieve some terminological clarity I will henceforth use the term 'emergency' to cover the events of the world that are perceived to be 'cases of great peril' whereas the term 'exception' is used to describe the exceptional legal and political measures taken to combat them.

Carl Schmitt's legal thinking has attracted increased academic attention in the wake of 9/11, likely because of the conflation of emergency situations and absolute sovereign power – and the totalitarianism it reminds us of given Schmitt's Nazi sympathies. His work has been the topic of intense discussion among legal scholars, philosophers and others, ever since 9/11 and the legal and political changes that followed (see, e.g. Vermeule 2009; Scheppele 2004; Scheuerman 2006a,b). In general the debate consists of two camps. On one hand we have those who see in the legal response to 9/11 a dangerous development, which carries with it borderline totalitarianism in the midst of so-called liberal democracy (the idea being that we are turning Schmittian and that we are therefore becoming Nazis). And on the other hand we have those who argue that these worries are wildly overstated, either because democracy and the rule of law is argued to be too well-founded to be threatened by a few minor legal changes, or because it is argued to be necessary to sometimes sacrifice certain liberties in order to defend liberal democracy as such (the idea being that we are either not becoming Schmittian at all, or that we are indeed becoming Schmittian, but that this fact is much less of a problem than the first camp would have it, or at the very least simply necessary). Finally, a popular strand of thought in both camps will consist in the argument that some of the proponents of the critical camp are under the influence of a typical overly intellectualized line of continental thinking. It is argued that what is at the bottom of radical critique is at best fanciful and empty conceptualizations (see, e.g. Scheuerman 2006b: 69; Vermeule 2009: 1100–1); too much speculation and too few facts; theoretization for the sake of theory alone; in so many words: metaphysics.

It is of course a disquieting situation, when arguments can be dismissed on ground of being too metaphysical, or too philosophical,[1] especially when the whole issue at stake is a metaphysical one. Whether we like it or not, political theology (regardless of the position one takes in, against or for it) *is metaphysics.* In the present context that means that it is underpinned by a specific concept of potentiality, which binds the metaphysics of terror together in a whole. The tough point that I shall have to defend in this final chapter is therefore that there is a metaphysical dimension to be investigated in the issue of the constitution of law, of sovereignty and of the state of exception, and that if we do not attempt to seriously tackle the problems that pertain to this metaphysical dimension, we are doomed to misconstrue the issue at hand. The point of taking up Schmitt on the study of political theology, apart from the fact that he coined the term, is that his way of conceptualizing sovereignty does offer some insight with regard to this metaphysical issue. As we shall see, however, Schmitt's view of the matter is limited in the end. I will therefore introduce the work of Agamben and most crucially Walter Benjamin, in order to steer the discussion in the right direction (of course Schelling will play a crucial role too).

Dictatorship

Perhaps because of the Schmittian tendency in the discussion, there is a crucial dogma to the debate, which to my knowledge has not been sufficiently challenged. I will refer to it as the dictatorship dogma. Dictatorship should not here be understood in the common-sense notion of some kind of authoritarian, totalitarian or otherwise non-democratic rule. Instead dictatorship should be understood as a very specific legal-political institution that dates back to the Roman Republic. This institution was praised among others by Machiavelli, who in his *Discourses* attributed to it a good deal of the reason why the Republic lasted for centuries (Machiavelli 1970: 195). Among more recent commentators Clinton Rossiter is particularly enthusiastic:

> If Macaulay's schoolboy knew 'who imprisoned Montezuma and who strangled Atahualpa', he knew even better the noble legend of Cincinnatus, the aged Roman farmer who was called from the plough by his embattled countrymen and given despotic authority to repel the threat of alien tyranny; and who, after sixteen days of absolute power, in which the enemy had been routed in disgrace and the state had been saved laid down the sword and again took up the plough. (Rossiter 1948: 16)

While this story of Cincinnatus is certainly a myth more than anything else (ibid.), the institution of Roman Dictatorship has been considered by many to be the ideal way of dealing with emergency situations. Three points are crucial in this regard: First of all the myth tells the story about how democratic institutions and separations of power meant a hindrance to action which should prevent a catastrophe, and of how it at times could be necessary to go beyond the normal institutions to fight off a threat. Second of all, the myth tells the story of how the solution to these problems is found in the condensation of power in one person. Finally, the myth paints the ideal picture of a solution to a central problem of exceptional measures. Namely the problem of how one gets rid of a temporary dictator, once he has solved the problem he was appointed to deal with. As the myth would have it Cincinnatus 'laid down the sword and again took up the plough' (ibid.).

The actual institution of dictatorship in the Roman Republic did in fact possess a lot of very strict mechanisms to make sure that the very wide scope of powers that were given to the dictator did not remain with him permanently. First of all a dictator could not hold office any longer than six months or the term of the magistrate who appointed him, whichever was shorter. He could not create new laws. Furthermore, only one dictator could be appointed each year (Rossiter 1948: 23; Gross & Ní Aoláin 2006: 17ff.). It is worth noting that over the course of the 300 years the institution of dictatorship was in force, from the birth of the Republic in 509 BC to the end of the Second Punic War in 203 BC, these restrictions were never broken (Rossiter 1948: 24).

That being said, it should be clear why Roman Dictatorship should come to serve as the model for the way many subsequent constitutional systems – especially democratic ones, their founders and their students – deal with exceptional legislation. If one could deal with the exception the way the Romans did, one could perhaps have the cake and eat it too. On one hand one could establish a system that relied on the rule of law, and on the other hand one could within that system have mechanisms that allowed for the rule of law to be set aside, if necessity arose.

The dogma of dictatorship, as I see it, does not entail a specific position with regard to democracy, the rule of law or even the dictatorship. It rather specifies the field within which the discussion takes place. For better or worse most arguments in legal, philosophical and sociological studies of the legal situation post-9/11 have precisely been debating whether it is necessary to give extraordinary powers to certain agents and institutions, and how one makes sure that the situation returns to normal once the emergency has disappeared. Necessity, concentration of power and return to normality. These are precisely the themes central to the dictatorship institution, and they are the themes to which the debates over the legal situation post-9/11 continue to return. Indeed, one could possibly ask: what else is there? The answer, I will propose here, is the same that I have been giving throughout these investigations. The thing that is missed in most assessments of our current political and legal situation is the work of the potentiality of the '+0'. In the particular field of political theology we will see that this element can have quite extensive and quite diverse effects.

In challenging the dogma of dictatorship we should take special care to be aware of the specific concept of necessity that we are dealing with. There are in fact several at play in the notion of dictatorship. Let us first of all note least important one. This is the concept which unfortunately receives the larger part of the attention. It even has its very own standardized Latin formulation: *Necessitas legem non habet* – necessity has no law. This notion of necessity is one that pertains to emergencies rather than exceptions – it is in other words the notion that once in a while the situation necessitates some cause of action, no matter what hindrance may be laid out by the law. With regard to this notion, I have already discussed the problems inherent in calling the situation of the war on terror a necessitating one. As I pointed out in the ontology above it is precisely not the actual violence or the threats of actual violence, but rather the potentiality of nothingness, which fascinates us in terror and terrorism. And as we saw in the psychological discussions that followed, it is the potentiality of terror that is crucial when we fear it, when we are struck with anxiety, and even when we are bored with it. There is nothing necessitating about terrorist threats, they do not force specific courses of action upon us. Instead, they open a field of potentiality and nothingness, which in many ways is more difficult to handle than a simple threat which necessitates a response, a counter-threat or something similar. This crucial point became particularly clear in the investigation of political cosmology above. The kind of actions which terrorist threats could be seen to necessitate, and indeed has been argued to necessitate in the past decade, precisely cannot serve as adequate responses. No matter how many actual advisors the Lord of Himeji Castle should choose to hang, no matter how many curfews and surveillance systems he installs, he will never be able to annul the potentiality for treachery or the potentiality that assassins or terrorists could avoid the curfew and hide from surveillance. Unlike normal threats that come from actual armies and actual politics, the crucial thing about the terrorist threat is that it is the potentiality itself which is at work. Against such potentiality the actualized responses that are available necessarily come out as overreactions – not simply in a moral sense, but in the ontological sense of being excessively actualized. The very same thing could be said for the acts of the various states, nations and armies that have been involved in the so-called war on terror.

But this alleged necessity of the situation is not the only one we are confronted with. There is also the necessity of governance itself. This is the idea that necessity is what not only *causes* but also *guides* governmental action in emergencies. It is the necessity of the exception rather than the emergency, to use the distinction introduced above. Here the claim about necessity is that what governments actually do in emergencies in a sense is necessitated; that there are certain things that must necessarily be done to confront emergency. In this case the example of the dictatorship institution in the Roman Republic will be illuminative. In the Roman Republic the executive power was vested with the magistrates, the highest of which were the consuls, who were always two in number. In the normal situation therefore, the Republic could always have a conflict at the top of the hierarchy of political power. This was a very useful mechanism to have in place as a means of keeping power in check, but precisely because of this, it was believed *necessary* to have the institution of dictatorship, which could streamline the use of power in tight situations. In the same way it is today still believed necessary to concentrate power in the face of emergency. Here we find one of the most pervasive notions of the debate. Some argue that one *should* concentrate power in the face of emergencies, others argue the one *should not* or that one should at the very least be careful when one does, but just about everyone agrees that the thing we are debating, with regard to emergencies and exceptions necessarily is the concentration of power. This precisely is the dictatorship dogma as I envision it. What I call into question by challenging this dogma is the very idea that it is necessary, or indeed at all possible, to concentrate power in this way. Instead of the ideas of necessity and contraction, which dominate the legal-political theology of the discussions of the war on terror, I propose that the central terms are potentiality and diffusion. In doing so I am following the lead of Giorgio Agamben, whose *State of Exception* precisely offers an argument to this effect – a fact which unfortunately has often been lost in the discussion of his work as both critics and proponents have tended to subsume it to the dictatorship model of necessity and concentration.

While terror forms a most problematic threat for sovereign power as we saw in the discussion of political cosmology above, it cannot be overlooked that it also serves as an opportunity. If there are certain tools in the fight against crime, dissidence, rebellion, etc. that a state apparatus should like to have available, then the threat from terrorism would certainly be the best imaginable argument it could possibly give to the public to legitimize those tools. But the viability of this argument for more or less populist political reasons does not mean that necessity is the crucial category to be investigated. And the more radical critique of the dictatorship model presented here suggests that even when the state, its institutions and the people in charge seize upon this opportunity, a concentration of power is not necessarily what follows. What follows could very well turn out to be something, which in many ways is much worse, namely a diffusion of power.

All of this relates to very classic notions of political philosophy of which I shall introduce only one. The concepts of necessity and concentration of power lead us almost immediately to the concept of anarchy that at the very least since Hobbes has been central to the theory of state. Traditionally it is exactly when weighed against anarchy that necessity and concentration of power look the most appealing. As the familiar argument goes, even the worst tyranny is better than anarchy and therefore we necessarily should accept some concentration of power to keep the chaotic and utterly destructive reality of anarchy at bay. This of course is the basic argument of statehood against the nomadic warmachine we discussed above. In my view, we should not accept this blackmail, but nor should we simply take the immediate counter-path and celebrate anarchy at the expense of the state. The question, we will be able to pose given the focus on potentiality and the diffusion of power introduced here, is if anarchy is really what confronts us on the 'other side of the law'.

By challenging the dictatorship dogma and by confronting the notions of necessity and potentiality and of concentration and diffusion we will be able to navigate the truly problematic metaphysical waters, we are placed in, when we try to tackle the problems of law, exception, justice and power in the time of the war on terror. The solution I suggest lies with taking seriously the political theology inherent in these issues, and as I will try to show this means that we must rely once again upon the notion of the excessive potentiality of nothingness.

Law must know necessity

In accordance with the method of last philosophy, we are following here, we should begin this investigation by taking a look at some of the empirical research that has been conducted of the legal situation post-9/11. In the present context we can of course only achieve a very cursory view, but even with this limited ambition we will still be able to see some overall and crucial tendencies. One very helpful tool in this regard is the collective work of Oren Gross and Fionnuala Ní Aoláin. In *Law in Times of Crisis*, they discuss three overall models for the ways in which the law deals with emergency situations. There are the *models of accommodation*, which in some way or other subscribe to the view that emergencies require extraordinary responses, and that the law therefore should accommodate for the additional pressure that is put on the state by extreme situations (Gross & Ní Aoláin 2006: 17ff.). To put the point succinctly the models of accommodation all argue that law must learn to know necessity. Then there is the *business as usual model*, which argues that one should never sacrifice liberties and rights in order to maintain security or even the survival of the state. As the business as usual model will have it, there is one law only, and it must be valid for all seasons (Gross & Ní Aoláin 2006: 86). In this model it is necessity which must come to know law. Finally, there are the models of *extra-legality*, which, contrary to both of the former models, share the view that emergencies in the end cannot be dealt with within the framework of law at all. It is believed that in order to confront the truly extreme cases of emergency that societies face from time to time, one must sometimes break the law to save the law (Gross & Ní Aoláin 2006: 110ff.). The models of extra-legality, which seem to enjoy Gross and Ní Aoláin's sympathies, therefore come to be the most clear-cut example of old adage that 'necessity has no law'.

We begin with the models of accommodation, according to which law must come to know necessity. Principles can be bent in many ways. Gross and Ní Aoláin provide accounts of three obvious possibilities: one can integrate mechanisms for accommodation into constitutional documents, one can formulate special emergency legislation or judges can interpret the law differently in the face of emergency. Of course it is also possible to combine the three. While there are differences between these models, they are similar in the central aspects that concern us here, and so we shall not spend too much time mapping out the differences. A few comments will be helpful though.

Throughout the history of regimes both democratic and undemocratic accommodation has been the dominant course of action in dealing with emergencies. Indeed, accommodation at times seems to be the default position within certain parts of the legal and philosophical debates. Eric Posner and Adrian Vermeule insist 'There is no reason to think that the constitutional rights and powers appropriate for an emergency are the same as those that prevail during times of normalcy' (Posner & Vermeule 2003–4: 607). Alan Dershowitz is another famous proponent of accommodation. His crucial point is that when faced with emergencies states and their agents, whether we like it or not, are going to take exceptional courses of action. Therefore he argues that it is preferable to have rules set in place to regulate how, when, where and on what grounds exceptional measures are taken (see Dershowitz 2006: 26).

Famous cases of accommodation include of course the USA PATRIOT Act (The Uniting and Strengthening America Providing Appropriate Tools Required to Intercept and Obstruct Terrorism Act). The Patriot Act is well known for Section 412's Provision to the Attorney General, which allows him to detain indefinitely any alien who is suspected of terrorism or whom the Attorney General believes, on reasonable grounds, is a danger to the National Security of the USA (Pub. L. No. 107–56, 115 Stat. 272. Section 412, Art 1–5). The Patriot Act also provides a wide range of measures for the US Police and Intelligence Agencies to conduct surveillance of the entire US population. The idea is well known and quite clear: because of the extreme danger posed to the security of the United States by the new terrorist threat, it is necessary to accommodate civil liberties to the situation. Following 9/11, this legislative move was mirrored by states across the globe. Indeed, the Security Council resolution 1373 obliged UN member states to implement certain measures without temporal or spatial restrictions. According to Andrea Bianchi 'these range from the prevention and repression of the financing of terrorism, the prevention and criminalization of acts of terrorism to international cooperation and the duty to ratify international anti-terror treaties' (Bianchi 2006: 1047). As later pointed out by the Security Council itself, in resolution 1535, resolution 1373 was an act that was truly out of the ordinary (Bianchi 2006: 1047).[2]

The historically most famous case of accommodation to emergencies, however, is the fatal history of Weimar Germany and article 48 of its constitution. The Weimar Constitution was born in a time of crisis. A war had been lost and rebellions from both left and right were abundant. Virtual anarchy reigned (Rossiter 1948: 34). These chaotic conditions provided Hugo Preuss and the other drafters of the constitution with ample grounds for the inclusion of an article such as 48 in the constitution, even though they were well aware of the dangers it harboured. The article consists of five sections: The first enabled the Reichspresident to intervene, with the aid of the military, in the affairs of the individual states of the German Republic, if they failed to fulfil their duties in accordance with the constitution. The second enabled the President to act to secure public order and safety, if they are seriously endangered, again with the aid of the army. In this regard the article lists a number of civil rights that may be revoked in such an event. The third section states that the President must keep the Reichstag informed about any measures taken in accordance with the first two sections, and that they are to be annulled at the request of the Reichstag. The fourth section gives the powers, given to the president in section 2, to the heads of the single states with regard to their territories, and the full wording of the fifth section goes 'A national law shall prescribe the details' (quoted in Rossiter 1948: 31). This law was, I dare say unfortunately, never formulated. It should be noted that the very fact that the Weimar republic stands as a prominent example of accommodation to emergencies itself has often been used as an argument against accommodation. (I will get back to the legal history of the Weimar republic below.)

It should be made clear, however, that accommodation is not only something that happens as a result of more or less grand political of constitutional debates. It also takes place in a way that is much less visible to the public eye. It happens all the time in the way the law is being interpreted and put to use. Gross and Ní Aoláin point out as a matter of fact that courts tend to 'go to war' with the state. In other words, judges are sensitive to the kind of criticism which would accuse them of impeding a war-effort, were they to rule in a certain way in relevant cases. But it is not only in times of war that interpretative accommodation takes place. For instance it has been shown by William Stuntz that the interpretation of the fourth and fifth amendments to the US Constitution in the US courts is influenced by the crime rate (Gross & Ní Aoláin 2006: 74). When the crime rate is on the rise judges will tend to put less emphasis upon the constitutional protection against unwarranted search and seizure (provided by the fourth amendment) and the right of a fair trial (provided by the fifth amendment).

Necessity must know law

The Business as Usual model gives away its crucial idea with its name. No matter what emergencies might occur the "business" of law should go on as usual. As Gross and Ní Aoláin argue the different models of accommodation are far more commonly accepted and in the end factually enacted than the Business as Usual model. In the end the reality of the model is probably that it is a phantasy. Still, there are a few examples that can at least help us point out its meaning. The most famous among them is *Ex Parte Milligan*.

The case of Lambdin P. Milligan dates back to the American Civil War. Milligan was accused of aiding rebels in Indiana; he was tried in a military tribunal and sentenced to death. Before the sentence was carried out he appealed the ruling to the civil courts and the case eventually was presented to the Supreme Court, which ruled that the military tribunal did not have jurisdiction over Milligan, and that he therefore should be released. By arguing in this way the Court made the point that although martial law[3] had been proclaimed at the time, Indiana was not a part of the zones of confrontation, and therefore martial law could not be in effect in that state. Hence, a military tribunal in Indiana could not have jurisdiction over civilians. In the words of Justice Davis, who concluded in the Court's decision 'The Constitution of the United States is a law for rulers and people, equally in war and in peace, and covers with the shield of its protection all classes of men, at all times, and under all circumstances' (Davis quoted in Gross & Ní Aoláin 2006: 92).

Such a formulation precisely captures the essence of the Business as Usual model. Predictably it has been the subject of both high praise, as a landmark for civil rights, and criticism, as an example of utter judicial irresponsibility (Gross & Ní Aoláin 2006: 94). Given the discussion we have followed in the chapter on cosmology (Chapter 3), concerning both the historical development and the spatial nature of war, it is not hard to see the problems critics would come up with. War is exactly a phenomenon which is most difficult, if not utterly impossible, to subject to spatial exclusion. But as those who praise the decision would argue, this only means that it is that much more important as a hallmark of civil rights.

But no matter how one views the idea of business as usual, the crucial point about this model is that it is indeed a rare occasion to find a strict adherence to it. As Dershowitz argues: 'every legal system has its "stretch points," its flexible areas capable of expansion and contraction depending upon the exigencies of the situation' (Dershowitz 2006: 119). The point is that even if one on the surface adheres to a strict interpretation of the Business as Usual model there will be plenty of legal loopholes through which one could make use of exceptional measures. Dershowitz quotes an interview he conducted before 9/11 with an unnamed deputy attorney general of the United States, asking if he would 'recommend invoking extraordinary powers of temporary detention' in the event of a terrorist attack on US soil. The deputy answered 'We wouldn't have to. There is enough play at the joints of our existing criminal law – enough flexibility – so that if we really felt that we had to pick up the leaders of a violent uprising, we could' (Dershowitz 2006: 119).

Necessity knows no law

Finally, we have the models of extra-legality. As the name would indicate the models of extra-legality differ from both of the former types in that they assume that real emergencies demand actions that go beyond law. Examples of extra-legal reactions by governments to emergencies are on one hand abundant, yet on the other hard to locate. A crucial reason for this is precisely the 'stretch points' pointed out by Dershowitz – very often governments will be able to find some kind of legal backing to their actions, no matter how obscure. A good example is the economic reforms under President Franklin Roosevelt as the economic crisis was at its peak in 1933 – the so-called New Deal legislation. In his proclamation of 6 March, he announced a national emergency, decreed a bank holiday and forbade the export of gold and silver. The authority on which Roosevelt acted was not his normal powers as President however, but rather section 5b of the 'Trading with the Enemy Act' of 1917, that is, a distinct piece of wartime legislation which had not been revoked (Rossiter 1948: 257; Gross & Ní Aoláin 2006: 76). Thus, Roosevelt's actions were not strictly speaking extra-legal (though they hardly could be said to be 'Business as Usual').

Still, as a matter of illustration there is one very prominent example that broaches the model of extra-legality. It takes us back to the start of the American Civil War and the so-called *Prize* cases. On 12 April 1861, confederate troops opened fire on the federal Fort Sumter, which was one of the bastions of the United States placed in the territory of the seceding states. The Fort surrendered on 14 April, and the day after President Lincoln called Congress together. But before Congress could convene 11 weeks later, Lincoln engaged in several acts of war. Among other things, he enlarged the army and the navy beyond their authorized strength, suspended *habeas corpus* and started a naval blockade against the Confederation (Hartz 2010: 72). The *Prize* cases were a number of cases that came before the Supreme Court, as a result of some of these actions. Specifically, they concerned several ships that had been taken as prize by Union blockading warships. The real issue for the court, however, was whether Lincoln had acted extra-legally, as he acted to go to war. The problem was that the US Constitution vests the power of going to war with Congress, and Congress had not yet been assembled to declare war as the ships were taken. According to the Court, Lincoln had in fact acted in accordance with the Law as he went to war, because of the Commander-in-Chief clause, which makes him the supreme commander of the US armed forces in times of war, and with regard to the specific case of *Prize* the court argued that at the time, war was already going on *as a matter of fact*. Thus in the decision of the Court, Lincoln had not in any way acted extra-legally. In a dissenting opinion, however, Justice Grier argued that while Lincoln had been morally right, and indeed legitimate in his actions, he had in nonetheless acted illegally. This latter position of the dissent provides a very fine example of the model of extra-legality. In the opinion of Grier, Lincoln did what was necessary, and broke the law to save the law – which precisely captures the essence of extra-legality as Gross and Ní Aoláin envision it.

Against necessity

Gross and Ní Aoláin make a compelling argument to the effect that the dominating way of dealing with the law in emergencies is highly problematic. As can be gathered from the examples I have discussed it is in the end quite hard to find instances where the law does not in some way accommodate emergencies. As a matter of fact, accommodation is the name of the game. The overall problem, they foresee in this fact, is the blurring of the lines between emergency and normalcy. They conduct an extensive study of the history of emergency legislation in the United States and in European countries and conclude:

> It is commonplace to find on the statute books legislative acts that had originally been enacted as temporary emergency or counter-terrorism measures, but that were subsequently transformed into permanent legislation. Indeed, the longer that emergency legislation, broadly understood, remains on the statute books, the greater the likelihood that extraordinary powers made available to government under this legislation will become part of the ordinary, normal legal system. (Gross & Ní Aoláin 2006: 176)

Gross and Ní Aoláin are certainly not the only ones to provide evidence of this. Plenty of legal, philosophical and historical studies have come to similar conclusions (see, e.g. Scheppele 2004; Scheuerman 2006a, b; Lobel 2002; Kohn 2003). The more we accommodate our legal systems, either by including of articles like 48 of the Weimar constitution, by introducing exceptional emergency legislation like the Patriot Act or by allowing judges and others enacting the law to interpret it differently, the less clear will the boundary be between rule and norm, between emergency and normalcy.

Crucially, it can be shown that, historically, it makes little difference if one introduces sunset clauses or if one tries to otherwise limit the influence the exceptional measures can have on the normal rule. While I cannot get into too many details in this regard a few examples will be helpful as we move along. First of all the history of the Patriot Act has been telling. Many of the most wide reaching provisions of surveillance were included with a sunset clause of four years. They were to expire at the end of 2005. Before that time almost all of these measures were either extended for ten years or made permanent (Gross & Ní Aoláin 2006: 179; Paye 2006: 162). Second of all, while the name of the act includes the word 'terrorism' the most frequent uses involve other crimes (Paye 2006: 156). In this way the exceptional measures of the Patriot Act became the norm. They were extended beyond their initial limitations and generally made permanent, and their use was quickly expanded beyond the very limited scope of their original intent.

The relation between France and Algeria provides an interesting story with a similar lesson. As a response probably to the extensive government by decree of Eduard Deladier and the Petain Government during the Occupation, the Fourth Republic placed the right to declare a state of emergency with the legislature, 'where it belongs' as Rossiter puts it (Rossiter 1948: 128). Still, as the troubles mounted in Algeria in the fifties these measures of control on emergency government action came under intense pressure. At first only in Algeria itself, where the army enjoyed a wide legal range to act to repress rebellion, because of the emergency regime that was instituted on 3 April 1955 (Gross & Ní Aoláin 2006: 192). But eventually this exceptional legal situation invaded upon the normality of mainland France. At the Battle of Algiers the practice of torturing prisoners was more or less openly admitted by General Jacques Massu, but over time torture became a practice used against the enemies of France within France itself (e.g. members of the Algerian resistance FLN, or the extreme-right-wing organization OAS). As Gross and Ní Aoláin argue this precisely goes to show just how difficult it is to put a *spatial* limitation on the use of exceptional measures – whereas the Patriot Act provides an example of how difficult it is to install *temporal* limitations. In France the state of exception was easy to accept as it pertained only to the situation in the colony Algeria, but inevitably these measures would be used in mainland France as well. The overall point is again that the clear-cut line of differentiation between exception and norm has a tendency to blur.[4]

The Weimar Constitution of course provides a most striking example that is all the more interesting for us, since Schmitt formulated his political theology in the time of the Weimar Republic. The debate with fellow jurist Hans Kelsen, who defended a strict legal positivistic outlook, is often considered a crucial part of this development. Where Schmitt argued for a very wide interpretation of article 48, stating that it makes little sense to assume that the state of exception, when announced by the president of the Reich, would be limited to the seven rights that are actually listed in article 48 (Schmitt 1994), Kelsen argued against him that this would mean the reduction of the entire constitution to article 48 (Kelsen 2008; see also McCormick 1997: 144). Thus Kelsen basically represented the same reservations Gross and Ní Aoláin formulate, namely that too much accommodation to potential emergencies would mean that the difference between exception and rule could disappear.

The history of the Weimar constitution tells us that Schmitt ended up being right as a matter of fact – even if, as some would still argue, Kelsen was right from a normative point of view. Article 48 was a powerful tool indeed, and it was often used during the turbulent years of the Weimar Republic – on more than 250 separate occasions (Rossiter 1948: 33). The way in which it was used was widely different however. In the early twenties under President Ebert it was used more than 130 times, mostly to quell communist rebellion, and rebellious states within the union, such as Saxony in 1923 (Rossiter 1948: 39–40).[5] Later on it was also used to solve the republics massive *economic* problems (Rossiter 1948: 46–8). And in the end article 48 was used as the sole source of law-making power. As Chancellor Brünings budget of June 1930 was rejected, the government collapsed. In the ensuing election both the Nazis and the Communists gained considerable ground in Parliament. This created the odd situation where the Social Democrats, who had contributed to Brünings fall by voting against his budget, felt forced to help him retake power after the election for fear that either of the more extreme parties would be able to take over government. They would not partake in any of his governmental actions however, and thus a legislative deadlock ensued (Rossiter 1948: 51). The result was that Brüning assumed the entire legislative responsibility by virtue of article 48 (ibid.).

The fact that Schmitt ended up being factually right in the debate with Kelsen, should tell us something important. The appeal to necessity – caused by an emergency and demanding swift action – as a matter of fact tends to have the argumentative upper hand, when it is posited in the debate with the appeal to the rule of law. This means that we should look elsewhere, if we wish to challenge the claims made in favour of wide-ranging emergency powers. For us this means that it is Schmitt's discussion with Walter Benjamin rather than the one with Kelson, which should interest us. We will go into greater detail with this surprising contact between a Communist Jew and a Catholic Nazi, once we have completed the review of the various relations between law and emergency.

Even if we set aside examples of deliberate constitutional and legislative accommodation, it would seem that accommodation to emergencies cannot be stopped anyway. As we saw Dershowitz point out above, most legal orders have plenty of stretch points that can be used by the executive, if it should be met with resistance from the legislative or the judiciary, when it is asking for exceptional measures. And in the case of the judiciary itself we saw Gross and Ní Aoláin argue that it tends to 'go to war' when the executive does. Indeed, interpretative accommodation is not at all limited to times of war. Here, the unpredictability of the practice of accommodation shows itself when we consider which cases turn out to be the relevant ones. Gross and Ní Aoláin point out that:

> One cannot read Fourth Amendment cases from the 1980s without sensing judicial attention to the pros and cons of the war on drugs – even when the cases did not involve drug crime. Crack dealers were the most salient crime problem a dozen years ago; now terrorists occupy that place. (Stuntz quoted in Gross & Ní Aoláin 2006: 238)

In the end it seems to be extremely difficult to counter the blurring of the line that separates emergency from normalcy and rule from exception.

To question these clear-cut distinctions and to argue that the differences are becoming increasingly blurred, means to adopt a position which is at least tangent to Benjamin's now famous assertion that 'the "State of Exception" in which we live is the rule' (Benjamin 1965: 84). What scholars like Gross, Ní Aoláin, Scheuerman, Kohn, Paye and others seek to show, is just how close we are coming to a situation where Benjamin's claim is factually true. They have of course been met with various forms of criticism, of which I will mention two. Alan Dershowitz has become famous for arguing that precisely because of the difficulties involved in keeping up a clear line of differentiation between normalcy and emergency, therefore we need to engage in much more extensive legislative and juridical accommodation. As the argument goes we are probably going to torture no matter what we do to try and stop it – therefore it is better to have the decisions that go into the use of torture out in the open (see, e.g. Dershowitz 2003).

Another line of critique has been presented by Adrian Vermeule. Vermeule's argument is particularly interesting as he basically agrees with much of what the critics are saying, that is, there is indeed a Schmittian element to the law, and the post-9/11 acts by the US government are a testimony to this fact. Only in his view there is not a whole lot that can be done about this fact (Vermeule 2009: 1149). He then adds that there is a different possible valence to the panics that cause legislators, executives, judges and people in general to accept *too much* accommodation in cases of emergency. Rather than focusing entirely upon the security panics, Gross and others are criticizing, he believes that we should also be wary of libertarian panics, which could cause us to accommodate *too little*. Indeed, he argues that one of the problems with critical scholars is that they might be taken in with the kind of libertarian panic that sees fascism and police states emerge everywhere as soon as we begin to accommodate even the slightest. As he foresaw in an article from early 2005 'The consequence of the modern [libertarian] panic may well be that the Patriot Act will not be renewed' (Vermeule 2005: 883). A few months later he could rest happily assured that his prophesy had turned out to be wrong, as the Senate on 29 July 2005, 'voted unanimously to make permanent virtually all the main provisions of the act' (Gross & Ní Aoláin 2006: 178).

In general I think that there is ample evidence provided by researchers such as Gross and Ní Aoláin and others to challenge one inherent dogma in the debate about emergency legislation, namely the idea that there can be a clear-cut separation between rule and exception, and between normalcy and emergency. The thing we should have learned from the discussion of the cases above is precisely that that exceptional legislation is, if not impossible, then at the very least very difficult to keep out of the normal sphere. Making this point does serve to challenge the dogma of dictatorship, I discussed above, but only in a limited way. What is challenged by the realization that we cannot keep up a clear line of separation between normalcy and emergence – that the exceptions we tend to make to the general rule in the face of emergencies themselves tend to become the rule – is specifically the third part of the dictatorship dogma. As we recall the dogma consists of three points: (1) Necessity – the idea that dictatorship is understood in terms of necessity. (2) Concentration of power – the idea that dictatorship functions as a concentration of power. (3) 'Laying down the sword' – the idea that the crucial feature of good constitutional dictatorship is that things return to normal after the emergency has passed. Most of the critical scholarship on the state of right, law and justice in the war on terror precisely seek to point out the naivety of the idea that we can fully 'lay down the sword', once we have taken it up, but they rarely do more than that.

This precisely leaves the first two parts of the dogma untouched. Necessity permeates the entire field we have portrayed. It is necessity, which forms the reason behind emergency measures, regardless whether they are taken in accordance with the model of accommodation or extra-legality. And furthermore necessity is what one argues *against*, if one follows the Business as Usual model. Here one will simply put the law above necessity, but thereby one is immediately positing that the crucial choice is between necessity and law. In this way all three models agree to the concept of necessity, they merely draw different consequences from it. As I see it, this is the issue we should take care to address.

There is no outside of the law . . .

The moment we begin to challenge the other two elements of the dictatorship model, we are in murky waters. By saying that the dogma is wrong, we could very likely be asked to come up with a better model. And it would seem that this is indeed impossible. In an important sense the tripartite division of the field, we have discussed above, must be seen as comprehensive. To see why, it can be helpful to consider the courses of action that are available in the event of a terrorist attack or a perceived terrorist threat. Either we could choose to simply do *nothing*, or we could choose to do *something*. If we do nothing, we are immediately adhering to the Business as Usual model. (Normally, this will be the course of action taken by the most of us, who will be expecting someone else to act on our behalf.) If we do something, we can still adhere to the Business as Usual model by interpreting the event (or the perceived threat) as something which can and must be dealt with within the framework of national and international law *as it is*. If we do not simply deal with the situation within the framework of the law as it is, we have again two possibilities: either we act outside the law or we accommodate the law to our action. It would seem that there really are no other options.

In a crucial way therefore legislators, jurists, governmental agencies cannot avoid positioning themselves in this field. From the standpoint of any of the branches of government, it is impossible to not position oneself in favour of one of either accommodation, Business as Usual or extra-legality. To put the point succinctly: there is no outside of the law. Choosing extra-legality would of course mean that one would be breaking the law, but it would not mean that one would be leaving the realm of law altogether. One would not enter the state of anarchy, but rather precisely retain a crucial relation to law. As the Grier dissent in the *Prize* case argued, one would be breaking the law to save the law. The point is that once one enters the realm of the law, there is no outside. To make use of a compelling analogy: we cannot leave the realm of language either, once we have entered it. It is only through language that we can make the distinction between the linguistic realm and the non-linguistic one, but once we have entered language and made that distinction, we cannot turn back. This is a comparison which Agamben puts to the point in *Homo Sacer*:

> We have seen that the sovereign decision on the state of exception opens the space in which it is possible to trace borders between inside and outside and in which determinate rules can be assigned to determinate territories. In exactly the same way, only language as the pure potentiality to signify, withdrawing itself from every concrete instance of speech, divides the linguistic from the nonlinguistic and allows for the opening of areas of meaningful speech in which certain terms correspond to certain denotations. Language is a sovereign who, in a permanent state of exception, declares that there is nothing outside language and that language is always beyond itself. (Agamben 2004: 21)

In *Homo Sacer* Agamben argues in most striking fashion that our relation to law is a lot like our relation to language. Once we are in it, we cannot get out. Even the most extreme cases of being excluded from the law – being outlawed, 'friedlos' or paradigmatically 'homo sacer' – are revealed to be the points where the law shows its most imminent capacity to include and capture. To Agamben being outlawed does not mean that one is excluded from the law, it rather means that one's extra-legal being – one's life in the most basic biological form – is included in the law. In this way there is no escaping the realm of law.

This analogy between law and language, gives us the clue to the Schellingian move we should make to bring hope the point we are after in these investigations of political theology. Just as we, in the political ontology of terror, found that there is a surplus element to the language of terror – as we recall the formula was 'expression + expressiveness = 1 + 0 – so too there is a surplus element at work in the political theology of terror. Saying that there is no outside of law, in terms of the models of emergency legislation we have been working with, would amount to saying: 'accommodation + extra-legality + business as usual = 1'. One can weigh the use of these models against each other, but in the end there is no course of action that takes us outside of them. Still, and this is the crucial wager, we make, when we challenge the overall model of dictatorship: just like the speaker, who is speaking about terrorism, continually says too much – continually invokes an excessive nothingness – so too will the power which positions itself in either of the models of accommodation or extra-legality or Business as Usual, find itself invoking an excessive element of nothingness. There is no outside of the law, but there is precisely *nothing* on the other side of the law. This does not mean that there is a fourth possible model, which we have overlooked, nor does it mean that the treatment in principle of one of the models is lacking somehow (even though there certainly is a lot more to be said in concrete about each of them). Instead, it should be taken to mean that the formula we are looking to understand is 'accommodation + extra-legality + business as usual = 1 + 0'.

In order to bring out this other side of the law, Agamben's much debated work *State of Exception* is exceptionally useful. It provides on the one hand an alternative to the dogma of dictatorship which we have seen dominate the entire field in which the models of accommodation, extra-legality and Business as Usual are placed and discussed. On the other hand it can help us see precisely why it is the element of '+0' which is at work in this alternative.

. . . but there is an other side

Agamben's book is often taken to be about Schmitt, which should probably be attributed to the fact that part of the debate about emergency legislation post-9/11 has been shaped by a renewed interest in the German jurist (e.g. in 'Our Schmittian Administrative Law' (Vermeule 2009), 'Carl Schmitt and the Road to Abu Ghraib' (Scheuerman 2006a) or 'Carl Schmitt's Dark Shadow' (Gross & Ní Aoláin 2006: 162ff.)). While Schmitt is an important figure in the book, it certainly also challenges the central idea of Schmitt's thought. As we recall, Schmitt's point that 'Sovereign is the one who decides on the exception' is easily understood in the way that 'The Boss', 'The Chief', 'The Top Dog' is the one who decides whether the rule applies or not. The problem with this seemingly self-evident understanding of the Schmittian definition of sovereignty is that it places the understanding of political theology under the heading of the model of the

Roman Dictatorship. The problem lies with the assumption that there is indeed *someone*, who can be identified as 'The Boss', 'The Chief' or 'The Top Dog'.

The most compelling part of Agamben's *State of Exception* is the effort to change this picture. It is not, as many would seem to believe, any kind of argument that we are all living in totalitarian systems and not real democracies – indeed, the honest reader would have a hard time finding that sort of argument anywhere in the book.[6] In a way the book is both far more and far less provocative. It is far less provocative in the sense that Agamben has precious little to say about the things we have been discussing so far. The Patriot Act is mentioned once (Agamben 2005a: 3), and then dropped for the remainder of the book. Agamben does provide an overlook of some of the institutions of emergency government that have been in place in the twentieth century, but this part of the book is rather superficial. The book is far more provocative, however, in terms of what it actually seeks to tell us. Agamben's crucial point about the state of exception is that we have absolutely no idea what we are talking about – even those of us who devote ourselves to intense studies of emergency procedures in general have no idea what we are saying, when we utter the words 'State of Exception'. In this sense we should read the book as an effort to provide a theory about the exception that directly challenges the commonly accepted dogmas of *necessity* and *concentration of power*, which, explicitly or implicitly, continue to dominate the field. Thus the crucial claim of *State of Exception* can be put very succinctly: The state of exception is not a dictatorship, it is not a quasi-dictatorship, in fact it has nothing to do with dictatorship at all.

In order to challenge the notion of dictatorship, Agamben investigates the emergency institution which emerged in Rome in the years after the Second Punic War. As we recall, the mechanism of dictatorship lasted from the founding of the Republic in 509 BC to the end of the Second Punic War in 203 BC. That dictatorship was abolished after the Second Punic War does not mean that emergencies were no longer experienced by the Roman Republic, nor does it mean that it no longer possessed legal mechanisms to deal with them. But it did mean that these mechanisms changed drastically. The new legal way of dealing with emergencies was found in the institution called *iustitium*.

After the Second Punic War, Rome was the reigning superpower in the world. The borders were far removed from the city of Rome itself, and the wars in which Rome was engaged changed in nature, in the sense that they were no longer defensive wars in which the survival of the city-state itself was at stake, but rather continual wars (of a more aggressive kind) at the borders (Gross & Ní Aoláin 2006: 239). Thus, the dictatorship – in general a defensive mechanism – was no longer needed. Furthermore, the Senate gained considerable control of power in the republic, and it was certainly not interested in allowing periods of dictatorship to take place, in which it would be delegating all power to one man. Therefore, in times of (perceived) emergency, the Senate would, rather than having the Consuls elect a dictator, make a resolution of the last resort (senatus consultum ultimum), after which iustitium, would be announced (Gross & Ní Aoláin 2006: 240).

'The term *iustitium* [. . .] literally means "standstill" or "suspension of the law" ' (Agamben 2005a: 41). Where the dictatorship was meant to concentrate all power of the republic in the hands of one man, iustitium rather called for *all* magistrates to enact their *imperium*, without constraint from the law. And not only that, it also meant that all the ex-dictators, ex-consuls, ex-censor should act *as if* they were again in possession of their imperium (Agamben 2005a: 42). Even ordinary citizens were to act *as if* they were magistrates. The actions of one Scipio Nasica, an ordinary Roman citizen, stand as a paradigmatic example of iustitium. As iustitium had been announced but the Consuls refused to act against a certain Tiberius Gracchus, Nasica called out 'He who wishes that the state be safe, let him follow me' and killed Gracchus (Agamben 2005a: 44). About this act Cicero later said that 'Nascia acted as if he were a Consul' (Agamben 2005a). The point about iustitium is, in other words, that it is best understood as a stoppage of law, in which anyone can and should do what he can to save the republic.

The difference between dictatorship and iustitium should thus be clear. When the dictatorship was in function a new seat of power emerged in Rome, a seat of power which concentrated almost all power in the republic. In iustitium, no new magistrate came into being, no new seat of power emerged. Instead, 'it is a matter of, under exceptional conditions, putting aside the restrictions that the law imposes on the action of the magistrates' (Agamben 2005a: 45). In this way the iustitium model, which Agamben suggests, challenges one of the inherent dogmas of dictatorship: It is not at all given that the natural response to emergencies is found in the concentration of legal power in one person. A more precise way of understanding what is actually going on in emergency legislation would often be to see it as a diffusion of such power. The crucial problem of emergency legislation is not the debate over too much or too little concentration of power. Rather, it should be seen as the problem of the vacuity of law.

If we follow the logic inherent in the idea that the state of exception is a legal vacuum rather than a legal concentration, we will further be able to see how the dogma of necessity is challenged. This will become evident once we consider the crucial problem that the Romans experienced with the legal institution of iustitium.

The crucial problem with the institution of iustitium was, not surprisingly, what legal sense one should make of the acts that were undertaken under the state of iustitium. These actions could not be said to break the law, because in iustitium the law does not forbid anything. And they could not be said to uphold the law either, because there was no legal rule to follow. What legal sense can one give to acts undertaken in a legal vacuum? Agamben gives a suggestion: 'If we wanted at all cost to give a name to a human action performed under conditions of anomie, we might say that he who acts during the iustitium neither executes nor transgresses the law, but *in-executes* it' (Agamben 2005a: 50). It is with this peculiar notion of in-execution that we find the link, which brings the discussion of the legal responses to emergencies into the field of Schellingian ontology that we have been investigating.

In the normal situation of law, all actions can be said to have some straightforwardly meaningful legal sense. Actions can be lawful or illegal, or they can be legislative acts of creating law, and executive acts of applying law (Agamben 2005a: 50). But the acts undertaken in iustitium are none of these. In the eyes of the law they do nothing other than enact the very lack of law, which is in place in iustitium. With regard to the law, acts undertaken in iustitium are in-actions in a way that is similar to the dancer, who is not-dancing. These acts can of course all be said to be the actual doing of something. The dancer who is not-dancing may be standing or sitting, but for our understanding of him as a dancer, it is the peculiar not-dancing, which is telling. Likewise an act such as Scipio Nasica's was an *actual* killing of Tiberius Gracchus, but in a strictly legal sense it would be wrong to say that it was a murder, since the rule determining certain acts as murder was not in function. On the other hand, it would also be wrong to say that it was *not* a murder, since the very same rule, which should have been in place to proclaim Nasica guilty, should also have been in place to proclaim his innocence. Instead, Nasica's act is best understood as the enactment of the very absence of a rule which could distinguish murders from other acts of killing. Nasica's act could thus be described as a non-murder.

This also means that Nasica's act cannot simply be said to be a case of anarchy. The state of exception is not simply a state of nature, where no-one is bound by any law or power. Instead, acts in the state of exception are undertaken in the very peculiar time of the suspension of law. There is a law, in virtue of which the act could be given a specific legal sense, only this law is not in function. Thus, when it is said that the act is one that enacts the absence of a rule that distinguishes murder from other killings, it should be emphasized that this is absence in the form of potentiality. That there is no rule in place through which Nasica's act could be said to have legal meaning, does not simply mean that the law is missing in an absolute sense, it means that the act has the legal sense of: there could have been a law in force which would have made sense of the act. In this way it is the in-execution or the *in-actment* of the law. In this precise sense the state of exception should be seen as the legal formation of nothingness-as-potentiality. And for this precise reason the crucial legal modality concerning exceptional legislation need not be necessity. If I am right the real problem lies with potentiality.

The claim that was made above about the 'other side' of the law can now be clarified. The other side of the law is not an outside in the sense of illegality, nor is it an outside in the sense of anarchy; it is rather an other side in terms of modality. Where the 'normal' side of the law is the side where actual law is in place and where arguments concerning necessity tend to determine the ways in which we relate to law, the 'other' side of the law is law in its state of pure potentiality. The other side of the law is precisely 'the law+0'.

Does anyone know the law?

In several articles Slavoj Žižek has commented on the curious notion that 'even what's secret is a secret in China' (see, e.g. Žižek 2008a,b). Thus 'many troublesome intellectuals who report on political oppression, ecological catastrophes, rural poverty, etc. (e.g. a Chinese woman who sent her husband, who lives abroad, clippings from a local Chinese newspaper), got years in prison for betraying a state secret, even if they are not aware of doing anything wrong' (Žižek 2008a: 1). In Žižek's argument, a secret law would be the best possible tool in the hands of despotic rulers. He points to Kant's transcendental formula of public law, which clearly defines the problem: 'All actions relating to the right of other men are unjust if their maxim is not consistent with publicity' (Kant quoted in Žižek 2008a: 1). Indeed, it is a fundamental presupposition of the rule of law that the law *can possibly* be known. Yet the problem of ascribing legal sense to the actions committed in iustitium points to a legal space in which knowledge of the law is radically impossible. The crucial difference with regard to the situation Žižek describes in China is, of course, that in China there are *some* people who are capable of knowing the law, even though most people do not. After all, that is what it means to say that something is a secret. In this way, Žižek's discussion of the legal situation in China remains under the heading of Roman Dictatorship. The secret law is merely a tool in the hands of those who know the secret, to suppress dissidence. But when Agamben argues that iustitium should be seen as the model for the modern state of exception, he is effectively arguing that this knowledge as such is impossible. In the end *no one* can know the law in its state of suspension – not because it is hidden, but because it is in the state of not being in force as law.

Lincoln could of course be said to have acted legally when he went to war against the confederation, because the Supreme Court effectively confirmed the legality of the actions in the *Prize* cases, or because of the fact that Congress ratified the actions as soon as it convened. Furthermore, if one were to indulge in a form of counterfactual writing of history, and assume that the majority of the Court had decided that Lincoln's actions were illegal, we would still be in the same situation. The specific legal meaning of Lincoln's actions would have been perfectly knowable (only in this counterfactual example they would have been known to be illegal). The crucial problem is that regardless whether we are in the actual or the counterfactual situation, this legal sense is only known *to us*, and only because of the fact that the Supreme Court in the meantime has made a legal decision on the matter. At the time of Lincoln's actions, it would have been much more problematic to ascribe such legal sense to them.

I would suggest a similar understanding of the legal short circuits that occur, when a statute which is intended specifically for a situation of war or rebellion is used to curtail an economic crisis, such as the acts of Roosevelt during the New Deal legislation, or the acts of Brüning or Papen towards the end of the Weimar Republic, where a legal statute begins to take the shape of an excuse for certain acts rather than a rule governing them. Dershowitz' argument about legal 'stretch point' only serves to underscore this point – the only problem with his position being that he seems unwilling to take into account the possibility that formulating new rules to 'get the tough decisions out in the open' might simply mean the introduction of even more stretch points that could be used in surprising ways further down the road. The best example again is the fact the vast majority of usages of the Patriot Act have been in cases with no bearing on terrorism (Paye 2006: 156). But the decision by the UK Government to use its anti-terrorism legislation to freeze the funds of the Icelandic Landisbanki in October 2008 should certainly be considered in the same vein (Darling 2008: section 9). What these more recent examples show is again the point that it can be extremely difficult, if not simply impossible to know what the law will be in the light of the post-9/11 anti-terrorism legislation. We cannot know in advance when and where this legislation, which in every way is exceptional, will be relevant or simply used.

It is the ontological ground of this insight, which we are slowly uncovering by taking up the notion of iustitium. The point is neither that we are descending into anarchy – that law as such is disappearing around us – nor is it that we are finding ourselves in a veiled dictatorship. The point is rather that we are dealing with actions of potential law. The actions in the *Prize* cases and in the more recent cases were actions taken in a zone where legality was reduced to the state of potentiality. *After* the fact of the act, it can be inscribed into a system of legal rules, but at the time of the act, the act itself must remain strangely autonomous.[7]

American legal scholar Adrian Vermeule has made the argument that this is in fact a necessary feature of emergency legislation. 'Emergencies cannot realistically be governed by ex ante, highly specified rules, but at most by vague ex post standards' (Vermeule 2009: 1101). Vermeule makes this argument to point out that this really is the best we can do, in terms of emergency legislation, and furthermore that it is good enough. While it may be true that it is the best we can do within legal thinking, that does not give an answer, it merely stipulates the impossibility of finding one. Indeed, finding this answer may be more of a metaphysical or political question than a juridical one, but to say that we are done with the question, because it is possible to ascribe a legal sense to the act after the fact is to make the task at hand too easy. Or to be precise: it is to make it completely impossible. Accepting this line of thought would make us quite like the man who was searching for his wallet under a streetlight, even though he had lost it further down the road, because of the fact that it was only under the streetlight that he could see.

Vermeule's point does however bring about the crucial temporal structure which is at work in the impossibility of knowing the law in the state of emergency. It is in a sense imprecise to say that we cannot know the law in the state of exception. The better way of putting the point is to say that it is impossible to know what the law *will have been*. In the future of the act we will be capable of asserting what the legal meaning of the act was in the past. In this way the meaning of the law in the state of exception is at once lost in the past and in the future. In the state of exception there is law, but never in the sense of contemporaneity. Again therefore we can find the precise Schellingian sense of our times. As I argued in Chapter 3, the one thing we are missing today is the capacity to be contemporary. We are constantly fluctuating between past and future, but genuine contemporaneity seems hard to come by. Under the heading of political theology this problem comes up precisely as the impossibility of knowing what the law will have been.

Schelling's point about the original act of God in creation was that it consisted of the transition from the will that *passively* does not will anything, to the will that *actively* wills, but does not will anything – it actively wills nothingness. What we should take care to note here is that this says something specific about the origin of an act; namely that there is at first no particular content to the act. There is no 'what' to the act only a 'that'. The origin of an act is the mere fact *that* an act is undertaken. It is only secondarily, after he has initiated the act, that God can be said to discover *what* he is actually doing. The meaning of an act, its intention, its aim, its means, follow only secondarily upon the first pure instance of the act – the pure fact that an act is initiated. In a similar vein the Schellingian concept of *human* freedom would be that it primordially is a pure groundless act. That 'Wollen ist Ursein' means that human freedom does not consist in a capacity to rationally evaluate our own motives etc., before we act. Human freedom means that we can act, pure and simple. It is only after we have acted that we can begin to give meaning to our actions.

The point of Schelling's concept of freedom is thus that at bottom freedom is neither nature nor spirit. Freedom is in a sense completely autonomous. In a quite disturbing sense, it is precisely because of our freedom that we are incapable of knowing the original meaning of our action. It is precisely not because some metaphysically more fundamental thing – such as nature or spirit or God – is predetermining our actions behind our back that we cannot know the true meaning of what we are really doing. Rather, it is because of our radical freedom that we cannot know origin of our actions. To Schelling it is precisely for this reason that the question of freedom is so pertinent to us. Precisely because our freedom is the enigma of our actions rather than the secure ground under them, therefore it constitutes a problem that at one and the same time is compelling and uncanny.

In continuation of this we should understand the very fact of an act as a call to be understood. Thus, even though 'Wollen is Ursein', the will itself can never stand alone; it must be followed by a reason, which strives towards an explication of *what* the will wills, when it wills. It is for this reason that freedom must be central to philosophy. The task Schelling envisaged for philosophy from the *Essay on Freedom* and onwards was to investigate how human beings through history could come to terms with the abyss of their own freedom.

The political theology we have presented with the aid of Agamben's discussion of the state of exception should be understood as the political reformulation of Schelling's theological philosophy of the will. In its origin the act has no legal sense. It only receives its legal name, after it has been inscribed in the law. Likewise in Schelling where reason precisely is the thing that always arrives too late, and can thus only understand the meaning of the act post factum. But just as Schelling envisages a task for philosophy which goes beyond the mere inscription of the act by reason into a system of rational ends, so too should we not simply be satisfied with the idea of ascribing legal meaning post factum.

All of this means that we have a new name for the other side – the '+0' – of the law. It is precisely the thing we encounter, when we try to understand the contemporaneity of the law in the state of exception. That this 'thing' at one and the same time can be interpreted as the origin of human freedom, and as the impossibility of knowing the law, goes to say that there are two paths to follow, once we have encountered it. There is on the one hand the impossibility of being contemporary and on the other hand perhaps the act of being contemporary as a way of achieving the impossible.

Auctoritas and potestas

The former of these paths can be deciphered by introducing the concepts of *auctoritas* and *potestas*[8] that Agamben uses to describe the relation between the original compulsive act and its endowment with legal meaning. Where potestas could be said to signify legal power or right, which in the Roman Republic originated with the Roman people and was delegated to the magistrates (Agamben 2005a: 78), auctoritas relates specifically to the capacity of enactment. Auctoritas originates in the verb augeo, which means to perfect or to augment, but as it has been shown by French linguist Emilie Benveniste it originally 'denotes not the increase of something which already exists but the act of producing from one's own breast; a creative act' (Agamben 2005a: 76). In this way the act of auctoritas corresponds to the original free act as it is understood by Schelling.

With the introduction of these terms the crucial difference between dictatorship and the state of exception come into clearer view. In dictatorship we precisely have a concentration of potestas in one body, or one seat of power. While this can certainly be problematic enough, an investigation of dictatorship does not really serve to describe the real problems inherent in the contemporary political order. The political danger threatening modern democracies is not so much the threat of a concentration of legal power in one specific place, but rather that there is an opening of spaces in which the legal order is in suspension, that is, waiting for authority to act and set in motion after which is can be bestowed with *ex post* legality.

The problem we have uncovered is not simply that auctoritas is a necessary part of the law. It is not simply that there is a legally indeterminate element inherent in the structure of the law. Indeed, it might be said that this indeterminacy is a necessary condition of any law and any system of law, in so far as it relies upon the capacity to judge – that is, the capacity to ascribe a meaning to an act in the wake of the act taking place. The problem is rather that there is a delicate balance between auctoritas and potestas, which can be dismantled. If auctoritas comes so far ahead of potestas, if the authority which enacts the law becomes so autonomous from the legal power which determines its meaning that there is nothing left to do for the law, but to ratify the acts that have been undertaken with authority, *then* we are in a situation where the state of exception is threatening to become permanent. The argument Agamben provides with regard to the rule of law is that this is only a meaningful concept in so far as there is some balance between the law itself and the authority which enacts the law. And it is precisely when the situation arises where it is completely impossible to know the contemporaneity of the law that this balance disappears.

But as I argued above there is also another path to be followed once we have formed the notion of the impossible contemporaneity of the law – that is, the +0 of the law that we have diagnosed so far. Perhaps it is precisely when we are confronted with the other side of the law that we can finally achieve a genuine relation to it. The first step on this path consists in the realization that Schmitt was wrong, even though he should be lauded for coining the notion of political theology. The temporal glitch we have encountered – the lacking of contemporaneity – is precisely the reason why the political theology, we are pursuing here, does not in the end fit with notion of sovereignty formulated by

Schmitt. No matter how much veneration Agamben himself seems to have for it, the Schmittian conception must be overturned – a point which Agamben does seem to acknowledge in his own convoluted way (see, e.g. Agamben 2005a: 58). The way to do this is to take up the thinking of Walter Benjamin.

Sovereign impotence

Perhaps the most overlooked point about Agamben's *State of Exception* is the fact that it is not really a Schmittian book at all. Unfortunately, the received opinion seems to be that the book defends the view that we are living in Schmittian times – that is, times in which power is being condensed in the hands of one sovereign agent (or at least very few of them). We have already seen just how wrong this view is as a reading of Agamben – and how lacking it is, as a diagnosis of the legal-political problems we are facing after a decade of anti-terrorism politics and legislation. The crucial problem we are facing, the problem which precious few are debating, is the problem of the diffusion of law, not the concentration of legal power; it is the problem of potentiality of law rather than a necessity that transcends law.

The crucial chapter of *State of Exception* is the chapter 'Gigantomachia Concerning a Void', in which Agamben uncovers the links between the intellectual developments of Benjamin and Schmitt respectively. He ends up giving Benjamin the upper hand just like I will be doing here, but he does so for other reasons than mine. While I agree with Agamben's insight that Benjamin is crucial for our understanding of the relation between the law and the state of exception, I do not agree that the final key to the puzzle is the conflation of law (in the state of exception) and life that Agamben accentuates by pointing to a letter from Benjamin to Gershom Scholem, in which he writes 'the Scripture without its key is not Scripture, but life' (Benjamin quoted in Agamben 2005a: 63). Rather than seeking out the conflation between law and life I will seek a more dialectic (i.e. Schellingian) way of putting Benjamin's insights – one that fits the overall perspective offered here.

In *Critique of Violence* (Benjamin 1965) Benjamin discusses the relation between violence (Gewalt) and law. He sets out by taking up what could be called the standard outlook of political philosophy, where the law is conceptualized along the lines of either natural law or positive law, and argues that the only way violence can be conceptualized within these boundaries is as a *means to an end*: Violence is either law-creating or as law-preserving. Specifically, neither natural law nor positive law is capable of conceptualizing a form of violence which destroys law. As Benjamin argues, wars and other similar grand scale events of violence, which certainly can be a threat to existing juridical orders, are precisely not forms of violence that destroy law, but rather forms of violence that create new law. Wars, revolutions and most general strikes all tend to have the foundation of a new legal order as their result.

Much in line with what we have argued about the concept above, Benjamin thus seems to presuppose that anarchy is in fact a meaningless concept. There is no outside of the law in the simple sense that law ends and anarchy breaks out. Wherever law ends in the conventional sense there will certainly tend to be plenty of violence, but that is not because of the lack of law, it is rather because at these points law is either being preserved or created anew. Perhaps surprisingly therefore, the task Benjamin sets himself in the *Critique of Violence* is to investigate if it is at all possible to conceptualize a form of violence which does not immediately result in the creation or preservation of law. This would be a form of violence without relation to law at all; it would in Benjamin's understanding be the only form of violence that might be law-destroying (Benjamin 1965: 59).

In order to conceptualize this form of violence, Benjamin gives the understanding of violence as a means a twist. He does not deny that violence is always a means, but he argues that violence sometimes is a means *without* end. As long as violence is seen as a means to an end, the end can and must be understood in some notion of law and legitimacy, but if violence is considered as a means without end, then we might have a notion of violence that is law-destroying. It is at this point that Benjamin's conceptualizations in *Critique of Violence* begin to resemble the Schellingian dialectic of potency.

Where Schelling's dialectic of potencies describe a wavering back and forth between excess and lack, between past and future, Benjamin's describes the wavering back and forth between ends and means. In natural law the means are measured by the legitimacy of their ends, in positive law the ends are measured by the legality of their means. But as Benjamin points out both of these systems subscribe to the dogma that legitimate ends can be achieved with legal means and that legal means can be used to achieve legitimate ends (Benjamin 1965: 31). There is no real outside to this system. All actions can be inscribed with some meaning in terms of legality and legitimacy. Actions may be illegal or illegitimate, but that does not put them outside of the system of the legality of means and legitimacy of ends.

But there is an *other* side to this system. When Benjamin seeks to formulate a notion of violence as a means without end, we should precisely see it in the sense of the +0, we have excavated in our discussion of the legal regime post-9/11.

Just like the relation between potentiality and actualization for Schelling precisely does not describe a kind of Aristotelian finalized system in which potentialities are either actualized or not, so too does Benjamin seek to find an understanding of the relation between ends and means that can tell us how and why this system does not describe a finalized whole – or to be precise: in which this whole is itself marred by a crucial and all-important incoherence. This crucial incoherence in the system of ends and means is not some transcendent principle or idea (that would simply be another end), nor is it life unfolding itself in a multitude of ways (that would simply be inscribed as means). Rather, the incoherence of the system of means and ends should be understood precisely as the means without end – as means that insist in their 'being means'. In Schellingian terms the means without end are of course the potency of the potentiality that is real without actualizing itself. The dancer who does not dance is precisely realizing a means without end.

Benjamin carries out his investigation of the notion of violence as a means without end by introducing two new concepts: mythical and divine violence. Mythical violence is violence as pure manifestation. It is the form of violence which says 'I have means, and I am not afraid to use them'. Benjamin argues that this form of violence serves to found states and legal orders. Mythical violence is the form of violence which creates a realm within which there can be law-making and law-preserving violence. In a sense therefore, mythical violence is the form of violence which works to make us forget that there could be anything other than violence as a means to an end.[9] Mythical violence is a pure manifestation of means and in this sense it does not have an immediate end, but the purity of this manifestation does itself serve an end; it serves to ground a system of violence and law where all means are tightly knit to their ends.

The construction of Himeji Castle could be a good example of mythical violence. However, it would precisely *not* be the many imposing defensive mechanisms in the castle, the architectural structure, the gates, etc. that would count as mythical violence. Those mechanisms are on the contrary very good examples of law-preserving violence. Instead, the specific mythical violence of Himeji is the very expression inherent in building such an imposing structure, which simply says: 'This can be done'. It is a pure expression of means.

Likewise most terroristic violence should be understood as mythical violence. In Benjaminian terms terrorist violence should be seen as an attempt at mythical violence which fails of ground a new system of ends and means – or perhaps we should simply see it as mythical violence 'by proxy'. It is violence which serves to say 'this can be done', it is a manifestation of power, but without a space of law that is founded as a result. Instead, it invites a response in the form of mythical violence by the state. On the other hand certain terrorists in fact do succeed in founding a new legal order – recent examples would be Menachem Begin of the Irgun movement or Nelson Mandela of the ANC.

Divine violence is argued by Benjamin, in typical poetic fashion, to be the precise opposite of mythical violence in every way 'If mythical violence is law-making, divine violence is law-destroying; if the former sets boundaries, the latter boundlessly destroys them; if mythical violence brings at once guilt and retribution, divine only expiates; if the former threatens, the latter strikes; if the former is bloody, the latter is lethal without spilling blood' (Benjamin 1965: 59). Divine violence operates in the same space as mythical violence. Like mythical violence it functions in the realm of pure means without end. But where mythical violence is the kind of manifestation that inaugurates the wavering back and forth between means and ends, between law-making and law-preserving violence,[10] divine violence seeks to dismantle it. Making out precisely what divine violence is, and what it might consist in, is somewhat more difficult than is the case with mythical violence.

The closest Benjamin comes to giving a concrete example of divine violence within the human sphere is the discussion of the proletarian general strike (Benjamin 1965: 50ff.). Throughout the essay Benjamin discusses the strike, and the workers' right to strike, as a curious phenomenon in the realm of law. It is a curious phenomenon, because it is one of the few areas where the state monopoly on the legal use of violence is broken. The strike is a form of violence, which certainly does not belong to the state, but the right to strike is nevertheless guaranteed by law (Benjamin 1965: 36). Benjamin argues that this probably is due to the fact that the strike as such is a form of in-activity 'Nicht-Handelns' (Benjamin 1965). To strike after all simply means to organize not working – a point which should not be lost on us. The parallel with our not-dancing dancer should be clear. Strikes are the not-dancing dancer turned into a political protest. The strike is a form of in-activity, which most forcefully makes the reality of being a worker present. Still, most strikes will tend to fall back into the wavering back and forth between means and ends, as they precisely function as a means *to an end*. The nurses could go on strike because they want to be compensated fairly for their work, the school-teachers might very well do the same to demand better working conditions and so on.

But in the case of the general strike, where all of society is not-working at once, we might have a collective phenomenon, which corresponds to Scipio Nasica's non-murder. It would not merely be a group of people protesting with some specific goal in mind, it would rather be a generalized in-actment of society as such, and with it perhaps an in-execution of the prevailing juridical-political order. Not all general strikes are of the same kind, however. Benjamin here draws upon George Sorel, who argued that the general strike in turn could be understood in two different ways: as political or as proletarian. In the *political* general strike the aim of the striking masses is to establish a new state in place of the existing one. Accordingly, the violence of a political general strike is mythical. It seeks to establish a new way in which the dialectic of law-preserving and law-creating violence can be in function. In the genuine proletarian general strike however, there is no such goal. As Benjamin argues it is only the latter, which can be said to really escape the end-means relation, because it does not merely seek better conditions for workers, but a different 'work' altogether (Benjamin 1965: 51).

One could perhaps argue that the proletarian general strike is a misconceived notion, and that it will always turn out to have been some form of political general strike; one could argue that all general strikes would tend to form a new state, if they succeed in overturning the present one. But the conceptual point, Benjamin makes, would still remain. If there is a space of human activity in which states are founded by virtue of some form of mythical violence, then it is also possible that other acts than pure manifestations of power are possible within this space. The point is however that we cannot yet know what this means. It is in this sense we should understand Benjamin's concluding comment that the critique of violence is the philosophy of its history (Benjamin 1965: 63). And it is at this point Schelling's projection of the task for a future philosophy begins to resemble Benjamin's. Investigating the history of violence means investigating the realm of action, where human beings try to come to terms with their own freedom. In this sense it may very well be that there has not yet been a single instance of divine violence in the history of mankind, but the task which Benjamin lays out consists not in proving that divine violence has taken place, but rather in showing that it can take place and perhaps at some point to invent *how*.

To sum up, mythical and divine violence should be taken as descriptions of various ways in which human action (violence) can take place on the 'other side' of the law. They are various ways in which human beings can act in relation to the entire system of legality and legitimacy, of ends and means. For better or worse mythical violence is the form of violence that always turns out as an *enactment* of this system. It qualifies it and gives it a mythical foundation. Divine violence on the other hand is the true *in-actment* of such a system. It exposes the very mythical foundation for what it is: a myth. Where mythical violence taps into the other side of the law in order to make us forget that there could ever be such an other side – that there could ever be anything but law-preserving and law-creating violence – divine violence seeks to remind us of what mythical violence wants us to forget.

This short presentation of Benjamin's reflections from *Critique of Violence* can serve to cast new light on our discussion of political sovereignty. First of all we can put a different light on the work of Schmitt. Agamben is right to point out: 'The theory of sovereignty that Schmitt develops in his *Political Theology* can be read as a precise response to Benjamin's essay. While the strategy of "Critique of Violence" was aimed at ensuring the existence of a pure and anomic violence, Schmitt instead seeks to lead such violence back into a juridical context' (Agamben 2005a: 54). In this way Schmitt's definition of sovereignty is turned upside down compared to the way it is usually read. Rather than serving as a way of defining the sovereign's action in relation to the rule of law Schmitt's definition is taken to define sovereign action in relation to the state of exception. Where the standard reading of Schmitt takes him to be arguing that the Sovereign is (and should always be) capable of announcing the state of exception and set aside the law, which is the understanding the theory of sovereignty is put in, when focus is placed on Schmitt's debate with Kelsen and the other positivists, the reading proposed here, which puts focus on the discussion with Benjamin, takes Schmitt to be arguing that the sovereign should be able to make sure that the state of exception is never completely separated from the law. Crucially (this may seem to be a provocative point) it is this version of Schmitt that is the really dangerous one. It is at this point that Schmitt turns out to in fact be much more in line with the notions of liberal democracy and the rule of law that so many critics wish to defend against him, and it is at this precise point that we should take care to renounce him.

Turning Schmitt upside down here means that focus is not placed on the spectacular scandal that the rule of law may be set aside by some form of sovereign decision – an act of auctoritas, or, as we know it by now, mythical violence. Reading Schmitt in conjunction with Benjamin means that something quite different is at stake. Here Schmitt's argument should rather be read in the way that sovereignty is the authority, which guarantees that there can be no divine violence. Schmitt's idea is that all human action in the space I am here characterizing as the +0, or as the other side of the law, must be controlled by the sovereign. His theory of sovereignty has the objective of arguing that there can be no other actions in this space than mythical violence and terrorism. But this also means that a problem emerges for Schmitt's position. Can there really be a sovereign, who can make sure of this?

The crucial term here is of course that of the decision in Schmitt's theory. The sovereign is the one who *decides* whether the law applies or not. In the common way of understanding Schmitt's work, this decision is viewed from the angle of the rule of law itself. The thing that is threatened by Schmitt's idea of sovereignty is perceived to be our normal state of legality – a fact which should be no surprise since much of the renewed interest in the work of Schmitt relates to the fear that anti-terrorism legislation might threaten this rule of law. Still, if one does not take the point of view of the rule of law, but rather that of the 'other side' of the law, Schmitt's concept of the decision is instead about what kind of action can be permitted in this anomalous space. What scares Schmitt more than anything else are in other words precisely the things that could take place on the other side of the rule of law – at this point his Hobbesian tendencies are most prevalent: the only things he can imagine at this other side are sovereignty and anarchy (and we should add terrorism). Therefore he is willing to sacrifice most of the content of the juridical order to save it from the threat he believes Benjamin's idea of divine violence is posing. In this sense it is not as much the need for someone to have final say over the rule of law that is stipulated in his infamous definition of sovereignty. It posits not so much a need, as it nurtures a frail hope. By arguing that *the sovereign* is the one who decides on the exception, Schmitt is nurturing the hope that *the exception* can be kept in check by the sovereign.

Following Agambens reconstruction of the debate, Benjamin offers at this point a counterargument in the *Origins of the German Tragic Drama*: The sovereign, who decides on the exception, is precisely the one who is 'incapable of making a decision' (Benjamin 1978: 52). Agamben's reconstruction is unfortunately a bit compact here, but a minor expansion will help clarify things. The German tragic drama, which Benjamin is describing, has its historical origin in the baroque, which to some may seem as a rather arbitrary theme for our discussion of political theology. As a discussion of sovereignty as such, however, and particularly as a discussion of Schmitt's theory of sovereignty, this baroque origin is crucial, because it would be the baroque sovereign that should come to be the ideal for Schmitt in the *Nomos of the Earth*. Here, in one of his most historically detailed books, he describes and discusses the European order formed under baroque sovereignty in the years from the peace of Westphalia until the end of the nineteenth century (Schmitt 2003: 144–5). The greatest achievement, so Schmitt claims, of baroque sovereignty was that it was able to control war. It could not make war impossible, but it could abolish wars of annihilation (Schmitt 2003: 147ff.). The baroque order of sovereignty was one in which the soil of Europe was divided into sovereign states that would often go to war, but when they did they would also consider each other as equals in going to war. Therefore, the baroque sovereigns of Europe were enemies that were capable of making peace with each other, and therefore the system of baroque sovereignty was one in which anarchy could be kept at bay. To Schmitt it was important to point out that keeping anarchy at bay should be understood quite literally. It was done by drawing lines on the world map. The first were the so-called amity lines that supplied the principle, by virtue of which the system of baroque sovereignty was able to provide centuries without wars of annihilation (i.e. anarchy). This principle simply was the clear separation of the old and the new world. In the old world of Europe treaties were expected to be upheld; in the new world in the colonies war was unbound. 'Beyond the line was an overseas zone in which, for want of any legal limits to war, only the law of the stronger applied' (Schmitt 2003: 93).

In light of the fact that Schmitt would later formulate this kind of argument in the *Nomos of the Earth*, Benjamin's argument that the baroque sovereign is the one who cannot make a decision becomes all the more striking. It should be clear that Benjamin is not trying to argue that the sovereign is incapable of deciding with regard to the realm of law. The baroque sovereign was certainly capable of deciding in that realm – he and later sovereigns are all capable of suspending the rule of law in favour of some emergency regime. Instead the sovereign's incapacity to decide pertains to the realm in which Schmitt's debate with Benjamin takes place, namely the other side of the law, the 'law+0'. And in this realm it should in fact be quite self-evident that Schmitt's sovereign is completely incapable of making a decision, because the sovereign decision is a decision about the exception *to the rule*. The sovereign is capable of deciding that an exception should be made to the rule, but once the rule is suspended, the sovereign is not really capable of deciding anything else. He can use all his might to strike down upon dissidents, terrorists, demonstrators and others that might annoy him, but he can make no further decisions, because there is nothing more to suspend. The sovereign is thus capable of dealing with any action that takes place somehow and somewhere within the rule of law and within the realm of ends and means. All means that pertain to the human sphere can have their legality annulled, and all ends can be called illegitimate, when the sovereign decides that the rules which govern legality and legitimacy are suspended. But the forms of violence that take place in the realm of means without end are precisely not affected this suspension.

Again our example with the ruler of Himeji Castle will be illustrative. The moment the idea of 'terrorism' has gained a solid footing in his mind, that is, the moment he begins to think of every meal as potential poisoning and of every advisor as a potential deceit, this ruler will certainly be able to assert his power over life as it is actually being lived inside and outside the castle – he would be capable of ordering random search and seizures, curfews and he would be capable of revoking any legal rights, his citizens might have acquired – but he would precisely not be able to *decide* that the potential threat should disappear. Like Nero he could very well end up setting the world on fire without ever being able to find peace.

Divine freedom

Following this line of thought Benjamin offers a different counterargument to Schmitt than the one provided by Kelsen. This is crucial because Kelsen's argument against Schmitt seems to be all too easily overcome by appeals to necessity. As long as we only argue against the Schmittian position from the side of the rule of law, we will theoretically and politically constantly be overrun by the appeal to necessity or arguments to the effect that legal niceties can be all right when things are normal, but in this particular situation in which we are finding ourselves today (and if it is not Islamist or red terrorists, it will probably be something else), we must accept what is necessary for an immediate and stern response. The lesson which we should learn from Benjamin's position in the debate with Schmitt is the ridiculous nature of this kind of response. The immense apparatus of anti-terrorism legislation, anti-terrorism police and ultimately the war on terror, should more than anything serve to tell us about the incapacity to decide, which haunts our contemporary political order. The crucial problem of political theology in the war on terror is thus perhaps not the problem of the relation between the state and the citizen, but rather the problem of the states relation to itself.

Similar to the conclusions we have made in the political psychology and the political cosmology above, we find in the political theology a certain wavering. In the political psychology we found the general political state of mind in the times of the war on terror to be a wavering back and forth between anxiety and boredom. In the political cosmology we found a temporality of the war on terror in which we are constantly wavering back and forth between past and future. In the political theology we find a constant wavering back and forth between dictatorship and the state of exception. Confronted with a terrorist threat state power tends to tighten its grip in the attempt to concentrate power, thus imitating in some way the ideal of Roman Dictatorship, but what results from this attempted tightening very often is a diffusion of political power, and thus the polar opposite of dictatorship: the state of exception.

In the end no-one is capable of controlling the anomalous space that is opened up with the suspension of the rule (of law). The problem of political power is therefore not that certain forces in society are capable of taking too much power, but rather, and perhaps more problematically, that precisely when a concentration of power is attempted, a displacement and a diffusion of power results. The crucial point Benjamin makes against Schmitt is that if Schmitt has a point that the insistence upon the strict adherence to the rule of law is naïve, the Schmittian dream of the sovereign power which is capable of taking charge and setting things straight is even more naïve. It is not (only) naïve because it underestimates the effects done to the rule of law by its temporary suspension (which would be Kelsen's argument), but more importantly because it overestimates the capacity of power to be condensed and concentrated. While legal scholars like Gross and Ní Aoláin certainly have an empirical point when they point out that emergency regulations and states of exception tend to become permanent in some form or other, the point they are missing is that this does not lead us on a straight line towards ever more strongly concentrated centres of power. Instead, is pushes us towards a realm where the centres of power themselves are incapable of knowing what they really can and cannot do.

This is a situation which on one hand should be considered to be much worse than an outright dictatorship. But perhaps it is also a situation in which we may find some kind of hope. Precisely because the 'state of exception' is not and cannot be controlled by either the realm of law or by sovereign decision, therefore we may still be able to nurture hope for the potentialities of human freedom. The lesson this investigation of political theology should teach us in this regard is the idea that there still is a narrow space of human action which we cannot yet determine. We do not yet know what human freedom really means. Therefore the task for any future philosophy must still be the Schellingian one: to investigate what we could do with our freedom.

Conclusion – All's Well That Begins Well

In *The Ticklish Subject* Žižek famously argued that the Cartesian subject has been the *persona non grata* in Western academia throughout most of the twentieth century. I would suggest that Žižek is only almost right here. Indeed, if there was one theme which has been even more unpopular than Cartesian subjectivity, probably since the death of Hegel, it would have to be the strong programme of metaphysics which seeks to know the whole in the sense of ontology, psychology, cosmology and theology.

The critique of metaphysics certainly unified most trajectories of twentieth-century thought. From Heidegger's destruction to Derrida's deconstruction; from American pragmatism and logical positivism to post-Wittgensteinian analytic philosophy; from the early Frankfurt School critical theory in Adorno and Horckheimer to later generations in Habermas and Honneth; from Foucaultian archaeology to Butler's queer theory; in natural and in social science, in the sciences of art, literature, language, history, culture, war, jurisprudence and most certainly in terrorism studies. In all of these fields, thinkers, and programmes we find the tiniest of common voices. A voice which says that a certain kind of thinking is no longer possible: metaphysics.

This voice says: Philosophy as the special kind of discourse which sought to investigate and understand everything through one single principle was perhaps possible at some point in the past, but with the advent of the modern specialized sciences of nature, man, and society, with modernist art and literature, with the division of the field of philosophy itself into a myriad of specialized disciplines, and most certainly with the political atrocities that dominated the experience of the twentieth century, it became scientifically improbable, institutionally and academically unfeasible, and politically atrocious to think that there could be meaningful metaphysics. Metaphysics is dead and it is not coming back.

I agree with all of this. Metaphysics is not a meaningful endeavour in the sense of a first philosophy which grounds all subsequent philosophical and scientific thought in general. But in a certain way the assumption that unites all of the above also seems to be that that there once was a time, where one could meaningfully, albeit naïvely, entertain metaphysical thought. Only that time is now over. Still, if metaphysics is impossible today, how could it then have been possible 200 or 2,000 years ago?

At his much anticipated introductory lecture in Berlin in 1841, Schelling made the point that 'at bottom, all philosophers believe and say in their hearts: philosophy should not exist anymore' (Schelling, PO, 93). With that he did not seek to produce an argument in anticipation of the anti-metaphysical tendencies of the twentieth century, but rather to describe a general tendency which pertained to *all* philosophy in his view. The idea that all philosophers seemed to share, thus goes Schelling's idea, is that once the work of philosophy is done, it is done. Once philosophy has answered the questions it poses itself, no-one needs to worry about those questions anyone. Indeed, this would be the one point which classic metaphysics and the critique of metaphysics agree upon: there once was a problem, and now it is not a problem anymore.

The point Schelling tried to make against this line of thought has already been broached. The task for philosophy is not to bring about the end of philosophy, but rather to make it begin. The task for philosophy is to investigate what freedom could possibly become, not to investigate what it already is. If we follow this idea to the end, then it could be argued that it was because time was not yet ripe for philosophy to begin, that Schelling's programme was doomed to fail and (more or less) be left in oblivion. At Schelling's time the notion of philosophy as a discipline which answered questions once and for all was perhaps still too strongly rooted for that other line of thought to be possible. If we accept this idea, the conclusion must be that it was metaphysics itself which made metaphysics impossible.

That thought puts us in an interesting position today. Given that we have been through the anti-metaphysical century, we may just finally have gotten rid of metaphysics as first philosophy. But that in turn means that the field is now – now finally – open for the real metaphysics to begin. If there is one thing that I hope to have shown in the present investigations, it is thus that philosophy as metaphysics, as genuine systematic metaphysics, is indeed possible. It is not possible *still*, but rather it is possible perhaps *for the first time*. The time for metaphysics lies ahead of us, not behind us.

A final note on collectivity

That being said we should take a moment to reflect upon the trajectories that have been laid out for us with this – if I may be so bold – new metaphysics. In the investigations above we have seen how the results that were achieved in the political ontology of terror have been crucial for each of the *Realphilosophische* fields of political psychology, political cosmology and political theology. Throughout these investigations we have been able to follow the paradoxical potency of the potentiality of nothingness – indeed it is this curious potency which binds all that has been said together in a system. But precisely because this potency is the paradoxical vanishing point rather than the stable Archimedean centre, therefore this system should be understood as the incoherent system of contemporary politics. The non-phenomenon at the bottom of this has been described as the '+0' we introduced in the discussion of the discursive linguistics of terror and more figuratively as the non-dancing dancer, who (perhaps reluctantly – after all that would be fitting) has been following us all along.

In the political psychology of terror we saw how the potency of nothingness can both take the shape of a potent nothingness that is the cause of anxiety and as an impotent nothingness which is becoming increasingly boring. In the political cosmology of terror we saw the potency of nothingness at work as the intangible excess that separates the striated space of state from the smooth space of war, and we saw it at work in the temporality of terror, where we are being held out between the extremes of the nothingness of the catastrophic future and the impossible catastrophe in our past. Finally, we found the potency of nothingness in the political theology of terror as the in-actment of the law, which does not amount to any kind of real anarchy, but instead functions as the potency of the potentiality that there could have been law.

In this way we have found the Schellingian coordinates of our contemporary metaphysics. As I argued in the introduction chapter the metaphysics of our time is 'Much Ado about Nothing'. An immense activity takes place in response to the crises of our time, yet for all the activity it would seem that nothing is really happening and most certainly nothing is changing. The metaphysics of terror is flat. It is one in which we precisely do not experience any kind of significant event, we rather find ourselves ever more deeply enmeshed in the most tragic oscillation between equally sad poles. Unfortunately the Presidency of Barak Obama, announced as it were as a river of change, provides the most striking example. With the signature on the National Defence Authorization Act on 31 December 2011 Obama not only confirmed the regime of indefinite detention without trial of suspects of terrorism, he signed it into law.[1] Thereby Obama wound up as yet another figure of oscillation between the poles of dictatorship and the state of exception. The fact that he was the President, who came into office as the champion of change who signed the bill, should not be lost on us. The most disheartening point about the metaphysics of terror is the fact that it would seem in this system to be increasingly difficult to even imagine what a significant Event, one that would effectuate genuine change, would look like.

The story we have been following has been one of constant failures. We have seen how the political metaphysics of terror is one where nothingness is at work, yet continually fails to make anything genuine happen. Thus, even though he has been the guiding figure of our investigations, it would seem that the one thing, we precisely have not been able to find, has been the non-dancing dancer. Even if the potentiality of nothingness he makes work has been the thing we have been following, we have also seen how our current metaphysics, the metaphysics of terror, is one in which nothingness precisely does not happen *successfully* for us in the way it does for the non-dancing dancer. Instead, we have again and again been confronted with a nothingness which unsuccessfully takes place. This diagnosis of our own time we have brought to bear is one of a constant fluctuation. Psychologically we are wavering back and forth between anxiety and boredom. Cosmologically we find ourselves in a constant fluctuation between past and future. Theologically we are helplessly caught between dictatorship and the state of exception. In this way the diagnosis we have found in the investigations above does follow the Schellingian dialectic of creation quite nicely. What we are presented with again and again is the indecisive oscillation, which characterized the being of God, as he oscillated between contraction and expansion trying to make things happen. But what we did not find was the kind of second creation, which could dismantle the logics of anxiety and boredom, past and future, dictatorship and exceptionality.

Still, the Schellingian ambition indicated in the closing comments in the political theology above should not be forgotten. Perhaps, the very fact that we have diagnosed a most depressing wavering back and forth between dictatorship and the state of exception should be taken as an opening of sorts. Precisely because sovereignty cannot take the shape Carl Schmitt was hoping for, precisely because the sovereign is the one who is incapable of making a decision, therefore we might be able to imagine a different kind of act in this anomalous zone. In so many words there is a zone of potential political freedom which emerges in the very gap of sovereignty. Such political freedom could in the words of Walter Benjamin be called divine violence, in the words of Schelling it would be captured in the question of the freedom of God. For our present purposes it would go too far to describe in full what this freedom is, indeed the philosophy describing this freedom might still only be to come, but what we should do is to give some indication of what it might turn out to be.

In order to do so I should like to turn to the sophism introduced by Lacan in his 'Logical Time and the assertion of Anticipated Certainty' (Lacan 2002: 161–75). The sophism involves a prison warden and three choice prisoners, to whom he announces that he is going to set one of them free. In order to decide who, he gives them a logical challenge. He presents to them five small disks, two black and three white, and says 'I will put one disk on the back of each of you, so that you will not be able to see the colour for yourself. You will then be allowed to walk around in the courtyard and see the colours of the others in silence. The one of you, who is able to first figure out his colour, should come to me at the exit and give me a logical explanation of why he thinks, he has the colour that he has, and he will be set free. But be warned: only a purely logical deduction will be accepted. A mere lucky guess or an explanation in terms of probability will only disqualify you.'

The prison warden now has three options at his disposal. He can give one prisoner a white disk and the two others black ones. He can also choose to give two prisoners white disks and the final one a black. And he can give all the prisoners white disks. In the two former instances the solution is fairly simple for the prisoners. In the final one, where they are all white, it gets quite a bit more complex, and for that reason equally more interesting for us. It will be helpful, however, to consider each of them in turn.

In the situation where both the black disks are used, a solution will be found almost immediately. As soon as the white sees two black disks, he will immediately know that he himself is white, as the warden only had two black disks. He will make his way to the door and be set free. In the situation where there are two whites and one black, no one will be able to immediately know his own colour. The two whites, however, will be able to do something. As soon as they see a white and a black disk, they will know that if they had themselves had a black disk, then the other one, who is white, would have immediately left for the exit, since he would have seen two blacks and therefore known himself to be white. Thus, since the white other does not immediately leave for the exit, they will both know that they cannot be black and must be white. In so many words: If one sees a black and a white disk, and the other white does not immediately leave, then one will know that one is white.

Now let us consider the final situation, where each of the prisoners is white. Here things get tricky. Let the prisoner doing the deduction be called A and the other two B and C respectively. A can then say 'if I were black, B would be able to deduce the following, *"If I were black like A, C would leave the place without hesitation, because seeing two blacks, he would know himself to be white. C did in fact hesitate, thus I must be white"*. But B did in fact not make such a deduction, because after having seen C hesitating to go out, B himself hesitated to go out. And vice versa with regard to C. Therefore, if I had been black, B and C should have made for the door together after having witnessed the initial hesitation of each other. But they did not, they both hesitated to leave, after having seen the other hesitate to leave. Therefore I cannot be black and must be white'. In the situation with three whites we can thus formulate the rule that: 'One must know that one is white when the others have hesitated twice in leaving' (Lacan 2002: 172).

This curious problem and its elegant solution do in many ways bring out the crucial philosophical themes we have been dealing with above. Especially, we should take care to note what the solution can tell us about in-activity, contemporaneity and collectivity.

Let us first consider the notion of *in-activity*. As I have said, it is the dual hesitation of the others that enables the prisoners to escape. In this way the solution lives off the very same notion of the potency of nothingness that we have been following throughout these investigations. To hesitate means precisely to not-do something. Thus, we are again confronted with the theme of the not-dancing dancer. Here, however, the crucial importance of not-doing-something is further accentuated as the others need to hesitate *twice*, before the prisoners can leave. Hesitating twice is what separates the situation with two white disks and one black from the situation with three whites. In the situation with two whites and one black, each of the whites only need to see the other white hesitate once (i.e. for a mere instance), but in the situation with three whites each of the prisoners need to see the others hesitate *and then hesitate again*. In this situation the prisoners not only have to detect the not-doing something of the others, they also have to be able to distinguish one not-doing something from another not-doing something. But how does one know that the others have stopped hesitating once and have now begun hesitating the second time? In the end I think there can be given no rule telling us how to do this. One cannot simply point out and say: 'See! There! Right there he stopped hesitating the first time, and now he is hesitating the second time.' And still, if we think about the situation the prisoners are in, I believe it is possible to imagine that they in fact could notice that the others were hesitating, not only once, but twice. To be sure there can be no actual thing or gesture, which would make them sure of this separation. In the end the only thing which could separate one nothingness from another, would precisely be nothing taking place between them. The other hesitates, he is not-going-out, and then nothing happens, and then he is hesitating again, he is not-going-out. Nothing happens, and in the middle of nothing happening, nothing happens, after which nothing continues to happen again.[3] The solution the prisoners offer plays on the idea, that we can in fact notice something like this in the other. As I have said, there can be no guarantee here, and certainly there is bound to be some doubt in the minds of the prisoners, as they are making the deduction. In short they would have to ask themselves: 'Just how long do I have to wait for the others to hesitate, before I can be sure that they have in fact hesitated twice?' This question brings us to the theme of contemporaneity.

To get a feel for the problem of contemporaneity, we can imagine that one of the prisoners thinks to himself: 'If I in fact *was* black, my two others would not need to formulate the same hypothesis, I have thought about, in order to conclude that I am white. They would not need to take their time to think about how their others would have reacted, if they were blacks. They would only need to hesitate once, in order to be able to conclude upon the hesitation of the other, that they were white. I on the other hand must first formulate the hypothesis, before I can draw the conclusion. But if they leave before I have made the hypothesis, I will not be able to formulate it, since my making a hypothesis is dependent upon their hesitation, and therefore I will not be able to determine my colour'. What we should infer from the possibility of such reflections is that the logic of the situation dictates a certain rush to make the conclusion. 'I hasten to declare myself a white, so that these whites, whom I consider in this way, do not precede me in recognizing themselves for what they are' (Lacan 2002: 168). Indeed, the 'Logical Time' Lacan unfolds would seem to necessarily entail 'The Assertion of Anticipated Certainty' stipulated in the headline. There is a natural rush to the conclusion built into the very logic of the situation. Once the others leave for the exit without me, I am lost and left to wonder whether they in fact hesitated twice or only once. This in a nutshell contains the problem of contemporaneity. The dual hesitation of the others must mirror the dual hesitation I myself am going through, as I arrive at my conclusion. If the deduction I described above is to work, the hesitations cannot simply be a matter of registering that the others are white and not leaving. Rather the two hesitations must entail a simultaneous thinking in each of the prisoners, where they simultaneously arrive at the same conclusion at the same time.

This contemporaneity is not at all a simple matter. Certainly it cannot merely be a matter of not being left behind. If the others should leave before me, one might think that they at least could feel certain of their conclusion, because they reached it in time as it were. But here a different kind of uneasiness would be lurking around the corner. As they leave together, certain in the knowledge that they have seen the others hesitate twice, they would have to wonder: Why is the third prisoner not leaving with us? We have each hesitated twice; he should be able to make his conclusion. The fact that one prisoner is too slow, could to the others mean that he simply is too stupid to figure out the logic entailed in the solution. But this possibility that the other might be stupid is not simply the possibility of one being left behind. Indeed, if I am black and the others just a bit 'slow', it could be that by the time I have done my calculations, and believe the others to have hesitated twice, then they have in fact only hesitated once. (They have in fact merely understood that if one of the others is black and the white other does not leave immediately, they must be white). In this case I am at a loss precisely because I arrive at my conclusion too quickly; I think the others have hesitated twice, and thus I conclude that I too am white, but in fact I am black and the others are dumb – and as a result they will be the ones who are able to solve the problem. In this way the demand of contemporaneity precisely means that *all* of the prisoners must in some way arrive at their conclusions together.

The problem inherent in the possibility that the other might be stupid would seem to be a problem each of the prisoners must be able to find a solution to. Indeed, this is an assertion that has been made by several commentators on the sophism. Alain Badiou claims as much in *Theory of the Subject* and Ed Pluth and Dominiek Hoens take op the same line of thought in 'What if the other is stupid?' (Pluth & Hoens 2004; Badiou 2009b: 254). Both of these discussions argue that the possibility of the other being stupid is a necessary problem, the prisoners must overcome. I would argue to the contrary that the possibility of stupidity is the one thing that is guaranteed to make impossible the solution to the problem. As long as I think that the others might be stupid, I would have to worry that I am making my conclusion too quickly – in this case they might only have hesitated once, while I take them to have hesitated twice. On the other hand, if I think that the others might leave before me, then I in fact fear that I myself am too stupid to reach the conclusion. If I fear that the other is lagging behind, I affirm his stupidity. If I fear that I will be too late in making my conclusion, I simply affirm my own.

The crucial point is here that it is not the actual stupidity of the others or myself which is problematic. Rather, the mere suspicion that stupidity may be in play is enough to derail the possibility of a solution. No matter how certainty is achieved that the others have indeed hesitated twice, as long as the possibility of stupidity in myself or the others is in some way entertained, the uncertainty that I might be too quick or too slow will continue to linger. What is needed for the situation to find a happy ending, therefore, is not simply that each of the prisoners assures himself that no one is stupid; what it needed is rather that the very question of stupidity must be annulled. The potential stupidity is enough for doubt to creep in.

This leads us to the final feature of the sophism which should concern us in the present context. This feature is collectivity. What the prisoners have to do is to find a way of being in the company of each other where the question of stupidity does not come up. How this would take place phenomenologically speaking, I think, cannot be known beforehand. Perhaps each of the prisoners look each other in the eyes as they hesitate to go out, perhaps they all smile at the same time, perhaps they start to smile even more as they move towards the exit. However it is achieved, the thing that is needed is the silent recognition in each of them that the others are intelligent and that they impossibly could be anything else. The point about contemporaneity is not simply that all the prisoners have to exit at chronologically the same time. Their exit must be done in a way that goes beyond three guys simultaneously walking through a door; they must exit together as a collective subjectivity in which each of the members have hesitated twice in leaving while affirming the intelligence of himself and the others as they too were hesitating twice.[4]

This final feature to the sophism has played a curiously underplayed role in the present investigations. Throughout the pages of this book, I have been using the word 'we' quite often. But in a crucial way the 'we', I have been talking about has been a very weak one. I have merely sought to indicate some notion of the general behaviour of societies, as they are confronted with and reacting to terrorism. In other words I have not in any serious or thorough way been touching upon the theme of what 'we' ought to do with our political future (or past). To be sure some indications of what I think have been given, but a precise definition and investigation of what it means for an 'us' to do something together have not been provided. This work presents an investigation of politics without collectivity. The lacking of collectivity on the pages of a book that would be about political phenomena is certainly a curiosity. Is not politics after all about collective action? It is, but I think I have provided reasons for why this in a sense had to be the case. The general diagnosis of the metaphysics of terror is that our current political metaphysics is one that is determined by oscillations between dual poles – between anxiety and boredom, between past and future, between dictatorship and the state of exception. In the Lacanian sophism we have been discussing over the last few pages this wavering is found again in the wavering back and forth between being too quick and too slow in making one's way to the exit. But what we have also seen is how this wavering can be described precisely as the lacking of a particular form of contemporaneity that implies an equally specific form of collectivity. In many ways it is the lacking of such collectivity that has been the unspoken background to everything, I have been arguing above.

Compared with the specific form of collectivity that we have revealed in the logic of the sophism, the moods of boredom and anxiety, we diagnosed in the political psychology of terror, are precisely forms of being alone in the world. These moods have of course been diagnosed as collective phenomena. They are something we can be said to share as we live in the times of the war on terror, but this 'we' is precisely not a 'we' of collective contemporaneity. Indeed, as we diagnosed in the political cosmology of terror the would-be 'we' engaged in this so-called war on terror is completely incapable of being contemporary. Instead, this 'we' is continually wavering back and forth between the impossible catastrophe of the past and the impossible yet certain catastrophe that looms in the future.

The crucial point, however, is that in the political theology terror we not only saw the problem of constant oscillation between dictatorship and state of exception; we also briefly touched upon a possible solution in the shape of Benjaminian divine violence. Interestingly divine violence is best expressed by Benjamin in the collective inactivity of a general strike. In this way it does in fact come quite close to the collective inactivity of the prisoners in the above sophism. Collectively hesitating could perhaps be said to be something quite different from a general strike, but in so far as both of these forms of action follow the trajectory of contemporaneity, collectivity and in-activity they at the very least pose the question once again about what our political freedom can be made out to be. As I have already suggested the future task of philosophy will be to further investigate this potentiality.

Such a task may be hopelessly naïve and old-fashioned at the same time. To many it would be difficult to even imagine the method of research or rules of inquiry one should follow in taking up such a task. I think the way ahead is both simple and necessary even if it may be unpopular. It goes, I believe, by the name of metaphysics.

Notes

Introduction

1 In *The Ages of the World* Schelling argues the same: '[O]nly in the system, in the organic connectivity of the living whole, can there be truth' (Schelling, AotW, 46).

2 According to Ernst Vollrath, the first formulation of this division of philosophical labour is found in Christian Wolff's so-called German metaphysics from 1720 (Vollrath 1962: 260).

3 Again the point is just as much Schellingian as it is Hegelian. Schelling says: 'Science is already in terms of the meaning of the word history' (Schelling, AotW, 112)

4 Alex P. Schmid and Albert J. Jongman counted no less than 109 distinct definitions in their study of the problem (Schmid & Jongman 1988: 5).

5 Certainly Carl Schmitt has not been the only one in the intellectual history of the West to argue that politics is primarily about conflict. Machiavelli, Hobbes and Marx would be obvious thinkers to name in that regard. As we shall see however, there is a reason why we must take particular interest in the jurist from the Weimar period, in spite or rather perhaps because of his involvement with the Nazi regime. The European experience with Nazism and the consequences it had for our notions of law and sovereignty will play an important role in Chapter 4.

6 The agenda has been presented most vividly in the collective work by Richard Jackson, Marie Breen Smith and Jeroen Gunning: *Critical Terrorism Studies: A New Research Agenda* (Jackson et al. 2009). The journal founded by the very same scholars is titled *Critical Studies on Terrorism*.

7 According to Žižek this point was in fact already contained in Marx's critique of ideology. Already in Marx ideology works on the side of 'doing' rather than 'knowing' in the formula 'they don't know it, but they do it'. It is thus not our beliefs about our practices that are ideological, but rather our actual doing what we do. In this way ideology functions very much like the Tibetan prayer wheels 'you write a prayer on a paper, put the rolled paper into a wheel, and turn it automatically, without thinking' (Žižek 1989: 32). The interesting point about Žižek critique of ideology is that it, because of this take on the matter, very often follows the trajectory of last philosophy, as it is prescribed here. Žižek's many analyses of film, opera, and other cultural phenomena precisely make the move from singular practices to their genuine metaphysical or at the very least universal significance, which again is very often interpreted in Hegelian or Kantian terms (if not in Lacanian ones).

8   Alain Badiou has given a very precise description of his own position in the recent
     magnum opus *The Logics of the Worlds*, which mirrors this Schellingian idea of
     the ground. He writes: 'Today, natural belief is condensed in a single statement:
     There are only bodies and languages' (Badiou 2009a: 1). He calls this position
     'democratic materialism', and with that he simply wishes to say that this is the
     materialist position which we all more or less agree to today. It is the worldview of
     everyday man, whom we have described before (see the discussion of Zupančič's
     notion of the 'psychotheology of everyday life' before). In Schellingian terms this is
     our generally accepted notion of *existence*. What Badiou does to arrive at his own
     position is precisely to add a Schellingian twist '*There are only bodies and languages,
     except that there are truths*' (Badiou 2009a: 4). This paradoxical formulation is in
     fact quite precise. It is in a similar way that one should understand the relation
     between ground and existence. There is only existence, except that there is the
     ground.

9   As has been argued by Marcela Garcia in her *The Significance of Aristotle in
     Schelling's Last Philosophy* (Garcia 2008), it was not until the very end of his
     philosophical career in *Presentation of the Purely Rational Philosophy* (Schelling,
     SW XI, 255ff.) that Schelling took a positive stance towards Aristotle.

10   Slavoj Žižek has argued however that Hegel exactly accomplishes a move quite
     similar to the Schellingian one, in that Hegel effectively lets the possible and the
     actual 'trade places' (Žižek 1998: 157ff.). There certainly is room for such a reading
     of Hegel's *Logic*. Still, it is in this regard interesting to note how Schellingian Žižek's
     Hegel at times seems to be. For example, when Žižek construes a Hegelian notion
     of the will, he does so in explicit Schellingian terms, that is, 'Rather than want
     nothing' (Žižek 2000: 103). And even more so regarding Žižek's crucial notion of
     a Hegelian 'Night of the World' (Žižek 2000: 29–30). This concept is from start
     to finish a reformulation of the Schellingian notion of an original contraction – a
     point which Žižek seems to be aware of (Žižek 2000: 34).

11   Hegel is even more arrogantly dismissive than usual when he directly considers the
     relation of potencies in the *Logic* (Hegel, Werke V, 381ff.). Hegel does not mention
     Schelling by name, but it is not difficult to see that he was the intended target.

12   This is a distinction which Giorgio Agamben (in *The Reign and the Glory*
     (Agamben 2008)) has traced back to the discussions on the problem of trinity in
     early Christian church fathers such as Hyppolytus and Tertullian, and which he
     argues to be the genealogical origin of our current form of governance. In this
     regard, it is interesting to note that Agamben in his genealogy of governance
     precisely takes up Schelling's idea of a *divine economy*. What Agamben refers to
     in this regard is Schelling's concept of a second creation in the Paulus-transcript
     of the lectures in Berlin (in 1841/2) on the *Philosophy of Revelation* (Schelling,

PO, 325; Agamben 2008: 24). Schelling also mentions the theological economy in the lectures published by his son in *Sämmtliche Werke* (Schelling, SW XIII, 340). As we shall see, however, the notion of a second creation is an important part of Schelling's thought already in the *Ages of the World* (Schelling, AotW, 243).

13 Žižek is one of many who has argued that this is far too simple a picture: 'With regard to the relationship between *Logic* itself and *Realphilosophie* Hösle again points out how their parallel is never perfect and stable: in the standard form of Hegel's system (Logic-Nature-Spirit), the triad of Logic (Being-Essence-Notion) is not reflected in the mere duality of *Realphilosophie* (Nature-Spirit); if, however, we transform *Realphilosophie* into the triad of Nature-finite Spirit-objective/ naturalized Spirit, the overall structure of the system is no longer a triad, but becomes quadruple. So we have either the overall triad, but without the perfect parallel between Logic and *Realphilosophie*; or the perfect triadic parallel, but with the overall dyadic split between Logic and *Realphilosophie*' (Žižek 2000: 82). The crucial point here, however, about the relationship between Schelling and Hegel, is that the argument regarding the first part of Hegel's system is unaffected by this insight. No matter how we construe the latter parts of the system, this construal does not challenge the autonomy of the first part.

14 To use a term that was introduced by Henrik Jøker Bjerre, albeit in a book on Kant: *Kantian Deeds* (Bjerre 2010). This way of putting the point does open some lines of confrontation with Hegelian thought that I cannot cover in full here. It suffices to say that a productive way of reading Hegel would be to insist that in Hegel the past is precisely not simply given as the past. The Hegelian past is always created in a form of retroactive restructuring. Hence the post-festum sage is never simply the kind of wise man, who is sitting after the fact telling right from wrong. The Hegelian past is not simply the things that have already happened; it is rather that, which must be made to be the past. It thus exhibits a structure that is quite like the twist, we know from an old chauvinist joke: A husband comes home to his wife and immediately yells: 'Quick! fetch me a beer before it starts.' The wife moans, but gets him his beer, which he immediately drinks up and says: 'Quick! get me another beer before it starts.' This time the wife looks really angry, but still she gets him the beer. He of course finishes it like the first one and repeats: 'Quick! Quick! Get me another beer before it starts.' At this point his wife has had it and begins to shout back: 'You lousy excuse of a man! You pitiful little insect! Are you simply going to sit there drinking beer all day while I do the work around here?' To which the husband replies: 'It has started.' One could argue that the proper Hegelian dialectical notion of the past is one that is retroactively restructured in the same way as the 'it' that is about to start (when we first hear the joke, we are supposed to think that it is a football match or something similar) and which

becomes retroactively redefined to having already meant something quite different once the jest of the joke is revealed. One could perhaps formulate an interpretation of Hegel's system, which relied upon this notion of retroactive restructuring at every level of the dialectic (which would be a way of following through on Alenka Zupančič's point that the *Phenomenology of Spirit* should be read as a comical work, Zupančič 2008a: 39). Such a move might shield it from the most damning aspects of the Schellingian critique, I have presented above. While that may be the case, it remains to be seen, as the formulation of such an interpretation lies beyond the scope of the present work.

15 The difficulties in translating the German 'Erkennen' into English, while bringing the essential processal meaning of the term to the fore, are well known. I have here chosen the somewhat cumbersome solution, 'cognize'.

16 Interestingly this position to a great extent mirrors Badiou's position in so far as much of his political and ethical thought discusses our situation *after the Event has taken place*. Here we are given the possibilities of fidelity and betrayal, the simulacrum and the disaster (Badiou 2002: 71).

17 No wonder then that Schelling was never able to finish *The Ages of the World*.

Chapter 1

1 Bernard McKenna and Neal Waddell have in 'Media-ted political oratory following terrorist events' surveyed the statements of politicians across the globe in 10,449 unique instances in the nine days following the London bombings of 7 July 2005. Condemnations were unsurprisingly one of the most popular themes (McKenna & Waddell 2007).

2 These specific words were uttered by Danish politician Villy Søvndal (who would later become the Foreign Secretary) following the attack on the Danish Embassy in Islamabad on 2nd June 2008.

3 Schmid was (together with Albert Jongman) the author of the now classic *Political Terrorism. A Guide to Actors, Authors, Concepts, Data Bases, Theory and Literature* (Schmid & Jongman 1988: 181). Paul Wilkinson has authored three works that should be mentioned here: *Terrorism and the Liberal State* (Wilkinson 1986), *Inquiry into Legislation Against Terrorism* (Wilkinson 1996) and *Democracy versus Terrorism* (Wilkinson 2001). David Rapoport is the author of the wave theory of terrorism (Rapoport 2006). Bruce Hoffman is the author of the much acclaimed *Inside Terrorism* (Hoffman 2006). Walter Lacquer has authored a series of books on terror and terrorism, of which *The New Terrorism* (Laqueur 1999) is the most interesting for our purposes. Jessica Stern has written what is often referred to as the authoritative source on the notion of 'new terrorism' namely *The Ultimate Terrorists* (Stern 1999).

4 Indeed, there have been terrorist organizations in recent years which have been able to achieve great results using terrorist tactics. Both sides of the Israeli–Palestinian conflict are a testament to this. On the one hand the Irgun movement led by Menachem Begin was an important factor in the establishment of the Israeli state. It used bombings and attacks on civilians to reach this goal, but that did not prevent Begin from later becoming the Prime Minister of Israel or from receiving the Nobel Peace prize together with Anwar Sadat of Egypt. On the other hand the kidnapping and killing of Jewish athletes at the Munich Olympic Games in 1972, by the organization Black September and the bombing campaigns by Hamas and Islamic Jyhad in more recent years could be said to have raised global awareness of the plights of the Palestinian people, even if all of these terrorist incidents were met by strong condemnations from all sides as they were undertaken (see Hoffman 2006: 173ff.).

5 Plenty of other books subscribing to the notion of new terrorism have been published since the early nineties. Important ones are Jessica Stern's *The Ultimate Terrorists* (Stern 1999), Walter Laqueur's *The New Terrorism: Fanaticism and the Arms of Mass Destruction* (Laqueur 1999). Paul Wilkinson, on the other hand, expresses a certain amount of scepticism with regard to the notion of 'New Terrorism' in his *Terrorism vs. Democracy* (Wilkinson 2001: 37).Yet in the very same work, when he attempts to project the future of the threat from terrorism, he explicitly warns against religious terrorism and the prospective of the use of WMDs (Wilkinson 2001: 179).

6 Aum Shinrikyo was led by the blind Chizuo Matsumoto, who had received the revelation that he was to be the leader of a new godly race that would be the only ones to survive the impeding Armageddon at the end of the century. He changed his name to the more spiritual Shoko Ashara and founded the cult in 1987 (Hoffman 2006: 119–20).

7 This is not a confusion that is unheard of as the same terms were used interchangeably in a report issued during the Clinton Presidency in 1997 (Capello 1997).

8 Many others follow this model, for example, Michael Walzer in *Arguing about War* (Walzer 2004: 146) and Brian Massumi in 'Potential Politics and Primacy of Preemption' (Massumi 2007: 5).

9 In fact article 51 of the UN Charter literally only affirms the 'inherent right of individual or collective self-defence if an armed attack occurs against a member' (UN Charter, art. 51). A literal reading of the 'occurs' is in general not accepted as law (Dershowitz 2006: 202). Instead the three mentioned criteria for the use of force as a form of legal self-defence seems to be in vogue. These criteria are derived from the *Caroline* case in which British entered US soil in order to combat a rebellion in Canada in 1837 (Schmitt 2002–3: 529).

10   It should be noted that Agamben, unsurprisingly, translates these passages quite
     differently than standard translations of Aristotle. Therefore I am giving his
     translations here.
11   A famous presentation of this notion is found in Ernesto Laclau and Chantal
     Mouffe's *Hegemony and Socialist Strategy* (Laclau & Mouffe 1985: x, 93ff.).

Chapter 2

1   Fukuyama himself did not make a great deal of the theme of boredom in the book.
     He mentions the concept twice on page 330, but otherwise he is mostly concerned
     with explaining and defending the idea *that* History (with a capital H) has ended,
     not the consequences thereof.
2   Tommy Brems Knudsen argues in 'The History of Humanitarian Interventions'
     (Knudsen 2009) that the humanitarian intervention is not a new phenomenon.
     He points out how the nineteenth century saw plenty of them. To Knudsen it was
     the absence of these actions during the Cold War that was the aberration. For our
     present purpose this only serves to strengthen our argument that a noticeable
     difference could be perceived between the eighties and nineties with regard to how
     problems were solved at the international political scene.
3   This is evidenced by all polls on the matter this author has seen, of which the
     internet resource Polling Report (www.pollingreport.com) provides quite a few.
     It can of course be speculated that lack of interest in terrorism in the later Bush
     years was simply due to the fact that the economic crisis was of a more recent date
     and hence more salient. Even if that were the case, however, it would not pose a
     problem for any of the arguments presented here, where we will be concerned with
     the ontological background to the emotional landscape of terror rather than the
     more contingent answers given to pollsters.
4   After 9/11 Beck saw fit to reintroduce the notion of risk society in 'The Terrorist
     Threat. World Risk Society Revisited' (Beck 2002) and 'The Silence of Words: On
     Terror and War' (Beck 2003).
5   In a work on political fear that precedes the war on terror – *The Politics of Everyday
     Fear* (Massumi 1993) – he does briefly mention the concept of anxiety, but only to
     dismiss it. 'The media affect – fear-blur – is the direct collective perception of the
     contemporary condition of possibility of being human […]. It is vague by nature.
     It is nothing as sharp as panic. Not localized as hysteria. It doesn't even have a
     particular object, so it's not a phobia. But it's not exactly anxiety either; it is even
     fuzzier than that. It is *low-level fear*' (Massumi 1993: 24).

6 Freud did not give an exact reference, which has led most authors who notice the Schellingian origin of Freud's formulation to simply take the definition as it is, without going further into the discussion Schelling himself provided. The definition is found in Schelling's twenty-eighth lecture on the philosophy of mythology, which he held in Berlin in 1842 and subsequently in 1845/6, and which was published in the second row of *Sämmtliche Werke*. It should be noted that Heidegger of course was very familiar with Schelling's work, but he seems to have missed this particular point

7 Since Heidegger is intently focused on hiddenness in his discussions of the concept of truth, where he makes a great deal out of the point that the Greek concept of truth (alethia) precisely means un-hiddenness or unconcealment, it does seem strange that he does not discuss 'un-hiddenness' in relation to das Unheimliche. But as we can see from the quote above (p. 112), Heidegger does indeed emphasize that there is nothing more to the concept of Unheimlichkeit than the feeling of not being at home.

8 The pseudonym author of the first part of *Either Or*.

Chapter 3

1 Conversely and briefly put, it is the task of the population to hate the enemy and the task of government to set political goals for war (Clausewitz 2008: 40–6).

2 It is hard not to notice the irony of this fact. Eyal Weizman reminds us of Herbert Marcuse's warning that criticism and contradiction could be equally subsumed and made operative as a tool in the hands of the powers one is criticizing (Weizman 2007: 211).

3 Or a Palestinian refugee camp like Jenin and Balata, where the IDF used similar tactics (Weizman 2007: 197).

4 It should be noted that the Katyusha rocket employed by Hezbollah is a very old and imprecise weapon. Thus most of the rockets struck harmlessly on open land. About one fourth hit populated areas and caused civilian casualties 'From July 12 until August 14, when the cease-fire went into effect, 43 Israeli civilians and 117 IDF soldiers were killed' (Israel 2008). In comparison, at least 500 Lebanese civilians were killed during the war (Bouckaert & Houry 2006: 3).

5 Joseph Stiglitz and Linda Bilmes have shown just how expensive in their collective work *The Three Trillion Dollars War* (Stiglitz & Bilmes 2008).

6 Let us add here the note that this of course does not mean that the suffering of the victims of 9/11 was nothing. And let us add that I do not aim to achieve any kind of insensitive provocation. Of course the suffering in relation to terrorism is

something – and indeed something quite important – the point is merely that with regard to our contemporary political cosmology it is the nothingness of 9/11 that is at work rather than the actuality of the death and suffering.

Chapter 4

1   In the end it is hard not to see these kinds of offhand dismissals as an eminent example of intellectual laziness. If something seems too strange at first impression, and if one does not wish to make the effort to inquire into its meaning, one can always find secure ground by calling it 'obscure', 'postmodern', 'metaphysical' or 'continental conceptualizations'. One can be sure to find many academics who will have been affected by the same kind of laziness, and who will therefore be eager to agree.

2   The different ways in which member states have implemented this requirement are of course widely varied. Andrea Bianchi provides an overview in 'Security Council's Anti-Terror Resolutions and Their Implementation by Member States' (Bianchi 2006).

3   Where the French State of Siege is often viewed as the model for the emergency legislation in civil law countries such as continental Europe and the South American countries, Martial Law is generally the model used in common law countries such as Great Britain and the United States (Rossiter 1948: 9; Gross & Ní Aoláin 2006: 30). The differences between common and civil law systems are of course crucially important for strictly legal discussions about emergencies and exceptional legislation, in the present context, where focus is on the more philosophical implications of these themes, I allow myself to bracket out these differences.

4   Finally, the war in Algeria had an important hand in the collapse of the Fourth Republic and the establishment of the Fifth. As the Pflimlin Government was invested on 13 May 1958, the French population of Algeria (the Pied Noir) rioted with the assist of French military commanders. On 23 May the rebellion spread to Corsica, and from there it seemed a matter of time before it would spread to mainland France. This resulted in the collapse of the Pflimlin Government. On 1 June 1958, de Gaulle (a popular man in the army) was made Prime Minister and was given Emergency Powers for six months (he himself had demanded two years) (Lustick 1993: 271). These powers included the capability to prepare the new constitution for the Fifth Republic, in which the right to declare an emergency situation is back with a powerful Presidential office (Gross & Ní Aoláin 2006: 195–7). Thus Article 16 empowers the President to take 'Any means

necessary' if the 'institutions of the Republic, the independence of the nation, the integrity of its territory or the fulfilment of its international commitments are gravely and immediately threatened and the regular functioning of the constitutional public authorities is interrupted' (quoted in Gross & Ní Aoláin 2006: 197).

5 There certainly also were right wing uprisings, such as Hitler's Beer Hall rebellion (also in 1923), but these were dealt with in a much less heavy handed way. As Rossiter points out, the reason for this discrepancy is obvious, since the state relied on the army to carry out its work in such matters, and the army was overwhelmingly a rightist, even reactionary, institution at the time (Rossiter 1948: 40).

6 A very telling example of the tenant of the book is found in his discussion of emergency legislation in Italy, where Agamben writes that law-making by decree is becoming an increasing threat to democratic institutions. The examples he gives are pieces of anti-terrorism legislation which were first presented as governmental decrees and then later ratified by the legislature. The decrees are the law-decree of 18 March 1978, n. 59, which was converted to the law of 21 May 1978, n. 191 (the Moro law), and the decree of 15 December 1979, n. 625, which was converted into the law of 6 February 1980, n. 15 (Agamben 2008: 18). While Agamben is focusing on the governmental and legislative practices which turn these kinds of acts into law, he does not say a word about the actual content of those laws, which were in fact quite spectacular in their time. For instance the law-decree of 15 December 1979 prolonged the potential time a person could be arrested preventively if he was suspected of terrorism, *beyond* the 12 years that was already set to be the limit by a law-decree from 1974 (Schimel 1998). Precisely, by *not* engaging very much in the details about the content of these laws, Agamben is trying to make us change our focus. His aim is to open a genuinely philosophical discussion about what the state of emergency in the first place could be. As he states in the very beginning of the book 'Although his [Carl Schmitt's] famous definition of the sovereign as 'he who decides on the state of exception' has been widely commented on and discussed, *there is still no theory of the state of exception in public law,* and jurists and of public law seem to regard the problem more as a quaestio facti than as a genuine juridical problem' (Agamben 2005a: 1).

7 In relation to the discussion of the *Prize* cases it should be noted that these are not *only* of historical interest to us today. The arguments of the court in relation to these cases have been instrumental in the legal cases that have followed in the wake of the war on terror and the internment of detainees at the Guantanamo Prison Camp. In many of the cases the US government precisely sought to establish an argument of precedence with reference to the *Prize* cases (Hartz & Ugilt 2011).

214   *Notes*

8 This is a conceptual pair, which offers a wide scope of interpretation. In the
   Nomos of the Earth, Schmitt discusses how the powers of the Emperor and the
   Pope were divided precisely in terms of the difference between auctoritas, which
   rested with the Emperor, and potestas, which belonged to the Pope (Schmitt 2003:
   61). In 'What is Authority?' and *On Revolution*, Hannah Arendt lamented the
   disappearance of the distinction from modern theories of state in a similar vein as
   Schmitt (Arendt 1977: 92). Agamben comments on how Arendt probably would
   have disliked finding herself in company with Schmitt in this regard. Both Schmitt
   and Arendt put great emphasis on the fact that in the Roman Republic *potestas*
   originated with the people, whereas the Senate alone had *auctoritas* (Schmitt
   quoted in Agamben 2005a: 75; Arendt 1977: 122, 1990: 178). In Arendt's book
   On Revolution, it is precisely this merely advisory yet nevertheless authoritative
   character of the Senate of Rome, which she praises. She believes that she can find
   a similar form of authority in the judiciary branch of the American Constitution,
   which possesses 'neither Force nor Will but merely judgement' (Arendt 1990: 200).
   Here she quoted Woodrow Wilson for describing Supreme Court as 'A kind of
   Constitutional Assembly in continuous session' (Arendt 1990: 200). The sense I am
   drawing from the concept of authority here is evidently a different one, and even
   though there is an interesting discussion to be had about the differences between
   the ways in which Agamben, Schmitt, Arendt and others understand the concept of
   authority, that is a discussion I shall have to take up at another time.
9 Conversely, much of Benjamin's essay consists in the discussion of phenomena that
   seem to contradict this point. Police violence, wars, strikes, language and criminal
   masterminds are all phenomena that in various ways question the integrity of the
   strict relation of means and ends.
10 Agamben refers to this wavering back and forth as a 'dialectic' (Agamben 2005a:
   53). It should be no surprise by now that I think this is an unfortunate move.

Chapter 5

1 The President certainly took the time to speak out against the provisions of the act
   that effectuated this regime (sections 1021 and 1022), and he threatened to veto
   earlier versions of the bill, but in the end the provisions that effectively suspend the
   right of Habeas Corpus of anyone associated with terrorism were enacted at the
   pleasure of the President (Obama 2011).
2 That is the effective situation B and C are put in A's hypothesis.
3 This idea is somewhat analogous to the initial move in the dialectic of creation, as it
   is laid out by Schelling in the *Ages of the World*. At first there is indifference, a bland

sea of nothingness and then at a point nothing happens in the midst of nothingness, a contraction in which nothing is being made the object of the then purely destructive divine will. Nothing is happening, and then, all of a sudden, nothing happens, and from that moment on everything is different.

4 One of the most promising concepts of collectivity of this sort is the notion of 'særklasse' that has been coined by the Danish philosophical collective Center for Vild Analyse (Centre for Wild Analysis). It was introduced in *Knoldesparkeren, Flottenheimeren og Glatnakken* (Thykjær et al. 2009), and it is the focal theme of their forthcoming book *Særklasse* (Thykjær et al., forthcoming).

Bibliography

General note

Aristotle's *Metaphysics* is cited using the Stephanus Pagination, for example (Aristotle 1047a). References to Kant's *Critique of Pure Reason* are made to the A- and B-versions using the acronym CPR, for example (Kant, CPR, A 573/B 602). The works of Hegel are cited from the Suhrkamp edition *Werke in 20 Bänden mit Registerband* edited by Eva Moldenhauer and Karl Markus Michel using the abbreviation *Werke* followed by the volume number in roman capitals followed by the page where appropriate. Thus the *Phenomenology of Spirit* is referenced, for example, as (Hegel, Werke III, 575). Schelling is cited from the *Sämmtliche Werke* published by his son KFA Schelling using the abbreviation SW followed by the volume number in roman capitals followed by the page where appropriate. Thus the *Philosophical Investigations into the Essence of Human Freedom and the Things that Relate to It* are referenced, for example, as (Schelling, SW VII, 350). The first two drafts of *The Ages of the World* (1811 and 1813) are cited using the edition published by Manfred Schröter in 1946 abbreviated as *AotW*, for example (Schelling, AotW, 25). Schelling's lectures on the *Philosophy of Revelation* are cited using the edition published by Manfred Frank with the abbreviation *PO*, for example (Schelling, PO, 325). Kierkegaard is cited using *Søren Kierkegaards Skrifter* abbreviated as SKS followed by volume number in roman capitals and page, for example (Kierkegaard, SKS, III, 181). With the exception of Aristotle, where I use the translation by Richard Hope (Ann Arbor, 1960), all translations of these works are my own.

Legal sources

107th Congress of the United States, AUTHORIZATION FOR USE OF MILITARY FORCE AGAINST IRAQ RESOLUTION OF 2002, Pub. L. No. 107–243, 116 Stat. 1498.

107th Congress of the United States, USA PATRIOT ACT, Pub. L. No. 107–56, 115 Stat. 272.

UN Charter.

Other sources

Agamben, G. 1999, *Potentialities. Collected Essays in Philosophy,* Stanford University Press, Stanford, CA.

—. 2004, *Homo Sacer: Sovereign Power and Bare Life,* Stanford University Press, Stanford, CA.

—. 2005a, *State of Exception,* University of Chicago Press, Chicago and London.

—. 2005b, *The Time That Remains. A Commentary on the Letter to the Romans,* Stanford University Press, Stanford, CA.

—. 2008, *Le Règne et la Gloire. Homo Sacer, II, 2,* French translation edn, Editions Seuil, Paris.

Althusser, L. 2008, *On Ideology,* Verso, London.

Andrejevic, M. 2006, 'INTERACTIVE (IN)SECURITY', *Cultural Studies,* 20(4–5), pp. 441–58.

Arendt, H. 1977, *Between Past and Future,* Penguin, London.

—. 1990, *On Revolution,* Penguin, London.

Aristotle. 1933, *Metaphysics Books I–IX. With an English translation by Hugh Tredennick,* Loeb Classica Library edn, Harward University Press, Cambridge, MA, London.

—. 1960, *Metaphysics,* Ann Arbor, MI.

Aristoteles. 1995, *Metaphysik,* Philosophische Schriften in sechs Bänden, Band 5 edn, Felix Meiner Verlag, Hamburg.

Badiou, A. 2002, *Ethics: An Essay on the Understanding of Evil,* paperback edn, Verso Books, London.

—. 2005, *Being and Event,* English translation edn, Continuum, London and New York.

—. 2009a, *Logics of Worlds,* Continuum, London.

—. 2009b, *Theory of the Subject,* English translation by Bruno Bosteels, Continuum International, London.

Bale, J. M. 1994, *The "Black" Terrorist International: Neo-Fascist Paramilitary Networks and the "Strategy of Tension" in Italy, 1968–1974,* UMI, Ann Arbor, MI.

Beck, U. 1992, *Risk Society. Towards a New Modernity,* Sage, London.

—. 2002, 'The Terrorist Threat. World Risk Society Revisited', *Theory Culture and Society,* 19(4), pp. 39–55.

—. 2003, 'The Silence of Words: On Terror and War', *Security Dialogue,* 34(3), pp. 255–67.

Becker, J. & Shane, S. 2012 29/5-last update, *Secret 'Kill List' Proves a Test of Obama's Principles and Will* [Homepage of The New York Times] [Online]. Available at: http://www.nytimes.com/2012/05/29/world/obamas-leadership-in-war-on-al-qaeda. html?_r=1&hp [2012, 6/6].

Benjamin, W. 1965, *Zur Kritik der Gewalt und andere Aufsätze,* Suhrkamp, Frankfurt am Main.

—. 1978, *Ursprung des deutschen Trauerspiels,* Suhrkamp, Frankfurt am Main.

Berkow, J. 2011, 2/5-last update, *Bin Laden Death Spikes Twitter Traffic Past Super Bowl Levels* [Homepage of Financial Post] [Online]. Available at: http://business. financialpost.com/2011/05/02/bin-laden-death-spikes-twitter-traffic-past-super-bowl/ [2012, 2/1].

Bianchi, A. 2006, 'Security Council's Anti-Terror Resolutions and Their Implementation by Member States', *Journal of International Criminal Justice,* 4(5), pp. 1044–73.

Biddle, S. & Friedman, J. 2008, *The 2006 Lebanon Campaign and the Future of Warfare: Implications for Army and Defense Policy,* Strategic Studies Institute, Carlisle, PA.

Bigo, D. & Tsoukala, A. (eds) 2008, *Terror, Insecurity and Liberty. Illiberal practices of liberal regimes after 9/11,* Routledge, London and New York.

Bjerre, H. J. 2010, *Kantian Deeds,* Continuum, London.

Bouckaert, P. & Houry, N. 2006, 'Fatal Strikes. Israel's Indiscriminate Attacks Against Civillians in Lebanon', *Human Rights Watch,* 18(3), pp. 1–50.

Bourke, J. 2006, *Fear. A Cultural History,* paperback edn, Virago, London.

Brackett, D. 1996, *Holy Terror. Armageddon in Tokyo,* Weatherhill, New York.

Buchheim, T. 1992, *Eins von Allen,* Felix Meiner Verlag, Hamburg.

Bush, G. W. 2002, *The National Security Strategy 2002* [Homepage of New York Times] [Online]. Available at: www.mtholyoke.edu/acad/intrel/bush/doctrine.htm [2010, 14/12].

Buzan, B., Wæver, O. & de Wilde, J. 1998, *Security. A New Framework for Analysis,* Rienner, London.

Capello, L. 1997, 'The Preemptive Use of Force: Analysis and Decision Making', *National Security Program Discussion Paper Series,* 97, pp. 1–85.

Choy, S. 2002, July 23-last update, *In the Spotlight: Aum Shinrikyo* [Homepage of Center for Defense Information] [Online]. Available at: www.cdi.org/terrorism/ aumshinrikyo.cfm [2010, 04/20].

Clausewitz, C. von 2008, *Vom Kriege,* Ungekürzter text edn, Ullstein, Berlin.

Closs Stephens, A. & Vaughan-Williams, N. (eds) 2009, *Terrorism and the Politics of Response,* Routledge, London and New York.

Coaldrake, W. H. 1996, *Architecture and Authority in Japan,* Routledge, London and New York.

Culler, J. 1976, *Saussure,* 2nd edn, Fontana Paperbacks, Glasgow.

Darling, A. 2008, 8/10-last update, *The Landisbanki Freezing Order. Financial Sanctions Notice* [Homepage of HM Treasury] [Online]. Available at: http://webarchive. nationalarchives.gov.uk/+/http://www.hm-treasury.gov.uk/fin_sanctions_ landsbanki.htm [2012, 12/2].

Deleuze, G. 1994, *Difference and Repetition,* Continuum, London and New York.

Deleuze, G. & Guattari, F. 2004a, *Anti-Oedipus,* Continuum, London and New York.

Deleuze, G. & Guattari, F. 2004b, *A Thousand Plateaus,* Continuum, London.

Department of Homeland Security. 2011, September 28-last update, *National Terrorism Advisory System* [Online]. Available at: www.dhs.gov/files/programs/ntas.shtm [2011, 18/12].

Dershowitz, A. 2003, 'The Torture Warrant: A Response to Professor Strauss', *New York Law School Law Review,* 48, pp. 275–94.

—. 2006, *Preemption. A Knife That Cuts Both Ways,* W. W. Norton and Co., New York and London.

Dillon, M. & Reid, J. 2001, 'Global Liberal Governance: Biopolitics, Security and War', *Millennium - Journal of International Studies,* 30, pp. 41–66.

Dolar, M. 2006, *A Voice and Nothing More,* MIT Press, Cambridge, MA.

Durkheim, E. 1981, *Die elementaren Formen des religiösen Lebens,* Suhrkamp, Frankfurt am Main.

Echevarria, A. 2005, *Fourth-Generation War and Other Myths,* Strategic Studies Institute, Carlisle, PA.

Falkenrath, R., Newman, R. & Thayer, B. 1998, *Americas's Achilles' Heel. Nuclear, Biological, and Chemical Terrorism and Covert Attack,* MIT Press, Cambridge, MA.

Freud, S. 1987, 'The Uncanny' in *Art and Literature,* ed. A. Dickson, The Pelican Freud Library, Vol. 14, Penguin, Hardmonsworth, pp. 335–76.

Fukuyama, F. 1989, 'The End of History?', *The National Interest,* 16, Summer, pp. 3–18.

—. 1992, *The End of History and the Last Man,* The Free Press, New York.

Furedi, F. 2005, *Politics of Fear,* Continuum, London and New York.

Gabriel, M. & Žižek, S. 2009, *Mythology, Madness and Laughter,* Continuum, London and New York.

Garcia, M. 2008, *The Significance of Aristotle in Schelling's Last Philosophy,* PhD-Thesis, Ludwig-Maximillian-Universität, Universidad de Navarra.

Gray, C. 2007, 'Irregular Warfare: One Nature. Many Characters', *Strategic Studies Quarterly,* 1(2), pp. 35–57.

Gross, O. & Ní Aoláin, F. 2006, *Law in Times of Crisis. Emergency Powers in Theory and Practice,* Cambridge University Press, Cambridge.

Guillaume, G. 1973, *Principes de Linguistique Generale,* Les Presses de l'Université Laval, Québec.

—. 1984, *Foundations for a Science of Language,* Excerpts from the manuscripts translated by Walter Hirtle and John Hewson, John Benjamins Publishing Company, Amsterdam/Philadelphia.

Gurr, N. & Cole, B. 2000, *The New Face of Terrorism: Threats from Weapons of Mass Destruction,* I.B. Tauris, London.

Habermas, J., Derrida, J. & Borradori, G. 2003, *Philosophy in a Time of Terror: Dialogues with Jürgen Habermas and Jacques Derrida,* University of Chicago Press, Chicago.

Hammes, T. 1994, 'The Evolution of War: The Fourth Generation', *Marine Corps Gazette,* 78(9), pp. 35–44.

Hartz, E. 2010, *The Zone of Twilight,* PhD edn, Center for Etik og Ret, Copenhagen.

Hartz, E. & Ugilt, R. 2011, 'The Problem of Emergency in the American Supreme Court', *Law and Critique,* 22(3), pp. 295–316.

Heidegger, M. 1969, *Identity and Difference,* Harper & Row, New York.

—. 1983, *Die Grundbegriffe der Metaphysik. Welt – Endlichkeit – Einsamkeit,* KlostermannSeminar edn, Vittorio Klostermann, Frankfurt am Main.

—. 1993, *Sein und Zeit,* 17. unveränd. Aufl. edn, Max Niemeyer, Tübingen.

—. 1998, *Was is Metaphysik?* Fünfzehnte Auflage edn, Vittorio Klostermann, Frankfurt am Main.

Henrich, D. 1971, *Hegel im Kontext,* Suhrkamp, Frankfurt am Main.

Herman, E. S. & O'Sullivan, G. 1989, *The Terrorism Industry: The Experts and Institutions That Shape Our View of Terror,* Pantheon, New York.

Hilberth, T. 2007, *Prolegomena zu einer Architektur der Sicherheit,* Arkitektskolen Aarhus Institut for Arkitektur og Æstetik, Aarhus.

Hobbes, T. 1997, *The Leviathan,* W.W. Norton & Company, New York.

Hoffman, B. 1999, *Terrorism and Weapons of Mass Destruction: An Analysis of Trends and Motivations,* RAND, Santa Monica.

—. 2006, *Inside Terrorism,* revised and expanded edn, Columbia University Press, New York.

Hogrebe, W. 1989, *Prädikation und Genesis,* 1st edn, Suhrkamp, Frankfurt am Main.

Hughes, S. 2007, *War on Terror, Inc. Corporate Profiteering from the Politics of Fear,* Verso, London and New York.

Huntington, S. P. 1996, *The Clash of Civilizations and the Remaking of World Order,* Simon & Schuster, New York.

Inbar, E. 2006, *Strategic Follie's: Israel's Mistakes in the Second Lebanese War,* Perspectives Paper 21, The Begin-Sadat Centre for Strategic Studies, Bar-Ilan University.

Israel, M.o.F.A. 2006, 14/9-last update, *Establishment of the Winograd Commission* [Homepage of the State of Israel] [Online]. Available at: www.mfa.gov.il/MFA/Government/Communiques/2006/Establishment%20of%20the%20Winograd%20Committee%2014-Sep-2006 [2011, 16/1].

—. 2008, *The Second Lebanon War (2006)* [Homepage of the State of Israel] [Online]. Available at: www.mfa.gov.il/MFA/Terrorism-+Obstacle+to+Peace/Terrorism+from+Lebanon-+Hizbullah/Hizbullah+attack+in+northern+Israel+and+Israels+response+12-Jul-2006.htm [2011, 16/1].

Jackson, R., Breen Smyth, M. & Gunning, J. (eds) 2009, *Critical Terrorism Studies: A New Research Agenda,* Routledge, London.

Jensen, R. B. 2004, 'Daggers, Rifles and Dynamite: Anarchist Terrorism in Nineteenth Century Europe', *Terrorism and Political Violence,* 16(1), pp. 116–53.

—. 2009, 'The International Campaign Against Anarchist Terrorism, 1880–1930s', *Terrorism and Political Violence,* 21(1), pp. 89–109.

Kaur, P. 2011, 23/7-last update, *Helvete på Utøya.* Available at: http://prableen.origo.no/-/bulletin/show/672218_helvete-paa-utoeya?ref=mst [2011, 08/12].

Kelsen, H. 2008, *Wer Soll der Hüter der Verfassung sein,* Ed. van Ooyen, Mohr Siebeck, Tübingen.

Knudsen, T. B. 2009, *The History of the Humanitarian Intervention. The Rule or the Exception?*, Conference Paper, The 50th Annual ISA Convention, New York.

Kober, A. 2008, 'The Israeli Defence forces in the Second Lebanese War: Why the Poor Performance?', *Journal of Strategic Studies*, 31(1), pp. 3–40.

Kohn, R. 2003, 'Using the Military at home Yesterday, Today, and Tomorrow', *Chicago Journal for International Law*, 4, pp. 165.

Kollewe, J. & Davis, R. 2011, 2/5-last update, *Osama bin Laden's Death Boosts Stock Markets* [Homepage of Guardian] [Online]. Available at: www.guardian.co.uk/world/2011/may/02/osama-bin-laden-stock-markets [2012, 2/1].

Lacan, J. 2002, *Écrits*, The First Complete Edition in English, W.W. Norton and Co., New York and London.

Laclau, E. & Mouffe, C. 1985, *Hegemony and Socialist Strategy: Towards a Radical Democratic Politics*, Verso, London.

Laqueur, W. 1999, *The New Terrorism: Fanaticism and the Arms of Mass Destruction*, Oxford University Press, New York and Oxford.

Lind, W. 2001, 'Fourth-Generation Warfare's First Blow: A Quick Look', *Marine Corps Gazette*, 85(11), p. 72.

—. 2004, 'Understanding Fourth Generation War', *Military Review*, 84(5), pp. 12–16.

—. 2009, *Draft FMFM 1-A*, The Imperial and Royal Austrro-Hungarian Marine Corps.

Lind, W., Nightengale, K., Schmitt, J., Sutton, J. & Wilson, G. 1989, 'The Changing Face of War: Into the Fourth Generation', *Marine Corps Gazette*, 73(10), pp. 22–6.

Lind, W., Schmitt, J. & Wilson, G. 1994, 'Fourth Generation Warfare: Another Look', *Marine Corps Gazette*, 78(12), pp. 34–7.

Lobel, J. 2002, 'The War on Terrorism and Civil Liberties', *University of Pittsburg Law Review*, 63, p. 767.

Lustick, I. 1993, *Unsettled States, Disputed Lands*, Cornell University Press, New York.

Lyotard, J. 1984, *The Postmodern Condition. A Report on Knowledge*, Manchester University Press, Manchester.

Machiavelli, N. 1970, *The Discourses*, Bernard Crick edn, Penguin, London.

—. 1992, *The Prince*, Translated by Robert M. Adams, W.W. Norton & Co., New York.

Massumi, B. 1993, *The Politics of Everyday Fear*, University of Minnesota Press, Minneapolis.

—. 2005, 'Fear! The Spectrum Said', *Positions*, 13(13/5), pp. 31–48.

—. 2007, 'Potential Politics and the Primacy of Preemption', *Theory and Event*, 10(2), pp. 1–34.

McCormick, J. 1997, *Carl Schmitt's Critique of Liberalism*, Cambridge University Press, Cambridge.

McKenna, B. & Waddell, N. 2007, "Media-ted Political Oratory Following Terrorist Events', *Journal of Language and Politics*, 6(3), pp. 377–99.

McNamara, J. 2009, 'Suspicious Activity Reporting (SAR)' in *Protecting Persons While Protecting the People*, eds C. Gal, P. Kantor & M. Lesk, Springer Berlin/Heidelberg, pp. 95–103.

Mouffe, C. (ed.) 1999, *The Challenge of Carl Schmitt*, Verso, London and New York.

Mouffe, C. 2005, *The Return of the Political*, Verso, London and New York.

Murray, A. & Zartaloudis, T. 2009, 'The Power of Thought', *Law and Critique*, 20, pp. 207–10.

Nandy, A. 1995, *The Savage Freud and Other Essays on Possible and Retrievable Selves*, Princeton University Press, Princeton, NJ.

Netanyahu, B. 1986, *Terrorism. How the West Can Win*, Avon Books, New York.

Nussbaum, M. 2007, 'The Supreme Court, 2006 Term, Foreword: Constitutions and Capabilities: "Perception" Against Lofty Formalism', *Harward Law Review*, 121(4), pp. 4–97.

Nussbaum, M. & Sen, A. (eds) 1993, *The Quality of Life*, Clarendon, Oxford.

Obama, B. 2011, 31/12-last update, *Statement by the President on H.R. 1540* [Homepage of the White House] [Online]. Available at: www.whitehouse.gov/the-press-office/2011/12/31/statement-president-hr-1540 [2012, 25/1].

Paye, J. 2006, 'From the State of Emergency to the Permanent State of Exception', *Telos*, 136, pp. 154–65.

Pluth, E. & Hoens, D. 2004, 'What If the Other Is Stupid? Badiou and Lacan on Logical Time' in *Think Again: Alain Badiou and the Future of Philosophy*, ed. P. Hallward, Continuum International, London, pp. 182–90.

Posner, E. & Vermeule, A. 2003–4, 'Accommodating Emergencies', *Stanford Law Review*, 56, pp. 605–44.

Rapoport, D. C. 2006, *Terrorism: Critical Concepts in Political Science*, Routledge, New York.

Rees, P. 2005, *Dining with Terrorists*, Pan Books, London.

Reid, E. 1993, 'Terrorism Research and the Diffusion of Ideas', *Knowledge and Policy: The International Journal of Knowledge Transfer and Utilization*, 6(1), pp. 17–37.

—. 1997, 'Evolution of a Body of Knowledge: An Analysis of Terrorism Research', *Information Processing & Management*, 33(1), pp. 91–106.

Reid, E. F. & Chen, H. 2007, 'Mapping the Contemporary Terrorism Research Domain', *International Journal of Human-Computer Studies*, 65(1), pp. 42–56.

Ritzau 2010, 19/12-last update, *Danskerne regner med et terrorangreb* [Homepage of Information] [Online]. Available at: www.information.dk/telegram/254225 [2010, 28/12].

Rossiter, C. 1948, *Constitutional Dictatorship. Crisis Government in the Modern Democracies*, Princeton University Press, Princeton, NJ.

Rumsfeld, D. 2002a, February 12th 2002-last update, *Department of Defence News Briefing. Transcript.* [Homepage of Federal News Service, Inc.] [Online]. Available at: http://www.defense.gov/transcripts/transcript.aspx?transcriptid=2636 [2010, 21/09].

—. 2002b, 'Transforming the Military', *Foreign Affairs*, 81(3), pp. 20–32.

Santner, E. 2001, *On the Psychotheology of Everyday Life*, University of Chicago Press, Chicago.

Saussure, F. de 1959, *Course in General Linguistics*, The Philosophical Library, New York.

Scheppele, K. L. 2004, 'Law in a Time of Emergency. States of Exception and the Temptations of 9/11', *University of Pennsylvania Journal of Constitutive Law*, 6(5), pp. 1001–83.

Scheuerman, W. E. 2006a, 'Carl Schmitt and the Road to Abu Ghraib', *Constellations*, 13(1), pp. 108–24.

—. 2006b, 'Emergency Powers and the Rule of Law After 9/11', *Journal of Political Philosophy*, 14(1), pp. 61–84.

Schimel, A. 1998, *Justice "de plomb" en Italie* [Homepage of Le Monde Diplomatique] [Online]. Available at: www.monde-diplomatique.fr/1998/04/SCHIMEL/10247 [2010, 8/6].

Schmid, A. P. & Jongman, A. J. 1988, *Political Terrorism: A New Guide to Actors, Authors, Concepts, Data Bases, Theories and Literature*, 2nd ed., revised, expanded and updated edn, North-Holland, Amsterdam.

Schmitt, C. 1994, *Die Diktatur. Von den Anfängen des modernen Souveränitätsgedankens bis zum proletarischen Klassenkampf*, 6. Auflage edn, Duncker und Humblot, Berlin.

—. 2003, *The Nomos of the Earth in the International Law of the Jus Publicum Europaeum*, Telos Press, New York.

—. 2007a, *The Concept of the Political*, expanded edn, University of Chicago Press, Chicago.

—. 2007b, *Political Theology: Four Chapters on the Concept of Sovereignty*, University of Chicago Press, Chicago.

Schmitt, M. 2002–3, 'Preemptive Strategies in International Law', *Michigan Journal of International Law*, 24, p. 513.

Shield, R. 2007, *Israel's Second Lebanon War: A Failure of Afghan Model Warfare?*, Naval War College, Newport, RI.

Silke, A. 2007, 'The Impact of 9/11 on Research on Terrorism' in *Mapping Terrorism Research*, ed. M. Ranstorp, Routledge, London, pp. 76–93.

Sloterdijk, P. 1983, *Kritik der zynischen Vernunft*, Suhrkamp, Frankfurt am Main.

Stenson, K. 2005, 'Sovereignty, Biopolitics and the Local Government of Crime in Britain', *Theoretical Criminology*, 9(5), pp. 265–87.

Stern, J. 1999, *The Ultimate Terrorists*, Harvard University Press, Cambridge, MA.

Stiglitz, J. & Bilmes, L. 2008, *The Three Trillion Dollar War*, W.W. Norton & Co., New York and London.

Suskind, R. 2006, June 19th-last update, *The Untold Story of Al-Qaeda's Plot to Attack the Subway* [Homepage of Time Magasine] [Online]. Available at: www.time.com/time/magazine/article/0,9171,1205478,00.html [2010, 21/09].

Theunissen, M. 1991, *Negative Theologie der Zeit*, Erste Auflage edn, Suhrkamp, Frankfurt am Main.

Thomsen, C. 2008, June 2nd-last update, *Massiv fordømmelse af terrorangreb* [Homepage of Politiken] [Online]. Available at: www.dr.dk/Nyheder/ Udland/2008/06/02/134432.htm [2010, 13/5].

Thykjær, S., Porsgaard, K., Bjerre, H. J. & Hansen, B. B. 2009, *Knoldesparkeren, flottenheimeren og glatnakken,* Informations forlag, Copenhagen.

Thykjær, S., Porsgaard, K., Hansen, B. B., Bjerre, H. J. & Ugilt, R., 2012, *Særklasse,* Informations forlag, Copenhagen.

Vermeule, A. 2005, 'Libertarian Panics', *Rutgers Law Journal,* 36, pp. 871–88.

—. 2009, 'Our Schmittian Administrative Law', *The Harvard Law Review,* 122, pp. 1095–149.

Vollrath, E. 1962, 'Die Gliederung der Metaphysik in eine Metaphysica Generalis und eine Metaphysica Specialis', *Zeitschrift für philosophische Forschung,* 16(2), pp. 258–84.

Wæver, O. 1995, 'Securitization and Desecuritization' in *On Security,* ed. R. Lipschutz, Columbia University Press, New York, pp. 44–86.

Walther, R. 2004, 'Terror, Terrorismus' in *Geschichtliche Grundbegriffe, Band 6,* eds O. Brunner, W. Conze & R. Kosellek, 1. Auflage dieser Studienausgabe mit beigefügten Korrigenda, Klett-Cotta, Stuttgart, pp. 323–440.

Walzer, M. 2004, *Arguing about War,* Yale University Press, New Haven.

Weizman, E. 2007, *Hollow Land. Israels Architecture of Occupation,* 1st edn, Verso, London and New York.

Wilkinson, P. 1986, *Terrorism and the Liberal State,* 2nd revised edn, MacMillan, London.

—. 1990, 'Terrorist Targets and Tactics: New Risks to World Order', *Conflict Studies,* 236, pp. 1–21.

—. 1996, *Inquiry into Legislation Against Terrorism,* Vol. 2, Secretary of State for the Home Department, The Secretary of State for Northern Ireland, London.

—. 2001, *Terrorism versus Democracy: The Liberal State Response,* Routledge, London.

Winograd, E., Gavison, R., Dror, Y., Einan, M. & Nadel, H. 2008, 30/1-last update, *Winograd Commission Final Report* [Homepage of Council on Foreign Relations] [Online]. Available at: www.cfr.org/publication/15385/winograd_commission_final_report.html [2011, 16/1].

Žižek, S. 1989, *The Sublime Object of Ideology,* 1st edn, Verso, London and New York.

—. 1996, *The Indivisible Remainder. An Essay on Schelling and Related Matters,* Verso, London and New York.—. 1998, *Tarrying with the Negative: Kant, Hegel, and the Critique of Ideology,* Duke University Press, Durham.

—. 2000, *The Ticklish Subject,* paperback edn, Verso, London.

—. 2002, *Welcome to the Desert of the Real! Five Essays on 11 September and Related Dates,* Verso, London.

—. 2003, 'The (Mis)uses of Catastrophes', *Distinktion – Scandinavian Journal of Social Theory,* 6, pp. 137–44.

—. 2008a, 'Legal Luck', *Unbound,* 4(1), pp. 1–14.

—. 2008b, *The Secret Clauses of the Liberal Utopia*, Springer, The Netherlands.

Zulaika, J. & Douglass, W. A. 1996, *Terror and Taboo: The Follies, Fables, and Faces of Terrorism,* Routledge, New York.

Zupančič, A. 2008a, *The Odd One In,* 1st edn, MIT Press, Cambridge, MA.

—. 2008b, *Why Psychoanalysis?* NSU Press, Aarhus.

Index

www.ingramcontent.com/pod-product-compliance
Lightning Source LLC
Chambersburg PA
CBHW050427280326
41932CB00013BA/2021